ESA
ESSENTIALS

Endangered Species Act

Murray Feldman and Sam Kalen

AMERICANBARASSOCIATION
Environment, Energy,
and Resources Section

Cover by Mary Anne Kulchawik/ABA Design

Printed in the United States of America

29 28 27 26 25   5 4 3 2 1

Contents

Preface

Fifty-plus years after its enactment, the Endangered Species Act (ESA) remains a bedrock of America's environmental laws and biodiversity goals, with both a domestic and international reach. As pressures on the nation's and the world's natural systems continue to grow—from, among other factors, development, climate change and adaptation, human migration, armed conflict, and the need and search for the resources to support a growing global population—species of fish, wildlife, and plants continue to be added to the ESA's list of endangered and threatened species.

The ESA embodies an important, legally enforceable determination by our country to protect, conserve, and recover those species and the habitats on which they depend. But disputes over how to do so and what the ESA requires are inevitable. In part, this is because of the ESA's broad reach. As the U.S. Supreme Court stated in its 1995 *Sweet Home* decision, "the Act encompasses a vast range of economic and social enterprises and endeavors." That reach cannot be understated. Activities from residential property development to national forest management of commodity and recreational uses, grazing or wind energy leases on Bureau of Land Management lands, energy generation and transmission, military training activities onshore and offshore, and so much more, even wildlife research and conservation itself, can implicate ESA regulatory requirements and processes.

The ESA, its implementing regulations, court decisions, and agency guidance collectively provide a robust body of law and direction for listed species and critical habitat conservation. Anyone concerned with or interested in what can, ought, or must be done to conserve imperiled species would benefit from the study and appreciation of the ESA. Likewise, if for no other reason than the serious nature of the constraints and penalties resulting from ESA violations, anyone engaging in activities that may affect a listed species or designated critical habitat should proceed with caution and understand what the Act prohibits or permits. For all those potentially interested, this book provides a basic overview of the ESA's major elements.

The book's chapters are separated into several sections and subsections to provide an overall framework for the more detailed discussion of particular ESA issues, with appropriate citations to case law, statutes, regulations, and representative secondary authorities. For more seasoned ESA practitioners, this volume may be used as a readily accessed quick reference to dive back into the key statutory provisions and case law holdings. For those less experienced, the book can help provide a working knowledge of basic ESA issues and concepts. While no *Essentials* book can address every specific issue that might arise, this volume provides a valuable starting point for further researching and exploring most ESA issues.

Following publication of the prior edition of this work in 2012, the law of the ESA has continued to grow and develop. This updated edition aims to capture the key areas and decisions that have illuminated the continued application and progress of the ESA since then. In this current time of dynamic regulatory change and potentially shifting balance of the courts and agencies in the review of administrative agency decisions and statutory interpretations, having a road map to the basic ESA foundations and past legal developments is a needed touchstone. We hope that you find this book helps serve that purpose.

Murray Feldman
Boise, Idaho

Sam Kalen
Ft. Collins, Colorado

Acknowledgments

The authors thank Sarah Orwig and her team at the ABA for the helpful review, assistance, and guidance in preparing this book for publication. And the authors are grateful for the ABA's peer reviewer comments. We are especially grateful for the research, drafting, and updating for this edition from Hannah Carrese and Katy Riker, colleagues of Murray Feldman and attorneys at Holland & Hart LLP. Their tireless efforts, always undertaken with good cheer and a detailed eye, made a lasting improvement to this book and ensured that the ESA's key developments and shifting regulatory landscape in the past decade and a half were appropriately captured. The authors also thank Tammy Feldman, teaching professor at the University of Michigan's Ross School of Business and former managing editor of the ABA *Antitrust Law Journal*, for her very thorough and helpful review of the final manuscript citations and formats.

About the Authors

Murray Feldman is a partner in the Boise, Idaho, office of Holland & Hart LLP. He represents clients in Endangered Species Act litigation and administrative proceedings on species listing, critical habitat designation, consultation, habitat conservation planning, and related issues. He has worked on ESA matters throughout the Pacific Northwest, Intermountain West, Alabama, Michigan, New York, and Texas ranging from the polar bear to the piping plover. His practice also includes National Environmental Policy Act, Clean Water Act, public lands, and climate change issues. Murray is a past chair of the Idaho Humanities Council, co-editor of *Idaho Wilderness Considered* (2016), a past trustee of the Foundation for Natural Resources and Energy Law, and a contributor to *The Codex of the Endangered Species Act, Volume II: The Next Fifty Years* (2024). He received his JD from the University of California, Berkeley School of Law, an MS degree from the University of Idaho College of Natural Resources, and a BS from the U.C. Berkeley College of Natural Resources.

Sam Kalen is the IU McKinney Family Chair in Environmental Law at Indiana University McKinney School of Law. From 2009 to 2024 he was at the University of Wyoming College of Law and most recently served at Wyoming as the William T. Schwartz Distinguished Professor of Law and Associate Dean. Professor Kalen is a nationally recognized environmental, energy, public land, and natural resources professor. He is a co-author of *Natural Resources Law and Policy* (4th ed. Foundation Press 2025) and of *Energy Follies: Missteps, Fiascos, and Success of America's Energy Policy* (Cambridge U. Press 2018), and he has authored numerous law review articles and book chapters. Prior to becoming a law professor, Mr. Kalen worked for a law firm in Washington, D.C., and served in the Solicitor's Office at the Department of the Interior.

Abbreviations

ALJ	administrative law judge
APA	Administrative Procedure Act
BA	biological assessment
BLM	Bureau of Land Management
BO	biological opinion
CCA	Candidate Conservation Agreement
CCAA	Candidate Conservation Agreement with Assurances
CFR	Code of Federal Regulations
CITES	Convention on International Trade in Endangered Species of Wild Fauna and Flora
DOI	Department of the Interior
DPS	distinct population segment
EA	environmental assessment
EIS	environmental impact statement
EPA	Environmental Protection Agency
ESA	Endangered Species Act
ESC	Endangered Species Committee
ESU	evolutionarily significant unit
FWS	Fish and Wildlife Service
HCP	habitat conservation plan
ITP	incidental take permit
ITS	incidental take statement
NEPA	National Environmental Policy Act
NMFS	National Marine Fisheries Service
NOAA	National Oceanic and Atmospheric Administration
RPA	reasonable and prudent alternative
RPM	reasonable and prudent measure
SPR	significant portion of its range
SHA	safe harbor agreement
USDA	United States Department of Agriculture
USFS	United States Forest Service

1 Executive Summary

1.1 Overview

The Endangered Species Act (ESA) is the "most comprehensive legislation for the preservation of endangered species ever enacted by any nation."[1] Congress's "plain intent" when enacting the ESA "was to halt and reverse the trend toward species extinction, at whatever the cost."[2] Today, the polar bear and Arctic seals are among the iconic symbols of the efforts to address the Act's conservation mandate and the regulatory implications of that mandate. Indeed, the words "endangered species" are so familiar in American life as to have become a cliché. "Ask [people] in the street what [they think] about the problem of disappearing species, and [they] may well reply that it would be a pity if the tiger or the blue whale disappeared," yet it is not apparent whether that sentiment is sufficient to cause the same people to alter their lifestyles.[3]

This book does not capture or explore the ESA's historical, scientific, sociological, political, or psychological underpinnings, or even provide a comprehensive survey of wildlife law in the United States.[4] It reflects a snapshot in time for a program that has

1. Babbitt v. Sweet Home Chapter of Cmtys. for a Great Or., 515 U.S. 687, 698 (1995).

2. Tenn. Valley Auth. v. Hill, 437 U.S. 153, 184 (1978).

3. Norman Myers, The Sinking Ark: A New Look at the Problem of Disappearing Species 3 (1979).

4. See Michael J. Bean & Melanie J. Rowland, The Evolution of National Wildlife Law (3d ed. 1997), for a detailed and thorough discussion of federal wildlife law, including the ESA; and for other useful books on the Act, see The Codex of the Endangered Species Act Vol. II: The Next Fifty Years (Lowell E. Baier, John F. Organ & Christopher E. Segal eds., 2024); Lowell E. Baier, The Codex of the Endangered Species Act Vol. I: The First Fifty Years (2023); Endangered Species Act: Law,

witnessed significant changes as new administrations are sworn in. Regulations, for instance, promulgated during the first Trump administration were reconsidered during the Biden administration, and now President Trump has indicated an interest in having many of those existing ESA regulations reconsidered once again. The reader should appreciate that some of these changes can occur and yet the structure and issues identified throughout this book ought to remain somewhat consistent. Also, the purpose of the *Essentials* series, and this book, is modest. The series is designed to introduce the reader to a particular statute and its overall regulatory structure and then offer citations and references that further inform the reader how the Act and its regulations have been implemented. The Act will remain a vibrant program warranting continued understanding as new species may become at risk because of climate change,[5] and as each new administration continues to explore how to implement the Act's various programs.

1.2 Purposes of the Endangered Species Act

By 1973, when the ESA became law, Congress already was acutely aware of the problem of human-induced species extinction.[6] Congress's earlier efforts, the 1966 Endangered Species Preservation Act[7] and the 1969 Endangered Species Conservation Act,[8] were insufficient to protect endangered wildlife.[9] Against this backdrop, Congress acted decisively. Finding that "species of fish, wildlife, and plants are of aesthetic, ecological, educational,

---

POLICY, AND PERSPECTIVES (Donald C. Baur & Ya-Wei Li eds., 3d ed. 2021); REBUILDING THE ARK: NEW PERSPECTIVES ON ENDANGERED SPECIES ACT REFORM (Jonathan H. Adler ed., 2011); STANFORD ENV'T LAW SOC'Y, THE ENDANGERED SPECIES ACT (2001); KATHRYN A. KOHM, BALANCING ON THE BRINK OF EXTINCTION: THE ENDANGERED SPECIES ACT AND LESSONS FOR THE FUTURE (1991); DANIEL J. ROHLF, THE ENDANGERED SPECIES ACT: A GUIDE TO ITS PROTECTIONS AND IMPLEMENTATION (1989).

5. *E.g.*, NOAA FISHERIES, *Climate Change Escalates Threats to Species in the Spotlight* (Aug. 29, 2024), https://www.fisheries.noaa.gov/feature-story/climate-change-escalates-threats-species-spotlight; *see also* Murray Feldman & Andrew Mergen, *The Role of Climate Change in ESA Decisions*, 53 ROCKY MTN. MIN. L. FOUND. J. 67 (2016).

6. For a discussion about the early concerns animating and surrounding the passage of the Act, see LEWIS REGENSTEIN, THE POLITICS OF EXTINCTION: THE SHOCKING STORY OF THE WORLD'S ENDANGERED WILDLIFE (1975).

7. Pub. L. No. 89-669, 80 Stat. 926 (1966).

8. Pub. L. No. 91-135, 83 Stat. 275 (1969).

9. *See* ROHLF, *supra* note 4, at 21–23.

historical, recreational, and scientific value to the nation and its people,"[10] Congress declared: "The purposes of [the ESA] are to provide a means whereby the ecosystems upon which endangered species and threatened species depend may be conserved, [and] to provide a program for the conservation of such endangered and threatened species."[11] To meet these underlying objectives, Congress established in the ESA a comprehensive suite of affirmative mandates, strict prohibitions, strong recommendations, and limited exceptions.

The U.S. Supreme Court has provided perhaps the most strident and oft-quoted summary of the ESA's breadth.[12] After reviewing the Act and its legislative history, the Court stated that "the plain intent of Congress in enacting this statute was to halt and reverse the trend toward species extinction, whatever the cost," and noted further that this conclusion is reflected "in literally every section of the statute."[13] Although the Court admitted that it might seem "curious to some that the survival of a relatively small number of three-inch fish among all the countless millions of species extant would require the permanent holding up of a virtually completed dam for which Congress has expended more than $100 million," the Court held in *Tennessee Valley Authority v. Hill* that the Act required "precisely that result."[14]

Since the Court's decision in *Hill,* Congress has substantively amended the ESA on four principal occasions (1978, 1979, 1982, and 1988). The rigidity of the Act's prohibitions has been tempered somewhat through the creation of several exceptions and exemptions[15] and the countervailing Supreme Court and circuit courts of appeals statements,[16] but the exceptions and statements

---

10. 16 U.S.C. § 1531(a)(3).

11. *Id.* § 1531(b).

12. Tenn. Valley Auth. v. Hill, 437 U.S. 153, 180 (1978).

13. *Id.*

14. *Id.* at 172–73. For the history of the Tellico dam controversy, see ZYGMUNT J.B. PLATER, THE SNAIL DARTER AND THE DAM: HOW PORK-BARREL POLITICS ENDANGERED A LITTLE FISH AND KILLED A RIVER (2013); KENNETH M. MURCHISON, THE SNAIL DARTER CASE: TVA VERSUS THE ENDANGERED SPECIES ACT (2007); *see also* Jason Nark, *How a Mistaken Identity Halted a Dam's Construction*, N.Y. TIMES, Jan. 4, 2025, at A13.

15. For discussion of the ESA's various exceptions and exemptions, see Chapter 4, Sections 4.3 and 4.8; Chapter 5, Section 5.4.5.4; Chapters 6 and 7; and Chapter 10, Section 10.7.

16. *E.g.*, Bennett v. Spear, 520 U.S. 154, 176–77 (1997) (The "obvious purpose of the requirement that each agency 'use the best scientific and commercial data available' is to ensure that the ESA not be implemented haphazardly, on the basis of speculation or surmise. While this no doubt serves to advance the ESA's overall goal of species preservation, we think it readily apparent that another

have not swallowed the rule. The ESA remains a "powerful tool"[17] for species protection and conservation, and quite possibly still warrants the sobriquet of being the "pit bull"[18] of all environmental and conservation programs. After all, it has served as the fulcrum for driving management decisions on millions of public and private acres, as well as for watersheds and river systems throughout the nation and offshore activities such as oil and gas development, wind energy, and military training exercises.

1.3 Basic Structure of the ESA

The ESA provides substantive protections to any species listed as endangered or threatened. Importantly, no protections are afforded unless and until a species is listed, whether or not it might be at risk of extinction. Key among these protections are the prohibition against any federal agency activity that might jeopardize a listed species or adversely modify or destroy its critical habitat,[19] the prohibition against any activities that would "take" a protected species,[20] the requirement that federal agencies develop programs to conserve and recover listed species,[21] and the obligation imposed on the federal government to cooperate with states and foreign governments to meet the purposes of

---

objective (if not indeed the primary one) is to avoid needless economic dislocation produced by agency officials zealously but unintelligently pursuing their environmental objectives.") (quoting 16 U.S.C. § 1536(a)(2)); Me. Lobstermen's Ass'n v. NMFS, 70 F.4th 582, 586 (D.C. Cir. 2023) (In a section 7 consultation biological opinion, the Service may not "when faced with uncertainty, give the 'benefit of the doubt' to an endangered species by relying upon worst-case scenarios or pessimistic assumptions." The "ESA and the implementing regulations call for an empirical judgment about what is 'likely.' The Service's role as an expert is undermined, not furthered, when it distorts that scientific judgment by indulging in worst-case scenarios and pessimistic assumptions to benefit a favored side.").

17. James C. Kilbourne, *The Endangered Species Act Under the Microscope: A Closeup Look from a Litigator's Perspective,* 21 Env't L. 499, 501 (1991).

18. Donald Barry, Address at ABA Section of Natural Resources, Energy, and Environmental Law, Workshop on Endangered Species (Apr. 6, 1990). *Cf.* Jonathan H. Adler, *Tarnished Gold: The Endangered Species Act at 50,* 18 FIU L. Rev. 385, 387 (2024) ("For all of the ESA's force and ambition, it is unclear how much the law has done to achieve its central purpose—the conservation of endangered species."); Daniel M. Evans et al., *Species Recovery in the United States: Increasing the Effectiveness of the Endangered Species Act,* 20 Issues in Ecol. 1 (2016).

19. *See* Chapter 5.

20. *See* Chapter 4.

21. *See* Chapter 3.

the Act.[22] The Act explicitly implements two international treaties respecting trade and conservation in wildlife and flora.[23] In some cases, federal agencies may avail themselves of limited exceptions to the Act's mandates,[24] and private parties may obtain a variety of permits allowing limited taking of protected species.[25] Finally, the ESA contains substantial criminal and civil penalties,[26] as well as a liberal citizen-suit provision, encouraging any person to act as a "private attorney general" to enforce the Act.[27]

Each section of the ESA attempts to work in tandem with the others to collectively achieve the Act's overarching conservation objective, although various provisions of the Act affect different people in differing ways and some requirements are relevant only to specific situations. The chapters in this book are organized with that in mind, grouping issues topically when appropriate, while adhering as closely as possible to the underlying organizational structure of the Act itself.

22. *See* Chapters 8 and 9.
23. *See* Chapter 9, Section 9.5.
24. *See* Chapter 5, Section 5.4.5.4, and Chapter 7.
25. *See* Chapter 6.
26. *See* Chapter 4, Section 4.7.1.
27. *See* Chapter 11.

2 Listing and Critical Habitat Designation

2.1 Overview

Congress described the Endangered Species Act (ESA) section 4[1] listing process as the "keystone" of the Act.[2] The ESA provides substantive protection to species only once they are listed as threatened or endangered pursuant to section 4. As Congress explained, "The protective measures to counter species extinction take effect when a species is listed."[3]

For purposes of the ESA, endangered and threatened species are defined as follows:

> The term "endangered species" means "any species which is in danger of extinction throughout all or a significant portion of its range other than a species of the Class Insecta determined by the Secretary to constitute a pest whose protection under the provisions of this Act would present an overwhelming and overriding risk to man."[4]
>
> The term "threatened species" means "any species which is likely to become an endangered species within the foreseeable future throughout all or a significant portion of its range."[5]

---

1. 16 U.S.C. § 1533.

2. H.R. Rep. No. 97-567, at 10 (1982), *reprinted in* 1982 U.S.C.C.A.N. 2807, 2810. For a detailed review of the listing process, see Benjamin Jesup, *Listing Determinations, in* Endangered Species Act: Law, Policy, and Perspectives 19 (Donald C. Baur & Ya-Wei Li eds., 3d ed. 2021). For a discussion of section 4 generally, see Daniel J. Rohlf, *Section 4 of the Endangered Species Act: Top Ten Issues for the Next Thirty Years,* 34 Env't L. 483 (2004).

3. H.R. Rep. No. 97-567, at 10 (1982), *reprinted in* 1982 U.S.C.C.A.N. 2807, 2810.

4. 16 U.S.C. § 1532(6).

5. *Id.* § 1532(20). Recent revisions to the Services' regulations have defined the term *foreseeable future,* providing that the "foreseeable future extends as far

Section 4 of the ESA vests the Secretary[6] with a "mandatory non-discretionary duty to list qualified species as endangered or threatened."[7] The Secretary may also list any species that so closely resembles in appearance a listed species that enforcement personnel would have difficulty differentiating between the two.[8] Not until recently have the Services been required to articulate any established policy for distinguishing between "endangered" and "threatened" species. But in connection with the listing of the polar bear as threatened, a district court held that the phrase "in danger of extinction" created sufficient ambiguity to qualify for deference under *Chevron U.S.A., Inc. v. Natural Resources*

---

into the future as the Services can make reasonably reliable predictions about the threats to the species and the species' responses to those threats." 50 C.F.R. § 424.11(d). The regulations add that "[t]he Services will describe the foreseeable future on a case-by-case basis, using the best available data and taking into account considerations such as the species' life-history characteristics, threat-projection timeframes, and environmental variability" and that they "need not identify the foreseeable future in terms of a specific period of time." *Id.* This definition generally comports with prior case law. *See* Alaska Oil & Gas Ass'n v. Pritzker, 840 F.3d 671, 681 (9th Cir. 2016) (accepting climate model as "rational and reasonable basis for evaluating the bearded seal's viability over 50 and 100 years," the "foreseeable future"); Safari Club Int'l v. Salazar (*In re* Polar Bear Endangered Species Act Listing & Section 4(d) Rule Litig.), 709 F.3d 1, 15 (D.C. Cir. 2013) (accepting that "FWS determines what constitutes the 'foreseeable' future on a case-by-case basis in each listing decision" and holding that a 45-year period was a reasonable interpretation of the term *foreseeable future*); Ctr. for Biological Diversity v. Lubchenco, 758 F. Supp. 2d 945, 962 (N.D. Cal. 2010) (upholding NMFS's decision not to list ribbon seal as threatened because NMFS's assertion that climate projections past 2050 were unreliable was reasonable basis not to assess foreseeable future beyond that date); W. Watersheds Project v. Foss, 2005 WL 2002473 (D. Idaho Aug. 19, 2005) (definition of "foreseeable future" varies depending upon species); Or. Nat. Res. Council v. Daley, 6 F. Supp. 2d 1139, 1150–51 (D. Or. 1998) (NMFS failed to correctly apply the "within the foreseeable future" standard because it predicated its listing determination on a finding that coho would not likely become endangered within two years, the interval between NMFS's finding that threatened listing was "not warranted" and the adoption of habitat protection measures by the state of Oregon). Most courts have accepted a "more likely than not" understanding of the term "likely" in connection with the "foreseeable future" language. *See* Me. Lobstermen's Ass'n v. Nat'l Marine Fisheries Serv., 70 F.4th 582, 595 (D.C. Cir. 2023) (courts and FWS have "read 'likely' to mean 'more likely than not'" in the section 4 context); *Alaska Oil & Gas Ass'n v. Pritzker*, 840 F.3d at 684 (same).

6. Throughout this book, the terms *Secretary, FWS, NMFS,* and *Service(s)* are used interchangeably, unless otherwise noted. The Secretary of Commerce (delegated to NMFS) is generally responsible for marine species, and the Secretary of the Interior (delegated to FWS) is responsible for all other listings.

7. H.R. Rep. No. 97–835, at 20 (1982), *reprinted in* 1982 U.S.C.C.A.N. 2860, 2861 (describing 16 U.S.C. § 1533(c)(1) ("The Secretary of the Interior shall publish in the Federal Register a list of all species determined by him or the Secretary of Commerce to be endangered species and a list of all species determined by him or the Secretary of Commerce to be threatened species.")).

8. 16 U.S.C. § 1533(e).

Defense Council, Inc., 468 U.S. 837 (1984),[9] prompting the Fish and Wildlife Service (FWS) to articulate a reasoned explanation for the difference between a threatened and endangered species.[10] In a document filed in the polar bear litigation, FWS emphasized that the distinguishing characteristic between an endangered and threatened species is temporal, and "depends upon the life history and ecology of the species, the nature of the threats, and the species' response to those threats."[11]

The actual lists of species determined to be endangered or threatened under the ESA are published in the Code of Federal Regulations.[12] In addition, FWS publishes a regular Candidate Notice of Review identifying species that are candidates for listing.[13] As a matter of policy, and in keeping with an ecosystem-based approach to the ESA, the Secretary will "group" listings on a geographic, taxonomic, or ecosystem basis whenever possible.[14] Although Congress noted that a purpose of the ESA is "to provide a means whereby the ecosystems upon which" the listed species depend will be conserved,[15] for many years the ESA was implemented with quite possibly a more limited focus on a species-by-species basis. Today, we recognize the importance of interrelated,

9. In *Loper Bright Enterprises v. Raimondo*, 603 U.S. 369 (2024), the Supreme Court overruled *Chevron*, holding that *Chevron*'s deference to agency interpretation of an ambiguous law that the agency is charged with enforcing contravened the Administrative Procedure Act (APA), which provides: "To the extent necessary to decision and when presented, the reviewing court shall decide all relevant questions of law, interpret constitutional and statutory provisions, and determine the meaning or applicability of the terms of an agency action." 5 U.S.C. § 706. *Loper Bright* detailed forms of deference that courts may still employ, most notably, deference under *Skidmore v. Swift & Co.*, 323 U.S. 134 (1944), to "interpretations and opinions" of the relevant agency "made in pursuance of official duty" and "based upon . . . specialized experience." *Loper Bright*, 603 U.S. at 394–95. The policy interpreting "in danger of extinction" that FWS produced in the polar bear litigation may not be suspect under *Loper Bright* because, in a subsequent case, the same district court held that *Chevron* did not apply to that policy and, further, that the policy was due deference under *Skidmore*. *See* Ctr. for Biological Diversity v. Everson, 435 F. Supp. 3d 69, 85 (D.D.C. 2020).

10. *In re* Polar Bear Endangered Species Act Listing and § 4(d) Rule Litig., 794 F. Supp. 2d 65, 79 (D.D.C. 2011), *aff'd*, 709 F.3d 1 (D.C. Cir. 2013).

11. *Id.* at 83.

12. 50 C.F.R. § 17.11 (fish and wildlife), § 17.12 (plants). This list includes species listed by FWS and NMFS; NMFS also separately publishes the list of endangered and threatened species under its jurisdiction at 50 C.F.R. §§ 223.102, 224.101.

13. *See* 88 Fed. Reg. 41,560 (June 27, 2023) (FWS's Candidate Notice of Review); *see also* 16 U.S.C. § 1533(b)(3)(C)(iii) (requiring the Secretary to "implement a system to monitor effectively the status" of candidate species).

14. 59 Fed. Reg. 34,273, 34,274 (July 1, 1994).

15. 16 U.S.C. § 1531(b).

interlocking, and overlapping ecological systems and the role they play toward sustaining the viability of species.[16]

Listing decisions, along with associated critical habitat designations,[17] are vital and often controversial activities that are governed by detailed statutory and regulatory guidelines.

2.2 What Is a Species?

The ESA broadly, if somewhat vaguely, uses the term *species* to define the universe of organisms that may qualify for listing as threatened or endangered; any species of fish, wildlife,[18] or plant[19] is eligible for listing consideration. The Act defines *species* as follows:

> The term "species" includes any subspecies of fish or wildlife or plants, and any distinct population segment of any species of vertebrate fish or wildlife which interbreeds when mature.[20]

Though perhaps not biologically or taxonomically correct, the ESA's definition of *species* implicitly recognizes scientific nomenclature as a starting point for determining eligibility for listing; Congress expressed a working comfort level with "taxonomic categories" at the subspecies level or above.[21] Nowhere in the ESA,

---

16. *See generally* Bradley C. Karkkainen, *Collaborative Ecosystem Governance: Scale, Complexity, and Dynamism,* 21 Va. Env't L.J. 189 (2002). Federal agencies have begun adopting such approaches. *See, e.g.*, NMFS Policy 01-120, *Ecosystem-Based Fisheries Management Policy of the National Marine Fisheries Service National Oceanic and Atmospheric Administration* (May 23, 2016, rev. Jan. 2024).

17. See Section 2.8 for a discussion of critical habitat designation.

18. The Act defines *fish or wildlife* as "any member of the animal kingdom, including without limitation any mammal, fish, bird (including any migratory, nonmigratory, or endangered bird for which protection is also afforded by treaty or other international agreement), amphibian, reptile, mollusk, crustacean, arthropod or other invertebrate[.]" 16 U.S.C. § 1532(8). The definition includes any part, product, egg, or offspring of the animal, and even its dead body. *See id.*

19. *Id.* § 1532(14), defining *plant* as "any member of the plant kingdom."

20. *Id.* § 1532(16). The term *species* is further qualified through regulation as not including "any species of the class Insecta determined by the Secretary to constitute a pest whose protection under the provisions of the Act would present an overwhelming and overriding risk to man." 50 C.F.R. § 424.02.

21. H.R. Rep. No. 95-1804, at 17 (1978), *reprinted in* 1978 U.S.C.C.A.N. 9484, 9485.

however, will one find any rigid adherence to a purely taxonomic definition of *species*.

The Services conclude that because "the Act does not attempt to define 'species' in biological terms,"[22] the term *species* may be applied "according to the best biological knowledge and understanding of evolution, speciation, and genetics."[23] Thus, in establishing the list of endangered or threatened species, the listing agencies may utilize such sources as the *International Code of Zoological Nomenclature,* but only to the extent "practicable."[24]

As discussed next in Sections 2.2.1 and 2.2.2, whether a particular group of vertebrate fish or wildlife is a "distinct population segment" or whether a species is threatened or endangered throughout "all or a significant portion of its range" has provoked attention and controversy.

2.2.1 Distinct Population Segments

In 1978, Congress amended the ESA definition of *species*.[25] The 1978 amendments provide that the term *species* encompasses "*any distinct population segment* of any species of vertebrate fish or wildlife which interbreeds when mature."[26] Congress did not

22. *See* 61 Fed. Reg. 4,710, 4,710 (Feb. 7, 1996) (discussing the term *species* in the context of whether "intercrosses" or "hybrids" may be protected under the ESA). Note that this proposed policy and rule was never finalized. *See* Fred W. Allendorf et al., *Intercrosses and the U.S. Endangered Species Act: Should Hybridized Populations Be Included as Westslope Cutthroat Trout?*, 18 Conservation Biology 1203, 1204 (2004).

23. 61 Fed. Reg. 4,710, 4,710 (Feb. 7, 1996). *See also* N.M. Farm & Livestock Bureau v. Dep't of the Interior, 952 F.3d 1216, 1224 (10th Cir. 2020) (noting of species that "[w]hen Congress has used technical words or terms of art [in a statute], the term must be given its technical or scientific meaning"). One recent example of the sometimes-fraught intersection between scientific definitions of species and the ESA is a morphological and genomic analysis finding that the snail darter, the subject of the first test of the ESA before the Supreme Court, *Tennessee Valley Authority v. Hill*, 437 U.S. 153 (1978), is taxonomically not a species but rather a subpopulation of another fish, the stargazing darter. *See* Ava Ghezelayagh et al., *Comparative Species Delimitation of a Biological Conservation Icon*, 35 Current Biology 398 (Jan. 20, 2025).

24. 50 C.F.R. § 17.11(c).

25. See Karl Gleaves et al., *The Meaning of "Species" Under the Endangered Species Act,* 13 Pub. Land L. Rev. 25, 30–31 (1992), for a detailed discussion of the 1978 amendments to the definition of *species*. *See also* J.B. Ruhl, *supra* note 2. The Act originally defined species to include taxonomic species, subspecies, and "any other group of fish or wildlife of the same species or smaller taxa in common spatial arrangement that interbreed when mature." Pub. L. No. 93-205, 87 Stat. 884, 886 (1973).

26. 16 U.S.C. § 1532(16) (emphasis added).

further clarify this amendment, but left it to the listing agencies to fill the definitional void and apply the ESA listing provisions to "distinct population segments" of vertebrate fish and wildlife.

One year later, in 1979, Congress considered but declined the opportunity to repeal, clarify, or modify its distinct population segment (DPS) language.[27] Instead, in a Senate report discussing the issue, Congress stated: "[T]he committee is aware of the great potential for abuse of this authority and expects FWS to use the ability to list populations *sparingly* and only when the biological evidence indicates that such action is warranted."[28] Whether a "sparing" use of the authority to list DPSs comports with the agencies' affirmative duty to list any species that otherwise qualifies as endangered or threatened is an unresolved question.[29] Nonetheless, the listing agencies have publicly committed to a sparing use of DPS listing authority[30] and have struggled somewhat to develop a sufficiently predictive policy for applying the DPS listing authority granted by Congress.[31]

The listing agencies have candidly summarized the key challenge in applying ESA coverage to DPSs: "It is uncontested that the term 'distinct population segment' is not mentioned in scientific literature, nor explicitly defined in the ESA."[32] And the

27. Gleaves et al., *supra* note 25, at 31–33.

28. S. Rep. No. 96-151, at 7 (1979), *reprinted in* Cong. Rsch. Serv., 97th Cong., 2d Sess., A Legislative History of the Endangered Species Act of 1973, at 1396–97 (Comm. Print 1982) (emphasis added).

29. *See* Gleaves et al., *supra* note 25, at 33 n.34; *see also* Humane Soc'y of the U.S. v. Zinke, 865 F.3d 585, 601–02 (D.C. Cir. 2017) (in designating gray wolves in the Western Great Lakes region as a DPS, FWS had arbitrarily and capriciously disregarded the impact extraction of that population would have on the legal status of the remaining population and observing that "[t]he Service's disregard of the remnant's status would turn that sparing segment process into a backdoor route to the de facto delisting of already-listed species, in open defiance of the [ESA's] specifically enumerated requirements for delisting").

30. *See* 61 Fed. Reg. 4,722, 4722 (Feb. 7, 1996) (noting that "the Services have used this authority relatively rarely," and that "of over 300 native vertebrate species listed under the Act, only about 30 are given separate status" as DPSs).

31. *See* Sw. Ctr. for Biological Diversity v. Babbitt, 926 F. Supp. 920, 926–27 (D. Ariz. 1996) (finding that FWS had arbitrarily selected which, among many, draft DPS policies it would follow in a particular case). Because the language appears ambiguous and it relies on agency technical expertise, pre-*Loper Bright* courts afforded the listing agencies deference when interpreting what constitutes a DPS. *See, e.g.*, Ctr. for Biological Diversity v. Zinke, 868 F.3d 1054, 1058 (9th Cir. 2017).

32. *Sw. Ctr. for Biological Diversity*, 926 F. Supp. at 926. *See also* FWS/NMFS Policy Regarding Recognition of Distinct Population Segments Under the Endangered Species Act, 61 Fed. Reg. 4,721, 4,722 (Feb. 7, 1996) ("[a]vailable scientific information provides little specific enlightenment in interpreting the phrase

Ninth Circuit has observed that "[t]here is no indication within the [ESA's] text that Congress intended to create a rigid limitation on the agency's discretion to define the statutorily undefined concept" of a DPS.[33] The listing agencies, therefore, have developed detailed DPS policy guidance informing their determinations of DPS status. This guidance is embodied in two *Federal Register* publications: the NMFS 1991 Policy on the Definition of Species under the Endangered Species Act[34] and the 1996 NMFS and FWS Joint Policy Regarding the Recognition of Distinct Vertebrate Population Segments Under the Endangered Species Act.[35]

The 1991 NMFS policy is applicable only to species of salmonids native to the Pacific.[36] NMFS has determined that a particular stock of salmon will qualify as a DPS only if that stock "represents an evolutionarily significant unit (ESU) of the biological species."[37] A stock qualifies as an ESU if it satisfies two criteria: (1) it must be substantially reproductively isolated from other conspecific population units, that is, units belonging to the same species and (2) it must represent an important component in the evolutionary legacy of the species.[38]

NMFS applied these criteria in the Columbia River Basin to list different seasonal runs of chinook salmon as separate ESUs.[39] In the late 1990s, NMFS determined that populations of steelhead trout occupying different reaches of the Columbia River also qualified as separate ESUs; it has since relisted those steelhead populations as DPSs, concluding that they are more appropriately

'distinct population segment'"). The Services occasionally repeat this concern when issuing DPS determinations. *E.g.,* Determination of Nine Distinct Population Segments of Loggerhead Sea Turtles as Endangered or Threatened, 76 Fed. Reg. 58,868, 58,869 (Sept. 22, 2011). In one case illustrating the difficulty of reconciling the DPS listing authority with existing scientific nomenclature, a court held that FWS/NMFS's 1996 joint DPS policy, to the extent it limited the DPS to one subspecies, was arbitrary and capricious. Sw. Ctr. for Biological Diversity v. Babbitt, 980 F. Supp. 1080, 1085 (D. Ariz. 1997).

33. Modesto Irr. Dist. v. Gutierrez, 619 F.3d 1024, 1032 (9th Cir. 2010).

34. 56 Fed. Reg. 58,612–18 (Nov. 20, 1991). For a more detailed discussion of NMFS's 1991 policy, see Gleaves et al., *supra* note 25, at 41–44.

35. 61 Fed. Reg. 4721–25 (Feb. 7, 1996).

36. 56 Fed. Reg. at 58,612. *See also Modesto Irr. Dist.,* 619 F.3d at 1030–31 (noting that NMFS only applies the 1991 policy to Pacific salmon).

37. 56 Fed. Reg. at 58,618.

38. *Id.* Note the Ninth Circuit's view that the 1991 policy establishes an ESU as the "functional equivalent" of a DPS. *Modesto Irr. Dist.*, 619 F.3d at 1028.

39. *See, e.g.,* 57 Fed. Reg. 14,653 (Apr. 22, 1992) (listing the Snake River spring/summer chinook salmon and the Snake River fall chinook salmon as two separate species).

listed under the 1996 joint policy because NMFS and FWS share jurisdiction over steelhead and because steelhead is "a type of salmonid with characteristics not typically exhibited by Pacific salmon."[40]

The 1996 joint NMFS/FWS DPS policy[41] provides guidance for determining whether any other (non-Pacific salmonid) group of organisms qualifies as a distinct population segment eligible for listing. The 1996 joint DPS policy lists three "principles"[42] that will be "considered" in making DPS determinations.[43] These principles are

- *discreteness* of the population segment in relation to the remainder of the species to which it belongs;
- *significance* of the population segment to the species to which it belongs; and
- *conservation status* of the population segment (i.e., whether the DPS is endangered or threatened).[44]

The joint DPS policy provides further guidance with respect to the first two principles, discreteness and significance. A

40. 71 Fed. Reg. 834, 834 (Jan. 5, 2006). In the 1990s steelhead listing decisions, NMFS concluded that applying the 1991 policy to list steelhead as ESUs was appropriate because the 1991 policy was "more detailed and applies specifically to Pacific salmonids." 62 Fed. Reg. 43,937, 43,939 (Aug. 18, 1997) (listing the upper Columbia River steelhead); *see also* 64 Fed. Reg. 14,517 (Mar. 25, 1999) (listing the middle Columbia River steelhead under ESU policy); 63 Fed. Reg. 13,347 (Mar. 19, 1998) (listing the lower Columbia River steelhead under ESU policy). For discussion about hatchery-raised fish and their effect on establishing ESUs, see *Trout Unlimited v. Lohn,* 559 F.3d 946 (9th Cir. 2009), and *Alsea Valley Alliance v. Evans,* 161 F. Supp. 2d 1154 (D. Or. 2001).

41. 61 Fed. Reg. 4,721 (Feb. 7, 1996).

42. *Id.* at 4,725.

43. *Id.* The policy arguably requires a positive finding on all three elements before a population segment qualifies as a DPS. The second principle will be considered "if" the first principle is satisfied, and the third principle will be considered "if" the first and second principles have been satisfied. *Id.* But courts have recently characterized a DPS as defined by the first two elements, with the third simply an additional consideration reflecting the ESA's purpose to provide "a program for the conservation of . . . endangered and threatened species." 16 U.S.C. § 1531(b); *see* Crow Indian Tribe v. United States, 965 F.3d 662, 671 (9th Cir. 2020) ("The FWS has defined the characteristics of a distinct population segment ('DPS') to be a segment that is both discrete from the remainder of the species and significant in relation to the remainder of the species."); Humane Soc'y of the U.S. v. Zinke, 865 F.3d 585, 600 (D.C. Cir. 2017) ("[T]he far more natural reading of the [1996] Policy is that it only requires a determination that the potential segment is threatened or endangered prior to listing, not prior to the designation of the segment itself.").

44. 61 Fed. Reg. at 4,725.

population segment is discrete if it is either (1) markedly separated from other populations of the same taxon as a consequence of physical, physiological, ecological, or behavioral factors, or (2) delimited by international governmental boundaries within which significant differences in control of exploitation, management of habitat, conservation status, or regulatory mechanisms exist.[45] Once a population segment has been determined to be discrete, the following factors may be considered to determine whether it is significant to its species:

- Persistence of the discrete population segment in an ecological setting unusual or unique for the taxon;
- Evidence that loss of the discrete population segment would result in a significant gap in the range of a taxon;
- Evidence that the discrete population segment represents the only surviving natural occurrence of a taxon that may be more abundant elsewhere as an introduced population outside its historic range;
- Evidence that the discrete population segment differs markedly from other populations of the species in its genetic characteristics.[46]

Recognizing the flexibility inherent in applying these criteria, the Services caution that it is not possible to describe in any blanket policy all of the classes of information that might influence the biological or ecological importance of determining a discrete or distinct population segment.[47] But at least the Ninth Circuit has

45. *Id.* The Services explicitly noted that only international boundaries, as opposed to state or local boundaries, were appropriate as a focus for a national program; the Services would decline to list entities that are not primarily of conservation interest at a national level. *Id.* at 4,723–24. For example, FWS has recently released a proposed revised listing decision for grizzly bears in the lower 48 states that modifies the geographic scope of the DPS. 90 Fed. Reg. 4,234 (Jan. 15, 2025). The population's discreteness is predicated on the international border with Canada, and the revised DPS would include not just specific recovery zones but, instead, all geographic portions of the currently listed lower-48 entity that contain suitable habitat and where grizzly bears are currently found or are likely to be found in the future as populations recover.

46. 61 Fed. Reg. at 4,725. *See, e.g.*, Ctr. for Biological Diversity v. Zinke, 868 F.3d 1054, 1058 (9th Cir. 2017). When the range of a species arguably is too small, a court might conclude that the Secretary acted arbitrarily in finding "significance." *See* Nat'l Ass'n of Home Builders v. Norton, 340 F.3d 835, 848–49 (9th Cir. 2003).

47. 61 Fed. Reg. at 4,725.

indicated that the policy is legally binding and afforded deference to the agencies' interpretation of the Act in the DPS policy, though it did so under the Supreme Court's now-obsolete *Chevron* holding.[48] A challenge to a DPS listing, therefore, typically involves determining whether the Secretary acted arbitrarily or capriciously in applying the DPS policy. In a challenge to the listing of the Arizona pygmy-owl as a DPS, for instance, the court affirmed FWS's discreteness determination for listing the species as a DPS "because the international border divides the [Arizona pygmy-owl from the northwestern Mexico pygmy-owl] and significant differences in conservation status exist between" the two populations.[49] The court was less sanguine, however, about FWS's "significance" determination, and held that the agency acted arbitrarily in concluding that the loss of the species would create a "significant gap in the range of its taxon or because it differed markedly in its genetic characteristics" from the other population.[50]

48. Nw. Ecosystem All. v. U.S. Fish & Wildlife Serv., 475 F.3d 1136, 1143 (9th Cir. 2007) (western gray squirrel). *See also Ctr. for Biological Diversity*, 868 F.3d at 1058 (affirming reliance on DPS policy under *Chevron*); *Trout Unlimited v. Lohn*, 559 F.3d at 954 (ESU and DPS policies entitled to deference); *Nat'l Ass'n of Home Builders v. Norton*, 340 F.3d at 852 ("Having chosen to promulgate the DPS Policy, the FWS must follow that policy."). Justice Kagan's dissent in *Loper Bright* used "distinct population segment" as an example of "a statutory phrase [that] has more than one reasonable reading." Loper Bright Enters. v. Raimondo, 603 U.S. 369, 453–54 (2024) (quoting *Nw. Ecosystem All.*, 475 F.3d at 1140–45). *See also Humane Soc'y of the U.S. v. Zinke*, 865 F.3d at 600 n.5 (holding that "the Service has the better and more natural reading of its Segment Policy" as not requiring a conservation status determination before DPS designation, and thus reserving judgment as to whether *Auer* deference would apply to FWS's interpretation of the DPS policy).

49. *Nat'l Ass'n of Home Builders v. Norton*, 340 F.3d at 842.

50. *Id.* at 852. The Services may not attempt to separate DPSs into further discrete categories based on their ranges and protect a DPS in only a significant portion of its range. When FWS attempted to delist the Northern Rocky Mountain gray wolf, a DPS, in a portion of its range, the court held that ESA does not allow the Service to "list a DPS, subdivide it, but then provide the mandated protections to only part of the DPS." Defs. of Wildlife v. Salazar, 729 F. Supp. 2d 1207, 1228 (D. Mont. 2010), *vacated as moot*, 2012 U.S. App. LEXIS 26769, at *4 (9th Cir. Nov. 7, 2012). *See also Humane Soc'y of the U.S. v. Zinke*, 865 F.3d at 601–02 (invalidating FWS rule designating a DPS of gray wolves and thus delisting a different sub-population of those wolves); WildEarth Guardians v. Salazar, 2010 WL 3895682 (D. Ariz. Sept. 30, 2010) (upholding challenge to determination that only a geographic range portion of the DPS of the Gunnison prairie dog should be listed because the Secretary of the Interior "cannot determine that anything other than a species, as defined by the ESA, is an endangered or threatened species").

2.2.2 Throughout All or a Significant Portion of Its Range

When considering whether a species requires listing as either threatened or endangered, the Services must determine whether the species is at risk "throughout all or a significant portion of its range." This "significant portion of its range" (SPR) language has been called "inherently ambiguous."[51] While the Secretary enjoys considerable discretion when applying this standard, the Secretary may not assume that a species' viability in a portion of its range obviates the need to list the species.[52] And until recently, the SPR determination has not been overly controversial or even subject to much discussion. Confronted with listing challenges to species, including the Northern Rocky Mountain gray wolf and the Gunnison prairie dog, the Department of the Interior Solicitor issued an opinion in March 2007 suggesting that FWS enjoys considerable latitude when listing or delisting a species based on geographic considerations.[53] But subsequent litigation questioned the 2007 opinion, which suggested that the Secretary could list a species other than as a DPS in only a part of its geographic range,[54] and the Department of the Interior withdrew the opinion in May 2011.[55] Therefore, when a species is at risk throughout either all or a significant portion of its range is an area of the law currently developing. Listing cannot be avoided simply because the species is not at risk everywhere,[56] but beyond that proposition remains

51. Defs. of Wildlife v. Norton, 258 F.3d 1136, 1141 (9th Cir. 2001). Notably, though the Ninth Circuit considered the ESA's SPR language inherently ambiguous, it did not defer to FWS's interpretation under *Chevron*; instead, the court relied on its own interpretation of the ESA. *See id.* at 1145 n.11.

52. *Id.* at 1145. Following the Ninth Circuit's decision in *Defenders*, other lower courts invalidated listing decisions. *See* Defs. of Wildlife v. Norton, 386 F. Supp. 2d 553 (D. Vt. 2005); Defs. of Wildlife v. Dep't of the Interior, 354 F. Supp. 2d 1156 (D. Or. 2005); Defs. of Wildlife v. Norton, 239 F. Supp. 2d 9 (D.D.C. 2002).

53. Solicitor Opinion M-37013 (Mar. 16, 2007).

54. *See* Defs. of Wildlife v. Salazar, 729 F. Supp. 2d 1207 (D. Mont. 2010); WildEarth Guardians v. Salazar, 2010 WL 3895682 (D. Ariz. Sept. 30, 2010). When the Service attempted to address the delisting of the DPS of gray wolves in the Rocky Mountain region, those efforts faltered and ultimately precipitated congressional action and a lawsuit challenging Congress's intervention. *See* All. for Wild Rockies v. Salazar, 672 F.3d 1170 (9th Cir. 2012) (rejecting challenge to congressional appropriation rider delisting gray wolf).

55. Solicitor Opinion M-37024 (May 4, 2011). A court subsequently dismissed as moot the Homebuilders' challenge to the 2007 opinion. Nat'l Ass'n of Homebuilders v. Salazar, 827 F. Supp. 2d 1 (D.D.C. 2011).

56. *Defs. of Wildlife*, 258 F.3d at 1141.

considerable discretion, despite the listing agencies' attempts to outline a detailed SPR policy.

In 2014, the Services adopted a detailed Policy on Interpretation of the Phrase "Significant Portion of its Range" in the Endangered Species Act's Definitions of "Endangered Species" and "Threatened Species."[57] The policy set out a two-step procedure as well as a refined interpretation of SPR. Under the two-step procedure, the Service would first determine whether the species was in danger of extinction, or likely to become so in the foreseeable future, throughout all of its range—that is, whether it was endangered or threatened throughout all of its range.[58] If so, it would list the species as endangered or threatened without any SPR analysis. If the Service did not find that the species was endangered or threatened throughout all of its range, it would move to the second step: determining whether the species was endangered or threatened throughout a significant portion of its range. In at least one listing decision, this policy led FWS to determine that a species was threatened throughout all of its range without addressing whether the species was endangered in a significant portion of its range.[59] A district court struck down this procedure in 2020, explaining, in part, that the ESA required the agency to determine whether a species was endangered by considering whether it was in danger of extinction throughout a significant portion of its range.[60]

The district court, however, did not disturb the Services' interpretation of SPR in the 2014 policy.[61] Under that interpretation, whether a portion of a species' range is "significant" depends upon two factors: "its contribution to the viability of the species" and whether it "is so important that, without the members in that portion, the species would be in danger of extinction, or likely to become so in the foreseeable future, throughout all of its range."[62] This inquiry is based upon the "biological importance of the portion of the range to the conservation of the species."[63]

---

57. 79 Fed. Reg. 37,578 (July 1, 2014).

58. *See* 16 U.S.C. § 1532(6), (20) (defining *endangered species* and *threatened species*).

59. Ctr. for Biological Diversity v. Everson, 435 F. Supp. 3d 69, 89–99 (D.D.C. 2020) (striking down the policy's two-step procedure in the context of FWS's decision to list the northern long-eared bat as threatened without assessing whether it was endangered in a SPR).

60. *See id.* at 93 (citing 16 U.S.C. § 1532(6)).

61. *See* Friends of Animals v. Williams, 2024 WL 3359507 (D.D.C. July 10, 2024), *appeal pending*.

62. 79 Fed. Reg. at 37,579.

63. *Id.* at 37,581.

The biological question then becomes "whether, *without that portion*," the representation, redundancy, or resiliency of the species "would be so impaired that the species would have an increased vulnerability to threats to the point that the overall species would be in danger of extinction (i.e., would be 'endangered') or likely to become so in the foreseeable future (i.e., would be 'threatened')."[64] This inquiry, the Secretaries explained, is separate and different from the inquiry into "significance" for purposes of determining whether to list a species as a DPS.[65] Because adopting the same standard would mean that all DPSs were endangered in a SPR, FWS indicated that the "threshold for significance" in the SPR context must be "higher than that in the DPS policy."[66]

2.3 Listing Criteria and Best Scientific and Commercial Data Available

In the ESA itself, Congress prescribed five criteria for the Secretary to consider when determining whether to list, delist,[67] or reclassify[68] species:

---

64. *Id.* at 37,582. "Range" is further interpreted to consist of "the general geographical area within which the species is currently found" and to include "those areas used throughout all or part of the species' life cycle, even if not used on a regular basis." *Id.* at 37,583. Lost historical range, while an important factor affecting the status of a species, is not considered a portion of its SPR. *See id.* Nonetheless, the policy purports to address the issue about historic range considered by the Ninth Circuit in *Defenders of Wildlife v. Norton*, 258 F.3d 1136, 1145 (9th Cir. 2001), and *Tucson Herpetological Society v. Salazar*, 566 F.3d 870, 876 (9th Cir. 2009), explaining that "the fact that historical range has been lost can be highly relevant to the conservation status of the species in its current range" and that the Services "also consider historical range during recovery planning." 79 Fed. Reg. at 37,584.

65. 79 Fed. Reg. at 37,581. *See* Nw. Ecosystem All. v. U.S. Fish & Wildlife Serv., 475 F.3d 1136, 1143 (9th Cir. 2007).

66. 79 Fed. Reg. at 37,581.

67. 16 U.S.C. § 1533(c)(2)(B)(i). *See* 50 C.F.R. § 424.11(e) (providing that a species will be delisted upon the Secretary's finding that the "best scientific and commercial data available" show (1) the species is extinct, (2) the species has recovered to a point where it no longer meets the definition of a threatened or endangered species, (3) post-listing decision information shows that the species does not meet the definition of an endangered species or a threatened species, or (4) post-listing decision information shows that the species does not meet the statutory definition of a species).

68. The status of a species under the ESA may be reclassified from "endangered" to "threatened," or vice versa. 16 U.S.C. § 1533(c)(2)(B)(ii)–(iii).

1. The present or threatened destruction, modification, or curtailment of the species' habitat or range;
2. Overutilization for commercial, recreational, scientific, or educational purposes;
3. Disease or predation;
4. The inadequacy of *existing* regulatory mechanisms; and
5. Other natural or man-made factors affecting the species' continued existence.[69]

Any one of these criteria, alone, might yield a supportable determination by the Secretary,[70] but courts have indicated an increasing willingness to closely examine the Secretary's findings with regard to the listing criteria.[71]

Two cases illustrate that any deviation from the five congressionally articulated listing criteria is improper. In *Biodiversity Legal Foundation v. Babbitt*[72] and *Southwest Center for Biological Diversity v. Babbitt*,[73] the District of Columbia federal district court determined that FWS improperly considered the adequacy of proposed future actions designed to ameliorate impacts on the Alexander Archipelago wolf and the Queen Charlotte goshawk, respectively. Because the ESA's listing criterion D (criterion 4 in the preceding list) specifically allows only consideration of

---

69. 16 U.S.C. § 1533(a)(1)(A)–(E); 50 C.F.R. § 424.11(c)(1)–(5) (emphasis added).

70. 16 U.S.C. § 1533(a)(1) (providing that a listing determination may be based on "any" of the five enumerated factors); 50 C.F.R. § 424.11(c) (determination may be based on "any one or a combination" of the factors). *See* Sw. Ctr. for Biological Diversity v. Babbitt, 215 F.3d 58, 60 (D.C. Cir. 2000) (list if any of five factors "sufficiently implicated"); *see also* Alaska v. Lubchenco, 825 F. Supp. 2d 209, 216–19 (D.D.C. 2011) (same regarding listing of beluga whale); Ctr. for Native Ecosystems v. U.S. Fish & Wildlife Serv., 795 F. Supp. 2d 1199, 1206–07 (D. Colo. 2011) ("individual consideration of each of the five factors does not suffice as the FWS must also consider the impact upon the species of all the factors together"). *But see* Friends of Blackwater v. Salazar, 691 F.3d 428, 436 (D.C. Cir. 2012) (indicating that, where consideration of other factors does not reveal a threat to the species, "inadequacy of existing regulatory mechanisms" is to be evaluated in the context of other listing factors and not independently).

71. *See, e.g.*, Greater Yellowstone Coal., Inc. v. Servheen, 665 F.3d 1015, 1028 (9th Cir. 2011) (rejecting as arbitrary and capricious FWS's explanation why "uncertainty regarding the impact of whitebark pine loss on the grizzly [a threatened species] counsels in favor of delisting now rather than, for example, more study"); N. Spotted Owl v. Hodel, 716 F. Supp. 479 (W.D. Wash. 1988) (holding that FWS had disregarded the expert opinion of its own biologists, and had failed to provide its own or any other expert analysis supporting its decision not to list the spotted owl).

72. 943 F. Supp. 23, 26 (D.D.C. 1996).

73. 939 F. Supp. 49, 52 (D.D.C. 1996).

existing regulatory mechanisms,[74] FWS was directed to reconsider its determinations.

Similarly, the District of Oregon federal district court held that NMFS must rely on "current regulatory structure," rather than on any hope that a state will in fact adopt and implement requisite conservation measures sufficient to protect the species.[75] In holding that NMFS improperly had relied upon plans for future conservation actions as the basis for its decision not to list a particular ESU of coho salmon, the court noted that the whole purpose of listing a species as endangered or threatened is to "compel" the changes needed to save the species.[76]

To promote conservation of unlisted species, as well as ensure consistency with respect to consideration of conservation efforts during the listing process, NMFS and FWS published a policy addressing the issue.[77] This policy provides that the two primary considerations in evaluating conservation efforts are (1) the certainty that the conservation effort will be implemented and (2) the certainty that the conservation effort will be effective.[78] Through this policy, the Services seek to encourage voluntary conservation efforts that sufficiently improve a species' status to make listing unnecessary.[79] When considering the adequacy of existing regulatory mechanisms for the delisting of the Yellowstone grizzly bear (a DPS of the North American grizzly bear), the Ninth Circuit suggested that conservation agreements might be acceptable tools to rely upon, but nonetheless avoided the issue by concluding

---

74. 16 U.S.C. § 1533(a)(1)(D).

75. Or. Nat. Res. Council v. Daley, 6 F. Supp. 2d 1139, 1152 (D. Or. 1998).

76. *Id.* at 1152. *See also* Friends of the Wild Swan, Inc. v. U.S. Fish & Wildlife Serv., 945 F. Supp. 1388, 1398 (D. Or. 1996) (holding that FWS cannot rely upon its own speculations as to the future effects of another agency's management plans to put off listing); Ctr. for Biological Diversity v. Morganweck, 351 F. Supp. 2d 1137 (D. Colo. 2004) (similar decision involving the Yellowstone cutthroat trout). *But see* Ctr. for Biological Diversity v. Haaland, 562 F. Supp. 3d 68, 85 (D. Ariz. 2021) (distinguishing *Oregon Natural Resources Council* and upholding decision to delist where delisting criterion provided: "States and Tribes will ensure regulatory mechanisms are in place to prohibit or regulate human-caused mortality of Mexican wolves in those areas necessary for recovery such that the Service determines that at least 320 Mexican wolves are likely to be maintained in the United States in the absence of Federal ESA protection").

77. Policy for Evaluation of Conservation Efforts When Making Listing Decisions, 68 Fed. Reg. 15,100 (Mar. 28, 2003). *See generally* Hadassah M. Reimer & Murray D. Feldman, *Give PECE a Chance: Evaluating Conservation Programs to Avoid Endangered Species Act Listings*, 56 Rocky Mtn. Min. L. Inst. 21-1 (2010).

78. 68 Fed. Reg. at 15,101.

79. *Id.*

that binding measures incorporated into land management plans (described as legally enforceable) are sufficient.[80]

In addition to providing the considerations upon which a listing decision must be based, Congress also determined what information or data the Secretary may use in making listing determinations. Specifically, Congress directed that the Secretary make listing determinations "solely on the basis of the best scientific and commercial data available."[81]

In the joint listing regulations promulgated by NMFS and FWS, the agencies highlight one particular subset of data that is excluded from the definition of *scientific and commercial data*: economic impact data.[82] In 1982, Congress amended section 4 of the ESA explicitly to overturn the Reagan administration's application, through Executive Order 12,291, of economic impact analysis to ESA listing decisions.[83] In addition to noting that "emotional reasons" and "improper biological data" are not appropriate considerations during the ESA listing process,[84] Congress also "specifically rejected" the application of economic criteria to any determination regarding the status of species.[85] Further, Congress clarified that the term "commercial information" as used in the Act means "trade data"[86] relevant to the trade in a particular species. Section 4's listing criteria, therefore, confirm the conclusion

80. Greater Yellowstone Coal. v. Servheen, 665 F.3d 1015 (9th Cir. 2011). In *Alaska v. Lubchenco*, 825 F. Supp. 2d 209 (D.D.C. 2011), the court upheld the Service's decision to list the beluga whale, affirming the Service's judgment that the existing conservation efforts lacked sufficient certainty in implementation and effectiveness.

81. 16 U.S.C. § 1533(b)(1)(A); 50 C.F.R. § 424.11(b). *See generally* Michael J. Brennan, David E. Roth, Murray D. Feldman & Andrew Robert Greene, *Square Pegs and Round Holes: Application of the "Best Scientific Data Available" Standard in the Endangered Species Act*, 16 Tul. Env't L.J. 387 (2003).

82. 50 C.F.R. § 424.11(b). In 2019, the Services revised the joint listing regulations to remove this prohibition on considering economic impacts. *See* 84 Fed. Reg. 45,020, 45,024 (Aug. 27, 2019). The prohibition was restored in 2024. *See* 89 Fed. Reg. 24,300, 24,305 (Apr. 5, 2024).

83. *See* H.R. Rep. No. 97-567, at 12 (1982), *reprinted in* 1982 U.S.C.C.A.N. 2807, 2820 (explicitly addressing Executive Order No. 12,291).

84. H.R. Rep. No. 97-567, at 22.

85. *Id. See also* H.R. Conf. Rep. No. 97-835, at 20 (1982), *reprinted in* 1982 U.S.C.C.A.N. 2860, 2861 ("economic considerations have no relevance to determination regarding the status of species, and the economic analysis requirements of Executive Order 12291 . . . will not apply to any phase of the listing process"). As discussed in Section 2.8.2, economic considerations are relevant to decisions on designating critical habitat.

86. H.R. Rep. No. 97-567, at 20.

of one commentator who wrote that "the ESA demonstrates a fervent Congressional preference for scientific decision making."[87]

Congress did not illustrate what information satisfies the threshold of "best" scientific or commercial data available. To fill this perceived gap, the Secretaries determined through regulation which sources or types of data will be considered in making any revision of the endangered and threatened species lists.[88] For example, the Secretaries may review scientific or commercial publications, administrative reports, maps or other graphic materials, information received from experts on the subject, and comments from interested parties.[89] In a 1994 Notice of Policy Statement, the Secretaries acknowledged the variability in the quality and reliability of information contained in such a wide variety of sources;[90] the challenge, of course, is to identify and utilize the "best"[91] available information in making listing decisions.

To ensure that listing (and other) decisions under the ESA are based on the best available scientific and commercial data, the Services promulgated guidelines directing agency employees to

1. require that biologists evaluate all scientific and other

---

87. Holly Doremus, *Listing Decisions Under the Endangered Species Act: Why Better Science Isn't Always Better Policy*, 75 Wash. U. L.Q. 1029, 1056 (1997). In addition to ensuring that the Secretary limits review to the congressionally authorized listing criteria, courts also will determine whether the source of data is a lawful one. *See* Ala. Tombigbee Rivers Coal. v. Dep't of the Interior, 26 F.3d 1103 (11th Cir. 1994) (court enjoined use of scientific report prepared in violation of the Federal Advisory Committee Act), *rejected by* Cargill v. United States, 173 F.3d 323 (5th Cir. 1999).

88. 50 C.F.R. § 424.13.

89. *Id.*

90. 59 Fed. Reg. 34,270 (July 1, 1994).

91. The best "available data" does not mean that FWS must have "conclusive evidence," and in one case FWS was found to have acted arbitrarily and capriciously in requiring conclusive evidence to support listing. Defs. of Wildlife v. Babbitt, 958 F. Supp. 670, 680 (D.D.C. 1997). *See also* Sw. Ctr. for Biological Diversity v. Babbitt, 215 F.3d 58, 60 (D.C. Cir. 2000) (best available data requirement "merely prohibits [an agency] from disregarding available scientific evidence that is in some way better than the evidence [it] relies on"); Conner v. Burford, 848 F.2d 1441, 1454 (9th Cir. 1988) (agency must use presently available data); Humane Soc'y of the U.S. v. Pritzker, 75 F. Supp. 3d 1, 12 (D.D.C. 2014) (adopting a reasonable person standard from NMFS regulation rather than requiring conclusive evidence); Alaska v. Lubchenco, 825 F. Supp. 2d 209 (D.D.C. 2011) (noting that data need not be perfect and affording deference to the Service); Ctr. for Biological Diversity v. Lubchenco, 758 F. Supp. 2d 945 (N.D. Cal. 2010) (rejecting challenge to best available data); Oceana v. Evans, 384 F. Supp. 2d 203, 219 (D.D.C. 2005) (certainty not required). *Cf. In re* Polar Bear Endangered Species Act Listing and § 4(d) Rule Litig., 794 F. Supp. 2d 65, 108, 110 (D.D.C. 2011) (FWS not acting arbitrarily and capriciously in relying on best available science).

information that will be used to make any listing decision;
2. gather and impartially evaluate biological, ecological, and other information that disputes official positions taken by FWS or NMFS;
3. ensure that biologists document their evaluation of information that supports or does not support a position being proposed by the agency;
4. use primary and original sources of information as the basis for listing decisions or recommendations;
5. adhere to the time frames or "schedules" established by the ESA; and
6. conduct management-level review of documents developed by the Services to verify and assure the quality of the science used to establish official positions.[92]

In addition, FWS/NMFS policy provides for peer review, by "three appropriate and independent specialists," of pertinent data relating to a species under consideration for listing.[93] The listing agency must include a summary of the opinions of peer reviewers in any final listing rule or withdrawal of a proposed rule.[94]

In the end, the Secretary must base a listing decision on the best available data, even if inconclusive.[95] When the information is inconclusive, the Secretary is simply not legally obliged to find "better data."[96]

---

92. 59 Fed. Reg. 34,271 (July 1, 1994).

93. *Id.* at 34,270.

94. *Id.*

95. "An agency's decision may be based on the best scientific evidence available even if the administrative record contains evidence for and against its decision." Trout Unlimited v. Lohn, 559 F.3d 946, 958 (9th Cir. 2009). *See* League of Wilderness Defs./Blue Mts. Biodiversity Project v. Connaughton, 752 F.3d 755, 764 (9th Cir. 2014) ("so long as an agency considers all relevant data, it may rely on that available evidence even when," as with snorkel surveys to prove absence of bull trout, "it is imperfect, weak, and not necessarily dispositive"); Bldg. Indus. Ass'n of Superior Cal. v. Norton, 247 F.3d 1241, 1246 (D.C. Cir. 2001) (best available not best possible science); Sw. Ctr. for Biological Diversity v. Babbitt, 215 F.3d 58, 61 (D.C. Cir. 2000) (Secretary of the Interior was not obligated to conduct actual counts of Queen Charlotte goshawks, and may base a listing determination on population estimates). *But cf.* Tucson Herpetological Soc'y v. Salazar, 566 F.3d 870 (9th Cir. 2009) (data on population size and trends uncertain, court consequently rejected this evidence as proof of persistence of species throughout its current range).

96. *Sw. Ctr. for Biological Diversity*, 215 F.3d at 61. *See also* Am. Wildlands v. Kempthorne, 530 F.3d 991, 998 (D.C. Cir. 2008) (independent studies not required).

2.4 The Petition Process

This listing process can begin in two ways. The Secretary may initiate the section 4 listing process by publishing a proposed rule in accordance with the informal rulemaking procedures under the Administrative Procedure Act (APA). Alternatively, section 4 provides that any "interested person" may submit a written petition to the Secretary, urging the Secretary to list, delist, or reclassify a species.[97] A petition submitted to the Secretary under section 4 of the ESA is considered a petition for informal rulemaking under section 553(e) of the APA.[98]

Regulations promulgated jointly by NMFS and FWS specify the technical requirements of a valid listing petition,[99] as well as the types of substantive information a petition should contain to justify the petitioned-for action. Among other such requirements, a petition should

- clearly indicate the administrative measure (delisting, listing, etc.) sought;
- give the scientific and common names of the species involved;[100]

97. 16 U.S.C. § 1533(b)(3)(A); 50 C.F.R. § 424.14(a). Any person also may petition the Secretary to designate critical habitat or to revise the boundary of designated critical habitat. 50 C.F.R. § 424.14(a) (permitting petitions requesting any action authorized by 50 C.F.R. § 424.10).

98. 16 U.S.C. § 1533(b)(4). In 1994, after Congress restricted FWS's use of funds to list species, FWS issued a Petition Management Guidance document to address the processing of petitions. 61 Fed. Reg. 36,075 (July 9, 1996). The Ninth Circuit subsequently held that this guidance document conflicted with the Act. Ctr. for Biological Diversity v. Norton, 254 F.3d 833, 836 (9th Cir. 2001). *See also* Colo. River Cutthroat Trout v. Kempthorne, 448 F. Supp. 2d 170, 177 (D.D.C. 2006) (noting that the court in Am. Lands All. v. Norton, 242 F. Supp. 2d 1, 18 (D.D.C. 2003), had issued a nationwide injunction against the guidance). In 2016, the Services issued new rules governing the petition process. 81 Fed. Reg. 66,462 (Sept. 27, 2016). Among other changes, the revised petition process no longer requires the Secretary to acknowledge a properly filed petition within 30 days of receipt. *Id.* at 66,479; 50 C.F.R. § 424.14(f). Additionally, the Ninth Circuit invalidated a different provision of the 2016 rule which required the petitioner to provide notice to affected state fish and wildlife agencies 30 days prior to filing a listing petition. *See* Friends of Animals v. Haaland, 997 F.3d 1010 (9th Cir. 2021) (rejecting 50 C.F.R. § 424.14(b)). But that requirement remains extant in the joint listing regulations. *See* 50 C.F.R. § 424.14(b).

99. A valid petition must be clearly identified as a petition, must be dated, and must include the name, signature, address, telephone number, and the business or other affiliation of the petitioner. 50 C.F.R. § 424.14(c).

100. The petitioner may request that a species or subspecies be listed throughout its range, or the petitioner may explicitly request that a DPS be listed. At least one court has held that the Service must at least address the scope of the petition.

- contain a detailed narrative justification for the recommended measure including, if the petition is to change the listed status of a species, information on current population trends and threats to the species identified in section 4(a)(1);
- for petitions to revise critical habitat, provide descriptions and maps of the relevant areas as well as descriptions of the physical or biological features essential for the conservation of the species; and
- provide citations and supporting documentation in the form of scientific publications, letters, reports, and the like.[101]

This information provides the basis for the Secretary's first substantive decision following receipt of a valid petition, the so-called 90-day finding.

2.4.1 The 90-Day Finding

To the "maximum extent practicable," the Secretary must make a finding within 90 days of the receipt of a valid petition about whether the petition presents "substantial scientific or commercial information" indicating that the petitioned action may be warranted.[102] Not surprisingly, the phrase "maximum extent practicable" has generated vigorous debate. As one court put it,

---

Friends of the Wild Swan v. Babbitt, 12 F. Supp. 2d 1121, 1134 (D. Or. 1997) (holding that FWS arbitrarily and capriciously made a finding with respect to five DPSs of bull trout, when the petitioner had specifically requested that the entire range of bull trout be listed) (citing Sw. Ctr. for Biological Diversity v. Babbitt, 926 F. Supp. 920, 922 (D. Ariz. 1996) (noting that FWS had properly considered the narrow petition to list a subpopulation of the northern goshawk, and that FWS had expanded consideration to the entire species only when listing of the subpopulation was determined not warranted)). *See also* Defs. of Wildlife v. Babbitt, 958 F. Supp. 670, 674–75 (D.D.C. 1997) (after deciding that the petitioned-for listing of DPSs of lynx was not warranted, FWS expanded its consideration to the entire lynx population).

101. 50 C.F.R. § 424.14(c), (d), (e). The petition also may include information on recommended critical habitat. *Id. See generally* FWS, Public Advisory: Information to Consider When Submitting a Petition Under the Endangered Species Act, https://www.fws.gov/sites/default/files/documents/2025-01/endangered-species-act-public-petition-guidance-2025-01-17.pdf.

102. 16 U.S.C. § 1533(b)(3)(A); 50 C.F.R. § 424.14(h)(1). *Substantial information* is defined as "credible scientific or commercial information" that would lead "a reasonable person conducting an impartial scientific review" to "conclude that the action proposed in the petition may be warranted." 50 C.F.R. § 424.14(h)(1)(i).

the phrase is "facially ambiguous," and in fact "the only thing clear about [it] is its ambiguity."[103] The supplemental information accompanying the joint listing regulations states that the 90-day finding may be waived (i.e., determined not to be "practicable") "only if the devotion of staff resources to petition responses would interfere with actions needed to list other species in greater need of protection."[104] The determination of whether other species are in "greater need" of protection must be rooted in a "scientifically based priority system" and may not be based on whether a species is a "higher or lower life form."[105]

If a 90-day finding is practicable, the Secretary must determine either (1) that the petitioned action is not warranted, or (2) that the petitioned action may be warranted.[106] Either finding must be published in the *Federal Register,*[107] and a negative finding is subject to judicial review.[108] A positive finding that the petitioned action may be warranted triggers a new time period and a new decision point: "the 12-month finding."

2.4.2 The 12-Month Finding

Having made a 90-day finding that a petitioned action may be warranted, the Secretary then has 12 months from the original receipt of the petition (not from the date of the 90-day finding) to make the next critical determination in the listing process.[109] During this 12-month period, the Secretary must conduct a "review of the status of the species concerned,"[110] and within the 12-month period must make one of the following findings:

1. That the petitioned action is warranted;
2. That the petitioned action is not warranted; or
3. That the petitioned action is "warranted but precluded," meaning that the promulgation of a rule to implement the

---

103. Biodiversity Legal Found. v. Babbitt, 146 F.3d 1249, 1254 (10th Cir. 1998).

104. 49 Fed. Reg. 38,900, 38,900 (Oct. 1, 1984). *See also* H.R. Conf. Rep. No. 97-835, at 21 (1982), *reprinted in* 1982 U.S.C.C.A.N. 2807, 2862.

105. 1982 U.S.C.C.A.N. at 2862.

106. 16 U.S.C. § 1533(b)(3)(A); 50 C.F.R. § 424.14(h)(1).

107. 16 U.S.C. § 1533(b)(3)(A); 50 C.F.R. § 424.14(h)(1).

108. 16 U.S.C. § 1533(b)(3)(C)(ii).

109. *Id.* § 1533(b)(3)(B); 50 C.F.R. § 424.14(h)(2).

110. 16 U.S.C. § 1533(b)(3)(A); 50 C.F.R. § 424.14(h)(2).

> action is precluded because of other pending proposals to list, delist, or reclassify; and that expeditious progress is being made to list, delist, or reclassify qualified species.[111]

A determination that the petitioned action is not warranted must be published in the *Federal Register,*[112] and is also subject to judicial review.[113] A finding that the action is warranted requires the Secretary promptly to publish in the *Federal Register* a general notice and the complete text of the proposed regulation to implement the petitioned action.[114]

Often the most controversial of the three permissible 12-month findings is the finding that the petitioned action is warranted but precluded. A warranted-but-precluded finding may be supported only if (1) the Secretary has determined that the information available indicated that the petitioned action is warranted; (2) the immediate proposal and timely promulgation of a rule to implement the petitioned action is precluded by other pending listing decisions; and (3) expeditious progress is being made to list, delist, or reclassify other species.[115]

A petition resulting in a warranted-but-precluded finding is considered automatically resubmitted on the anniversary date of the finding;[116] within 12 months of the warranted-but-precluded

---

111. 16 U.S.C. § 1533(b)(3)(B)(i)–(iii); 50 C.F.R. § 424.14(h)(2)(i)–(iii). During the 12-month review period, the Secretary also may publish a "notice of review" soliciting information from interested persons regarding the status of the species involved. 50 C.F.R. § 424.15. Note that agency review of a petition to revise critical habitat largely follows this same process. *Id.* § 424.14(i).

112. 16 U.S.C. § 1533(b)(3)(B)(i); 50 C.F.R. § 424.14(h)(2)(i).

113. 16 U.S.C. § 1533(b)(3)(C)(ii).

114. *Id.* § 1533(b)(3)(B)(ii); 50 C.F.R. § 424.14(h)(2)(ii). See Section 2.5 for a discussion of the rulemaking process.

115. 16 U.S.C. § 1533(b)(3)(B)(iii); 50 C.F.R. § 424.14(h)(2)(iii). *See* Wildwest Inst. v. Kurth, 855 F.3d 995, 1005 (9th Cir. 2017) ("When we are dealing with the potential life or death of an entire species, the legitimacy and efficacy of this system (where we accept that certain listings are 'warranted but precluded') seems to be questionable policy. It means in substance that a species in peril needs some protective standards, but will get none."); Ctr. for Biological Diversity v. Kempthorne, 466 F.3d 1098, 1102 (9th Cir. 2006) ("warranted but precluded" finding can be invoked in narrowly defined circumstances); W. Watersheds Project v. U.S. Fish & Wildlife Serv., 2012 U.S. Dist. LEXIS 13771 (D. Idaho 2012) (upholding "warranted but precluded" finding for sage grouse). The sage grouse remains unlisted, though FWS has twice since proposed its listing, once in response to a court order. *See* Survivors v. Dep't of the Interior, 321 F. Supp. 3d 1011, 1020 (N.D. Cal. 2018) (reviewing history and ordering FWS not to withdraw its proposed sage grouse listing). *See generally* K. Molly Smith, *Abuse of the Warranted but Precluded Designation: A Real or Imagined Purgatory?*, 19 SE. ENV'T L.J. 119 (2010).

116. 16 U.S.C. § 1533(b)(3)(C)(i). *See* Oliver Houck, *The Endangered Species Act and Its Implementation by the U.S. Departments of Interior and Commerce,*

finding, the Secretary must again determine whether the petitioned action is warranted, not warranted, or (once again) warranted but precluded.[117] In 1988, Congress amended the ESA to require the Secretary to develop a system to monitor the status of all species in the warranted-but-precluded category and directed the Secretary to make "prompt use" of the Act's emergency listing authority to prevent significant risks to the well-being of these species.[118]

Still, the Services face a significant backlog of 12-month findings. In 2016, responding to this issue, FWS developed a prioritization methodology[119] that assigns each 12-month finding to one of five priority bins: (1) the species is critically imperiled; (2) strong data are already available about the status of the species; (3) new science is underway that would inform key uncertainties about the status of the species; (4) conservation efforts are in development or underway and likely to address the status of the species; or (5) the available data on the species are limited.[120] Generally, 12-month findings with a lower bin number have a higher priority than 12-month findings with a higher bin number.[121] The Service uses this methodology to schedule the 12-month findings on a National Listing Workplan.[122]

2.5 Informal Rulemaking Necessary for Listing Species

If the Secretary determines to list, delist, or reclassify any species, whether as a result of the petition process just outlined in Section 2.4 or on the Secretary's own initiative, the Secretary must adhere

64 U. Colo. L. Rev. 277, 285–87 (1993) (providing a detailed overview of the use of "warranted but precluded" designations, and describing the 12-month recycling of species listings deemed warranted but precluded as a "black hole for unlisted endangered species").

117. 50 C.F.R. § 424.14(h)(3).

118. 16 U.S.C. § 1533(b)(3)(C)(iii).

119. 81 Fed. Reg. 49,248 (July 27, 2016).

120. *Id.* at 49,249–50. *See* Ctr. for Biological Diversity, Inc. v. Haaland, 2021 WL 4169567 (N.D. Ill. Sept. 14, 2021) (assessing and approving these priorities).

121. 81 Fed. Reg. at 49,249.

122. *Id.* at 49,248.

to the informal rulemaking procedures outlined in the Act.[123] This rulemaking process begins with publication of a proposed rule in the *Federal Register*[124] and culminates between 90 days[125] and 18 months[126] later in a final rule that either implements or withdraws the proposed listing rule.[127] The following discussion outlines the process from a proposed to a final rule.

2.5.1 Proposed Listing Contents

The Secretary initiates the listing rulemaking process by publishing a "general notice" and the "complete text" of the proposed rule in the *Federal Register*.[128] By regulation, the Secretary must include the following information in the notice of the proposed rule:

1. A detailed description of the proposed action;
2. A summary of the data upon which the proposed rule is based;
3. A showing of the relationship of the data to the proposed rule; and
4. A summary of factors affecting the species.[129]

Persons interested in whether a particular future activity may affect or harm a species proposed for listing should pay particular attention to the "summary of factors affecting the species" section in the proposed listing. This information not only provides insight into the potential restrictions on certain activity but also may serve as an early starting point for development of measures necessary to permit certain types of "incidental take."[130] Likewise, as discussed elsewhere in this book, candidate species conservation agreements

---

123. 16 U.S.C. § 1533(b)(4), (5), (6), (8). Except as otherwise provided through these procedural sections, the rulemaking procedures of the Administrative Procedure Act also apply to any listing action. *Id.* § 1533(b)(4).

124. *Id.* § 1533(5)(A)(i); 50 C.F.R. § 424.16(c)(1)(i).

125. 16 U.S.C. § 1533(b)(5)(A) (proposed listing may not become effective until at least 90 days after publication of the proposed rule).

126. *See* Section 2.5.3.

127. 16 U.S.C. § 1533(b)(6)(A)(i); 50 C.F.R. § 426.17(a)(1), (2).

128. 16 U.S.C. § 1533(b)(5)(A)(i); 50 C.F.R. § 424.16(b).

129. 50 C.F.R. § 424.16(b).

130. See Chapter 6, Section 6.2 for a detailed discussion of incidental take permits.

may be fashioned to alleviate the factors negatively affecting the species, and it may be possible in some cases to eliminate the need for listing altogether.[131]

2.5.2 Notice and Comment

In addition to the blanket, constructive notice provided by *Federal Register* publication, the Secretary also must provide "actual notice" of a proposed rule to each relevant "state agency,"[132] as well as to the counties where the species is believed to occur. Any federal agencies, local authorities, and private organizations or individuals "known to be affected" by the rule are entitled to actual notice,[133] as are certain foreign nations[134] and any professional scientific organization the Secretary deems appropriate.[135] Finally, the Secretary must publish a summary of the proposed regulation in a "newspaper of general circulation in each area of the United States in which the species is believed to occur."[136]

After publication of the proposed rule in the *Federal Register,* the Secretary must allow public comment for at least 60 days and may extend or reopen the public comment upon a finding of "good cause."[137] In addition, the Secretary shall "promptly" hold at least one public hearing if any person requests one within 45 days of *Federal Register* publication of the proposed rule.[138]

As mentioned earlier, the procedural requirements of the APA also apply to ESA listing decisions. Therefore, "meaningful" opportunity to participate in the rulemaking process is required, and the opportunity to participate must occur "reasonably close

131. See Chapter 6, Section 6.5 for a detailed discussion of candidate conservation agreements with assurances.

132. 16 U.S.C. § 1533(b)(5)(A)(ii); 50 C.F.R. § 424.16(c)(1)(ii). *State agency* is no longer specifically defined in the listing regulations, but the regulations refer to such bodies as those "responsible for the management and conservation of fish, plant, or wildlife resources within" a state. 50 C.F.R. § 424.14(b), (c)(9).

133. 50 C.F.R. § 424.16(c)(1)(iii).

134. 16 U.S.C. § 1533(b)(5)(B); 50 C.F.R. § 424.16(c)(1)(iv).

135. 16 U.S.C. § 1533(b)(5)(C); 50 C.F.R. § 424.16(c)(1)(v).

136. 16 U.S.C. § 1533(b)(5)(D); 50 C.F.R. § 424.16(c)(1)(vi).

137. 50 C.F.R. § 424.16(c)(2). A criminal defendant's failure to comment on a proposed listing of the red-bellied turtle precluded him from later collaterally attacking the validity of the listing by introducing DNA evidence relative to the listing determination. United States v. Guthrie, 50 F.3d 936 (11th Cir. 1995).

138. 50 C.F.R. § 424.16(c)(3). At least 15 days' prior notice of the place and time of the hearing also must be published in the *Federal Register. Id.*

to the time in which the Secretary makes a decision."[139] The public also must be provided access to new information that is "critical to [the agency's] determination."[140]

2.5.3 The Final Rule

Within 12 months after publication of the proposed listing in the *Federal Register*,[141] the Secretary must take one of the following actions:

1. Publish a final rule implementing the proposed rule;
2. Publish a notice withdrawing the proposed rule, upon a finding that the evidence does not justify the action proposed; or
3. Extend the deadline for a final decision on the proposed listing by no more than six months.[142]

A six-month extension (option 3) is allowed only upon a finding by the Secretary that "there is substantial disagreement regarding the sufficiency or accuracy of the available data relevant to the determination."[143] Before the end of any six-month extension, the Secretary "shall" either publish a final rule or withdraw the proposed rule.[144]

---

139. Idaho Farm Bureau Fed'n v. Babbitt, 58 F.3d 1392, 1404 (9th Cir. 1995).

140. *Id.* at 1403 (citing Cmty. Nutrition Inst. v. Block, 749 F.2d 50, 57–58 (D.C. Cir. 1984)).

141. Congress amended the listing provisions in 1982 to "expedite" the listing process and thus reduced the allowable time frame for final action on a listing proposal from two years to one year from the date of the proposed listing. H.R. Conf. Rep. No. 97-835 (1982), *reprinted in* 1982 U.S.C.C.A.N. 2807, 2860. The Secretary is entitled to a 12-month period to finalize a proposed listing, even though the Secretary may have belatedly published the proposed rule. Or. Nat. Res. Council v. Kantor, 99 F.3d 334, 338 (9th Cir. 1996) (12-month period to finalize rule begins running on date of publication of proposed listing, not on due date of 12-month finding on petition to list).

142. 50 C.F.R. § 424.17(a)(1). For petitions to revise critical habitat, the Secretary can also publish a finding that such revision should not be made. *Id.* § 424.17(a)(1)(ii).

143. 16 U.S.C. § 1533(b)(6)(B)(i); 50 C.F.R. § 424.17(a)(1)(iv).

144. 16 U.S.C. § 1533(b)(6)(B)(iii). The Secretary's duty to finalize or withdraw a proposed rule, within the 12- or 18-month time period specified, has been termed a "mandatory, nondiscretionary duty," excusable only in the face of fiscal impossibility. Env't Def. Ctr. v. Babbitt, 73 F.3d 867, 870 (9th Cir. 1995) (court recognized that Secretary could not legally finalize the proposed listing of the red-legged frog because of congressional rescission of appropriated funds), *on remand*, Env't Def. Ctr. v. Babbitt, CV-95-2867-R (C.D. Cal. May 6, 1996)

In an instance where the Secretary promulgated a final rule well after the end of the 18-month maximum allowable time frame (seven years in that case), the Ninth Circuit held that the statutory time frames were an "impetus to act rather than a prohibition on action taken after the time expires."[145] In that case, *Idaho Farm Bureau,* the court held that the Secretary's much-delayed listing of the Bruneau hot springsnail was not invalid by virtue of its tardiness. Relying on the legislative history of the ESA and amendments that shortened the listing time frames, the Ninth Circuit held that although a citizen suit would have been possible to *compel* a listing decision within the allowable time frame,[146] "failure of an agency to act within a statutory time frame does not bar subsequent agency action absent a specific indication that Congress intended the time frame to serve as a bar."[147] The court noted the general rule that a regulation promulgated in violation of the APA is invalid, but held that the Secretary's rule in this case survived, because in some cases "equity demands the regulation . . . be left in place."[148]

A final rule listing, delisting, or reclassifying a species is not effective until 30 days after it is published in the *Federal Register,* unless otherwise provided for "good cause."[149] The final publication of a rule must contain a detailed description of the action being finalized; a summary of comments and recommendations

(ordering immediate listing of the red-legged frog within two weeks after lifting of the congressional spending moratorium on listing); Sierra Club v. Babbitt, 948 F. Supp. 56 (E.D. Cal. 1996) (lack of funding from Congress excused Secretary's failure to finalize listing of the Peninsular bighorn sheep).

145. Idaho Farm Bureau Fed'n v. Babbitt, 58 F.3d 1392, 1401 (9th Cir. 1985). *See also* Endangered Species Comm. v. Babbitt, 852 F. Supp. 32 (D.D.C. 1994) (violation of Secretary's duty to make supporting data available for public review did not invalidate final listing in light of the equities, the purposes of the ESA, and the relatively small prejudicial effect of lack of availability of data).

146. *Idaho Farm Bureau,* 58 F.3d at 1401.

147. *Id.* at 1400.

148. *Id.* at 1405. Conversely, courts have held that the Services cannot use the ESA's listing deadlines as excuses to withdraw proposed listings. *See* Ctr. for Biological Diversity v. Haaland, 530 F. Supp. 3d 853, 878 (D. Ariz. 2021) ("It would defeat the Congressional intent behind the ESA deadlines if the Service could decline to even consider a listing if it determined that it did not have sufficient time to do so under the ESA deadlines. And it would not be rational to abandon consideration of a listing based on the statutorily-mandated deadlines.").

149. 50 C.F.R. § 424.18(b)(1). A decision to delist a species or reclassify a species from endangered to threatened follows the same process and requires that the Service consider the same five factors as for a listing action. 16 U.S.C. § 1533(a)(1); 50 C.F.R. §§ 424.10, 424.11(c), (d), (e). ESA regulations indicate that a species may be delisted on the basis of the Services' analysis of four factors. *See supra* note 67; 50 C.F.R. § 424.11(e)(1)–(4).

received on the proposed rule; a summary of any data upon which the rule is based and its relationship to the rule; a description of any conservation measures available under the rule; and, if the final rule lists, delists, or reclassifies a species, or revises critical habitat, a summary of factors affecting the species.[150] In addition, NMFS and FWS policy requires the listing agencies to identify, at the time the species is listed, specific activities that will, or will not, likely result in a violation of ESA section 9.[151]

Once a species is listed, the Act directs the Secretary to engage in a status review of that species every five years.[152] The purpose of the review is to determine whether the species ought to be delisted or reclassified. Several district courts have held that this status review is a mandatory, nondiscretionary duty.[153] But the history of the Act does not yet demonstrate that delisting, and to a lesser extent reclassification, is a likely immediate response for many species.[154] For example, in a challenge to the delisting of the Yellowstone grizzly bear, the Ninth Circuit affirmed a lower court's decision vacating the Service's delisting rule, reasoning that the Service failed to explain adequately, in the face of uncertainty and merely parroting adaptive management, why food shortages did not pose a threat to the species.[155]

---

150. 50 C.F.R. § 424.18(a).

151. 59 Fed. Reg. 34,272 (July 1, 1994). In addition, the final listing rule must list a contact with the Service who will assist the public in determining whether particular activities constitute prohibited actions under section 9. *Id.*

152. 16 U.S.C. § 1533(c)(2); 50 C.F.R. § 424.21. *See also* NOAA & U.S. Fish & Wildlife Serv., 5-Year Review Guidance: Procedures for Conducting 5-Year Reviews Under the Endangered Species Act (July 2006).

153. *See, e.g.*, Ctr. for Biological Diversity v. Haaland, 2023 U.S. Dist. LEXIS 139815, at *19 (D.D.C. Aug. 11, 2023) ("[T]he only mandatory aspect of the status review provision is that one must take place every five years."); Fla. Home Builders Ass'n v. Kempthorne, 496 F. Supp. 2d 1330, 1332 (M.D. Fla. 2007). But "[r]egardless of what suggestion is made at the conclusion of the five-year review process, FWS has no corresponding duty to implement the proposal," so the decision on the five-year status review, once made, does not appear to be judicially reviewable. Am. Forest Res. Council v. Hall, 533 F. Supp. 2d 84, 90–94 (D.D.C. 2008).

154. *See* Jonathan H. Adler, *The Leaky Ark: The Failure of Endangered Species Regulation on Private Land, in* Rebuilding the Ark: New Perspectives on Endangered Species Act Reform 6, 10 (Jonathan H. Adler ed., 2011).

155. Greater Yellowstone Coal. v. Servheen, 665 F.3d 1015, 1026 (9th Cir. 2011). In January 2025, FWS issued a proposed rule rejecting Montana's and Wyoming's petitions to delist certain grizzly bear DPSs. *See* 90 Fed. Reg. 4,234 (Jan. 15, 2025). FWS also revised its listing for grizzly bear, complying with a settlement that required FWS to either revise that listing or delist grizzly bear throughout the lower 48 states by January 31, 2026. *Id.*; *see* Save the Yellowstone Grizzly v. U.S. Fish and Wildlife Serv., No. 4:23-cv-00363, ECF No. 26 (D. Idaho Feb. 22, 2024). The proposed rule retains the grizzly's status as a threatened

2.6 Emergency Listings

Since 1982,[156] an important alternative to informal rulemaking has been available to list species, designate critical habitat, or promulgate special rules. The Secretary may promulgate an emergency rule, effective upon publication, implementing one of these actions.[157] The Secretary may invoke these procedures to address "any emergency posing a significant risk to the well-being of any species."[158] The Secretary must merely publish the details of the emergency situation concurrent with publication of the emergency rule in the *Federal Register,*[159] and must give actual notice of the regulation to the state agency in each state where the species is believed to occur.[160] The rule is effective immediately upon publication in the *Federal Register* and remains in effect for up to 240 days.[161]

With respect to candidate species,[162] Congress has directed the Secretary to make "prompt use" of the emergency listing authority.[163] In the only major case construing the ESA's

---

species but revises the geographic extent of the grizzly bear DPS to include "all geographic portions of the currently listed lower-48 entity that contain suitable habitat and where grizzly bears are currently found or are likely to be found in the future as populations recover," an area including "all of Washington and portions of Idaho, Montana, and Wyoming." 90 Fed. Reg. at 4,234. FWS also proposed revising the grizzly bear 4(d) rule to allow additional take of "bears constituting a demonstrable but non-immediate threat to human safety and for bears committing significant depredations to lawfully present livestock, crops, or beehives." *Id.* at 4,254. Chapter 4, Section 4.3 includes further discussion of 4(d) rules for threatened species. The January 2025 proposed rule remains subject to change and may be modified.

156. Act of Oct. 13, 1982, Pub. L. No. 97-304, § 2(a)(2), 96 Stat. 1411, 1414 (codified at 16 U.S.C. § 1533(b)(7)).

157. 16 U.S.C. § 1533(b)(7); 50 C.F.R. § 424.20. Emergency listing is "expressly committed to the Secretary's 'discretion,' the exercise of which is not structured by any statutorily prescribed criteria or procedures." Fund for Animals, Inc. v. Hogan, 428 F.3d 1059, 1064 (D.C. Cir. 2005). Thus, courts have held that the ESA does not create a right to petition for an emergency listing. *See id.*

158. 16 U.S.C. § 1533(b)(7).

159. *Id. See, e.g.*, 87 Fed. Reg. 20,336 (Apr. 7, 2022) (emergency rule listing the Dixie Valley toad as endangered because of imminent development of a geothermal energy project using springs that were toad habitat).

160. 16 U.S.C. § 1533(b)(7).

161. *Id.*; 50 C.F.R. § 424.20(a). During the 240-day effective period of the emergency rule, the Secretary may promulgate a formal listing, using informal rulemaking procedures. 50 C.F.R. § 424.20(a). Alternatively, the Secretary must withdraw the emergency rule if, at any time following promulgation of the rule, he or she determines that substantial evidence does not exist to warrant the rule. *Id.* § 424.20(b).

162. See Section 2.7 for a discussion of candidate species.

163. 16 U.S.C. § 1533(b)(3)(C)(iii).

emergency listing procedures, the D.C. Circuit held that Congress unambiguously directed the Secretary to effect emergency listings "prophylactically," and that Congress intended the Secretary to, in a sense, "shoot first and then ask all of the questions later."[164] The court also held that something less than "substantial evidence" is required to support an emergency listing, and that the ESA contemplates a "somewhat less rigorous process of investigation and explanation for emergency rules than for normal rulemaking."[165] To date, no court has overturned an emergency listing, and whether the emergency listing procedures create an "almost entirely discretionary authority"[166] remains to be seen.

2.7 Candidate Species

Since 1979, the ESA has required the Secretary to establish "a ranking system" to assist in the identification of species that should receive priority review for listing.[167] Congress clarified this mandate in legislative history accompanying the 1982 ESA amendments, noting that species ranking should occur through a "scientifically based priority system," without regard to whether the species is a "higher or lower life form."[168] This candidate list also serves to stimulate public and private efforts to engage in voluntary conservation efforts that might avoid the need to list the species.

In 1983, FWS published notice of its Listing Priority Guidelines,[169] establishing three criteria for prioritizing listing actions: (1) the magnitude of the threat facing the species, (2) the immediacy of the threat facing the species, and (3) the taxonomic distinctiveness of the species.[170] The 1983 guidelines establish priorities *among species,* and more current guidance promulgated

164. City of Las Vegas v. Lujan, 891 F.2d 927, 932–33 (D.C. Cir. 1989).
165. *Id.* at 932.
166. *See* Houck, *supra* note 116, at 296 n.129.
167. Act of Dec. 28, 1979, Pub. L. No. 96-159, § 3(6), 93 Stat. 1225–1226 (1979) (codified at 16 U.S.C. § 1533(h)(3)).
168. H.R. Conf. Rep. No. 835, at 21, *reprinted in* 1982 U.S.C.C.A.N. 2860, 2862.
169. 48 Fed. Reg. 43,098 (Sept. 21, 1983).
170. *Id.* at 43,103.

by FWS establishes additional criteria to assign priorities to different *types* of listing actions,[171] as follows:

1. Highest priority is for processing emergency listing rules;
2. Second priority is for processing final determinations on proposed listings;
3. Third priority is for making determinations regarding current candidate species (either proposing to list a candidate species, or removing the species from the candidate list altogether); and
4. Fourth priority is to process administrative findings on petitions to list or reclassify species.[172]

The listing priority guidelines are intended to serve only as a "guide."[173] At least one court rejected the claim that listing priority guidance violates the ESA section 4 listing criteria,[174] and courts in particular cases have implicitly recognized the validity of the Secretary's application of the guidelines.[175]

With the number of species being added as candidates for listing by FWS, the listing process has become hindered by a lack of sufficient agency resources. This in turn has led to litigation, and eventual court decrees or settlements establishing a process for how FWS will respond to outstanding petitions to list a species

---

171. 64 Fed. Reg. 57,114 (Dec. 10, 1999). In 1996, the Service eliminated maintaining a separate list for category 2 and category 3 species. 61 Fed. Reg. 64,481 (Dec. 5, 1996).

172. 64 Fed. Reg. at 57,118–19. This listing priority guidance eliminates critical habitat designation from the guidance altogether. *Id.* at 57,115.

173. *See* 48 Fed. Reg. 43,098 (Sept. 21, 1983) (stating that "[t]he priority systems presented must be viewed as guides and should not be looked upon as inflexible frameworks for determining resource allocations"). In accord with this view, the Ninth Circuit has held that the Services may consider factors other than a species' listing priority number (LPN) in prioritizing listing. *See* Wildwest Inst. v. Kurth, 855 F.3d 995, 1007 (9th Cir. 2017) (FWS's "decision to list other species with the same or higher LPNs before the whitebark pine did not render its 'warranted but precluded' finding for the whitebark pine arbitrary and capricious, an abuse of discretion, or otherwise not in accordance with the law").

174. Biodiversity Legal Found. v. Babbitt, 146 F.3d 1249, 1252–53 (10th Cir. 1998) (addressing 1997 Listing Priority Guidance, 61 Fed. Reg. 64,475–81 (Dec. 5, 1996)).

175. Carlton v. Babbitt, 900 F. Supp. 526, 536 (D.D.C. 1995) (holding that FWS had "provided adequate support for their application of the guidelines to rank the Cabinet/Yaak Grizzly"). *But see* Forest Guardians v. Babbitt, 174 F.3d 1178 (10th Cir. 1999), *amending* 164 F.3d 1261 (10th Cir. 1998) (when faced with a nondiscretionary duty to designate critical habitat, the Secretary must do so "without regard to his preferred priorities").

as well as render a decision on whether to propose a species for listing. In 2011, petitions to list over 1,200 species were pending, and FWS had a backlog of numerous species on its candidate list. That year, in a significant settlement, FWS agreed to make initial or final decisions for hundreds of species in accordance with a schedule established in a pair of settlement agreements.[176] Still, petitions submitted as early as 1996 remain outstanding in FWS's docket. As of spring 2025, there are more than 500 species awaiting status review and consideration for listing under the ESA.[177] In January 2025, FWS entered into another settlement requiring it to abide by a schedule for making listing decisions on 76 species.[178]

2.8 Critical Habitat

Habitat protection undoubtedly is critical to the recovery and survival of vulnerable species, and the ESA contains several provisions designed to address species' habitat needs. One of those provisions is the designation of critical habitat. For many years, the designation of critical habitat received little attention, and indeed FWS had suggested that "[f]or almost all species, the Section 7 critical habitat adverse modification and jeopardy standards are the same, resulting in an unnecessary duplicative and expensive regulatory process."[179] But through litigation and continued attention to the critical habitat program, the section 4 critical habitat designation process has become a prominent component of the Act.

At the time a species is listed, a listing agency "shall [to the] maximum extent prudent and determinable"[180] designate any habitat of the species that is considered to be critical habitat.[181]

176. *In re* Endangered Species Act Section 4 Deadline Litig., 277 F.R.D. 1, 80 Fed. R. Serv. 3d 663 (MDL No. 2165, D.D.C. Sept. 9, 2011).

177. FWS, National Listing Work Plan for Fiscal Year 2024–2028 (May 2024).

178. Stipulated Settlement Agreement, ECF 72-1, Center for Biological Diversity v. Haaland, No. 1:20-cv-00573-EGS (D.D.C. Jan. 15, 2025).

179. 64 Fed. Reg. 57,114, 57,118 (Mar. 12, 1999). *Cf.* 77 Fed. Reg. 51,503, 51,504 (Aug. 24, 2012) (noting benefits of designation).

180. Forest Guardians v. Babbitt, 174 F.3d 1178, 1192 (10th Cir. 1999), *amending* Forest Guardians v. Babbitt, 164 F.3d 1261 (10th Cir. 1998) (holding that designation of critical habitat is nondiscretionary and that the Secretary's duty to act cannot be excused by a "generalized claim of inadequate resources").

181. 16 U.S.C. § 1533(a)(3); 50 C.F.R. § 424.12(a).

Critical habitat designations must be based on "the best scientific data available and after taking into consideration the economic impact, the impact on national security, and any other relevant impact" of the designation.[182] This is the singular instance in the ESA where the Secretary is specifically charged with considering the economic impact of a decision under the Act.[183] Also, if the benefits of excluding an area from designation outweigh the benefits of inclusion, an area may be excluded as long as the exclusion does not result in the species' extinction.[184] Whether or how the National Environmental Policy Act (NEPA) might apply to designations remains an open question, with courts reaching differing conclusions.[185]

The ESA defines *critical habitat* as the specific areas containing features essential to the conservation of the species, and that may require "special management considerations or protection."[186] Critical habitat is generally limited to the geographical area occupied by the species at the time it is listed, unless areas outside the occupied geographical area are "essential for the conservation of the species."[187] Considering critical habitat for the dusky

182. 16 U.S.C. § 1533(b)(2); 50 C.F.R. § 424.12(a). The Secretary has claimed broad discretion to determine what other impacts (other than economic and national security) are relevant. *See* Solicitor's Opinion M-37016, The Secretary's Authority to Exclude Areas from Critical Habitat Designation Under Section 4(b)(2) of the Endangered Species Act (Oct. 3, 2008).

183. *See* Bennett v. Spear, 520 U.S. 154, 172 (1997).

184. 16 U.S.C. § 1533(b)(2).

185. *Compare* Douglas Cnty. v. Babbitt, 48 F.3d 1495 (9th Cir. 1996) (NEPA does not apply to critical habitat designations), *with* Catron Cnty. Bd. of Comm'rs v. U.S. Fish & Wildlife Serv., 75 F.3d 1429 (10th Cir. 1996) (NEPA applies to critical habitat designations), *and* Cape Hatteras Access Pres. All. v. U.S. Dep't of the Interior, 344 F. Supp. 2d 108 (D.D.C. 2004) (NEPA applies to critical habitat designations). *But see* Otay Mesa Prop., L.P. v. Dep't of the Interior, 144 F. Supp. 3d 35, 69 (D.D.C. 2015) (summarizing debate and adopting position of Ninth Circuit that NEPA does not apply to critical habitat designations).

186. 16 U.S.C. § 1532(5)(A)(i).

187. *Id.* § 1532(5)(A)(ii). *See* Otay Mesa Prop., L.P. v. U.S. Dep't of the Interior, 646 F.3d 914 (9th Cir. 2011) (holding insufficient evidence supporting decision that area was "occupied" by the species). *Cf.* Home Builders Ass'n v. U.S. Fish & Wildlife Serv., 660 F.3d 983, 990 (9th Cir. 2010) ("There is no requirement that every area be classified as" occupied or unoccupied.); *see also* Ariz. Cattle Growers' Ass'n v. Salazar, 606 F.3d 1160, 1163 (9th Cir. 2010) (whether a species "occupies" an area is contextual and fact dependent, and a species can occupy an area even if the area merely contains some individuals where those individuals use the area with some frequency).The Ninth Circuit currently suggests that the standard for designating unoccupied habitat is higher than that for occupied habitat. Ctr. for Biological Diversity v. United States Fish & Wildlife Serv., 67 F.4th 1027, 1035 (9th Cir. 2023) ("the standard for designating unoccupied critical habitat is 'more demanding' than the standard for designating occupied critical habitat"; to meet the "essential" requirement, designation of critical habitat must

gopher frog in southern Mississippi, the Supreme Court has held that areas designated as critical habitat must be places where the species can currently survive; they cannot be places that could serve as habitat only with modification.[188]

Designation is a context-dependent inquiry; in making the determination as to what areas are essential to conservation of the species or which require special management considerations, the Secretary may consider "the appropriate quality, quantity, and spatial and temporal arrangements" of the critical habitat features "in the context of the life history, status, and conservation needs of the species."[189] The Secretary must consider essential "physical or biological features" such as roost sites, nesting grounds, spawning sites, feeding sites, wetlands, vegetation, soil type, and water quantity or quality.[190] Generally, such features include

- space;
- food, water, air, light, minerals, other nutritional or physiological requirements;
- cover or shelter;
- sites for breeding, reproduction, or rearing of offspring;
- habitats protected from disturbance or representative of the historic geographical distribution and ecological distribution of the species.

Once determined, the critical habitat must be delineated on a map,[191] and critical habitat may not be designated within foreign

---

be "necessary" or "indispensable" to survival or recovery, and not merely "beneficial" to or capable of "promoting" survival or recovery). But federal regulations no longer require the Services to consider unoccupied areas essential only where a critical habitat designation limited to occupied areas would be inadequate to ensure the conservation of the species. *Compare* 50 C.F.R. § 424.12(b)(2) *with* 84 Fed. Reg. 45,020, 45,053 (Aug. 27, 2019).

188. Weyerhaeuser Co. v. U.S. Fish & Wildlife Serv., 586 U.S. 9 (2018). Following *Weyerhaeuser*, the Services codified a new definition of "habitat": "For the purposes of designating critical habitat only, habitat is the abiotic and biotic setting that currently or periodically contains the resources and conditions necessary to support one or more life processes of a species." *See* 85 Fed. Reg. 81,411 (Dec. 16, 2020). A 2022 rulemaking rescinded that definition. *See* 87 Fed. Reg. 37,757 (June 24, 2022).

189. 50 C.F.R. § 424.12(b)(1)(ii).

190. *Id.* The Services previously referred to these features as "primary constituent elements."

191. *Id.* §§ 424.12(c), 424.18(a)(1).

countries.[192] The Services have now promulgated a series of rules that remove the preexisting requirement to publish in the Code of Federal Regulations a textual description of the boundaries for any designated critical habitat.[193]

2.8.1 Prudent and Determinable

Once a species has been listed as endangered or threatened, the Secretary "shall" designate critical habitat "to the maximum extent prudent or practicable."[194] NMFS and FWS jointly have defined the terms *prudent* and *determinable*. The Secretary may determine that designation of critical habitat is not "prudent," "based on the best scientific data available, after taking into consideration the probable economic, national security, and other relevant impacts" of the decision, in situations like the following:

1. The species is threatened by taking or other human activity, and identification of critical habitat can be expected to increase the degree of such threat to the species.
2. The present or possible future threat to the species' habitat or range is not a threat to the species.
3. For species occurring primarily outside the United States, areas within the United States provide no more than negligible conservation value.
4. No areas meet the definition of critical habitat.[195]

---

192. *Id.* § 424.12(g). *See also* Pub. L. No. 108-136, § 318(a), 117 Stat. 1433 (2003) (codified at 16 U.S.C. § 1533(a)(3)(B)(i) (re-designation of Department of Defense lands and adding consideration of national security)).

193. This change began with the rulemaking published at 77 Fed. Reg. 25,611 (May 1, 2012) and concluded with the rulemaking published at 86 Fed. Reg. 38,573 (July 22, 2021). The changes together mean that maps rather than textual descriptions establish the official boundaries of designated critical habitat. 86 Fed. Reg. at 38,573. This change does not affect the designation process.

194. 16 U.S.C. § 1533(a)(3); Sierra Club v. U.S. Fish & Wildlife Serv., 245 F.3d 434, 438 (5th Cir. 2001).

195. 50 C.F.R. § 424.12(a)(1). The current regulations expand on earlier regulations, which permitted a determination of imprudence only where (1) the species is threatened by a taking or other human activity, or (2) designation of critical habitat would not benefit the species. *See* NRDC, Inc. v. United States Fish & Wildlife Serv., 719 F. Supp. 3d 1, 21 (D.D.C. 2023) (no reasoned explanation for failure to designate).

In a 2008 Solicitor's Opinion, the Department of the Interior further elaborated on FWS's authority to exclude areas from critical habitat designation.[196]

Likewise, critical habitat is not "determinable" when one or both of the following situations exists:

1. Information sufficient to perform required analyses is lacking.
2. The biological needs of the species are not sufficiently well known to permit identification of an area as critical habitat.[197]

The agencies initially sought to avoid several critical habitat designations by concluding that the designation would not be prudent, but the trend in the case law suggests that today any attempt to avoid a designation under the not-prudent rationale will be scrutinized carefully by a court.[198]

2.8.2 Economic Analysis

The designation of critical habitat is one unique area of the Act where Congress expressly contemplated the consideration of

196. Solicitor's Opinion M-37016, The Secretary's Authority to Exclude Areas from Critical Habitat Designation Under Section 4(b)(2) of the Endangered Species Act (Oct. 3, 2008).

197. 50 C.F.R. § 424.12(a)(2).

198. *See Sierra Club*, 245 F.3d 434, 436, 443, 447 (5th Cir. 2001) (invalidating decision not to designate habitat for gulf sturgeon); NRDC v. U.S. Dep't of the Interior, 1133 F.3d 1121, 1125–26 (9th Cir. 1997) (FWS's refusal to designate critical habitat for the coastal California gnatcatcher was not supported, and FWS's conclusory statements with regard to increased threats associated with such designation were unsupported by the record. Likewise, the court found unpersuasive the Service's finding that designation of critical habitat on private lands would not benefit the species, nor could critical habitat designation be avoided because another program provided superior protections.); Conservation Council for Haw. v. Babbitt, 2 F. Supp. 2d 1280 (D. Haw. 1998) (Service failed to properly consider evidence concerning the benefit and threat of designating critical habitat; the fact that listed plants were located on private land was insufficient basis for failure to designate critical habitat.). A similar hard look might occur when the Service determines that designation is not determinable. *See* Forest Guardians v. Babbitt, 164 F.3d 1261, *amended opinion at* 174 F.3d 1178 (10th Cir. 1998); Ctr. for Biological Diversity v. Evans, 2005 WL 1514102 (N.D. Cal. June 14, 2005) (northern right whale). Courts have yet to grapple with the expanded list of considerations that might make critical habitat designation imprudent, but they have remained consistently skeptical of determinations that designation is imprudent. *See, e.g., NDRC*, 719 F. Supp. 3d at 21 (compelling designation of critical habitat for the endangered rusty patch bumblebee).

economic impacts.[199] But precisely how that should occur was left open to agency implementation. The Office of Management and Budget has suggested that the proper methodology requires comparing the current state of affairs, a baseline, with a post-designation state of affairs. Another methodology, dubbed the "co-extensive" approach, "would take into account all of the economic impact of the [designation], regardless of whether those impacts are caused co-extensively by any other agency action (such as listing) and even if those impacts would remain in the absence of the [designation]."[200] The difference between these competing approaches surfaced because of an argument that the listing of the species itself and the accompanying no-jeopardy standard imposes the same economic consequences as a designation. The Ninth Circuit has endorsed FWS's use of a baseline analysis.[201] In new regulations, the Services has done the same, requiring that "[p]rior to finalizing the designation of critical habitat," the Secretary "consider the probable economic, national security, and other relevant impacts of the designation upon proposed or ongoing activities" and qualitatively or quantitatively "compare the impacts with and without the designation."[202] Still, because of the differing approaches, the Service generally discloses in its critical habitat economic analysis both the baseline economic impacts of protections afforded listed species absent critical habitat designation and the estimated economic impacts specific to critical habitat designation.[203]

199. *See* H.R. Rep. No. 97-567, at 12 (1982), *reprinted in* 1982 U.S.C.C.A.N. 2807, 2812 (explaining that the economic analysis required for critical habitat designation offers some "counterpoint" to the listing process); *see also* 50 C.F.R. § 424.19 (regulation governing impact analysis and exclusions from critical habitat).

200. N.M. Cattle Growers Ass'n v. U.S. Fish & Wildlife Serv., 248 F.3d 1277, 1283 (10th Cir. 2001).

201. Ariz. Cattle Growers Ass'n v. Salazar, 606 F.3d 1160, 1172–74 (9th Cir. 2010); Home Builders Ass'n v. U.S. Fish & Wildlife Serv., 616 F.3d 983, 992–93 (9th Cir. 2010).

202. 50 C.F.R. § 424.19(b).

203. *See, e.g.*, 86 Fed. Reg. 34,979, 34,990 (July 1, 2021) (critical habitat for Suwannee moccasinshell); 77 Fed. Reg. 71,042, 71,076 (Nov. 28, 2012) (critical habitat for the southern Selkirk Mountains population of woodland caribou). *See generally* Sheila Baynes, *Cost Consideration and the Endangered Species Act*, 90 N.Y.U. L. Rev. 961 (2015).

2.8.3 Critical Habitat Designation and Revision

As already discussed, critical habitat designation is an action that should occur concurrently with listing. If, however, the Secretary does not designate critical habitat concurrent with listing a species, the Secretary has 12 months within which to designate critical habitat to the maximum extent prudent.[204] Assuming the Secretary had previously determined not to designate critical habitat for a listed species, regulations implementing ESA section 4 allow any party to petition for critical habitat designation.[205] Such petitions are reviewed "in accordance with the Administrative Procedure Act," and the Secretary must "take appropriate action" in response.[206]

Likewise, a person may submit a petition seeking to have designated critical habitat revised, and the Secretary must make a finding, within 90 days of receiving the petition, as to whether the revision may be warranted.[207] Within 12 months of a 90-day finding that the petitioned revision may be warranted, the Secretary must publish notice of "how he intends to proceed."[208]

204. 16 U.S.C. § 1533(b)(6)(C)(ii); 50 C.F.R. § 424.17(b)(2).

205. 50 C.F.R. § 424.10 (permitting the Secretary to "designate critical habitat"); *id.* § 424.14(a) ("Any interested person may submit a written petition to the Services requesting that one of the actions described in § 424.10 be taken for a species.").

206. 50 C.F.R. § 424.14(j). The lack of specificity with regard to the Secretary's obligation upon receipt of a petition to designate critical habitat is probably justified in light of the fact that the Secretary would have, by necessity, already made a determination (either upon listing, or within 12 months thereafter) that critical habitat designation was not prudent and/or determinable. *See also* Sierra Club v. U.S. Fish & Wildlife Serv., 930 F. Supp. 2d 198, 210 (D.D.C. 2013) (FWS's "12-month determination in response to a petition to revise critical habitat for a species listed under the Endangered Species Act is unreviewable" by a court).

207. 16 U.S.C. § 1533(b)(3)(D); 50 C.F.R. § 424.14(i).

208. 16 U.S.C. § 1533(b)(3)(D)(ii); 50 C.F.R. § 424.14(i)(2). Options available include publication of a proposed rule designating critical habitat; finding that a statutory factor, such as economic impact or national security, overrides the need for species protection; or a determination that designation of critical habitat is not prudent or determinable. *See* Ctr. for Biological Diversity v. Evans, 2005 WL 1514102 (N.D. Cal. June 14, 2005). For an example of a critical habitat revision petition decision, see 64 Fed. Reg. 57,399 (Oct. 25, 1999) (NMFS decision to exclude certain areas from designated critical habitat for threatened Snake River spring/summer chinook salmon). *See also* Murray D. Feldman & Michael J. Brennan, *The Growing Importance of Critical Habitat for Species Conservation*, 16 NAT. RES. & ENV'T 88, 93, 134 (2001).

3 Conservation: Section 7(a)(1) and Recovery Planning

3.1 Overview

As the Endangered Species Act's (ESA) most tangible manifestation, the endangered and threatened species list itself may appear to be the goal of the Act. Others may believe that the ESA creates a list of endangered species to further the aim of allowing government regulation of activities affecting species on the list. Professor Houck addresses such perceptions as follows:

> It is not the Act's goal to catalogue [species], to identify their habitats, to review and alter jeopardizing activities, to give developers a difficult time, or perpetuate precarious populations on the brink of extinction. These aspects of the Act are but means to the end of "conserving" these species.[1]

As illustrated in the table at the end of this chapter, the goal of conservation transcends nearly every ESA statutory section. It corresponds with the ESA's ultimate goal to recover imperiled species. The conservation mandate in section 7(a)(1), consequently, relates to efforts to recover a listed species.[2]

This chapter discusses two of the mechanisms through which the ESA's conservation mandate may be fulfilled: section 7(a)(1) conservation obligations and section 4(f) recovery plans.

---

1. Oliver A. Houck, *The Endangered Species Act and Its Implementation by the U.S. Departments of Interior and Commerce,* 64 U. Colo. L. Rev. 277, 344 (1993).
2. *See* 16 U.S.C. § 1532.

3.2 Section 7(a)(1) Conservation Obligations

ESA section 7(a)(1) directs the Secretaries of the Interior and Commerce to review programs administered by their respective departments and to utilize such programs in furtherance of the purposes of the Act.[3] In addition, section 7(a)(1) obligates "all other federal agencies," in consultation with the Secretary of the Interior or Commerce (as appropriate), to "utilize their authorities in furtherance of the purposes of the ESA . . . by carrying out programs for the conservation of [listed species]."[4] Separate and distinct from the ESA section 7(a)(2) consultation and avoidance of jeopardy requirements,[5] section 7(a)(1) suggests independent obligations applicable to all federal agencies. Unfortunately, this obligation is not well understood.[6] Section 7(a)(1) and (a)(2) were combined in the ESA's original language, and they only became separated into two provisions (and arguably into independent obligations) after *Tennessee Valley Authority v. Hill*.[7] In fact, the United States occasionally argues that "section 7(a)(1) of the ESA does not require agencies to develop species-specific and location-specific programs for the conservation of listed species."[8] The breadth of section 7(a)(1), therefore, has been established mostly through

---

3. 16 U.S.C. § 1536(a)(1). For a very thorough discussion of ESA section 7(a)(1), see J.B. Ruhl, *Section 7(a)(1) of the "New" Endangered Species Act: Rediscovering and Redefining the Untapped Power of Federal Agencies' Duty to Conserve Species*, 25 Env't L. 1107 (1995).

4. 16 U.S.C. § 1536(a)(1).

5. *Id.* § 1536(a)(2). See Chapter 5 for a detailed discussion of ESA section 7(a)(2).

6. Joint regulations promulgated by NMFS and FWS to implement ESA's section 7(a)(2) consultation requirements address the 7(a)(1) conservation mandate peripherally and in the narrow context of federal action likely to adversely affect the listed species. See 50 C.F.R. § 402.14(g)(6) (providing that NMFS or FWS will formulate "discretionary conservation recommendations" that federal action agencies may implement to reduce or mitigate the impacts of federal actions).

7. *See* Pub. L. No. 93-205, 87 Stat. 892 (1973). Congress redesignated this provision as section 7(a) in 1978 and broke up the sentence with a period. Pub. L. No. 95-632, 92 Stat. 3752 (1978). As the Act was subsequently amended, the provisions then became separated. Pub. L. No. 96-159, 93 Stat. 1226 (1979); Pub. L. No. 97-304, 96 Stat. 1417, 1426 (1982) (as amended).

8. Fla. Key Deer v. Paulison, 522 F.3d 1333, 1141 (11th Cir. 2008). But, for instance, FWS states that federal agencies "have an affirmative responsibility for species conservation under section 7(a)(1)." 69 Fed. Reg. 24,084, 24,085 (May 3, 2004).

litigation,[9] as well as more recently through guidance from the Department of the Interior's Solicitor's Office.[10]

Whether section 7(a)(1) obligations are mandatory or voluntary has been considered by a few courts, which have generally concluded that the provision creates some mandatory, affirmative obligation on agencies.[11] Courts originally addressed section 7(a)(1) only in the context of agencies acting to carry out other "primary" agency missions; no court had established that an agency must initiate a separate program for the purpose of conserving listed species.[12] For example, courts interpreted section 7(a)(1) to authorize an agency to refuse to execute a new contract,[13] require an agency to implement alternative courses of action when significant conservation benefits may be achieved consistent with an agency's primary mission,[14] require an agency to show that it has minimized harm to listed species, "consistent with other obligations" of the agency,[15] and require an agency at least to consider section 7(a)(1) when undertaking other activities.[16]

In 1998, the Fifth Circuit seemingly expanded the section 7(a)(1) ESA conservation obligation. In *Sierra Club v. Glickman,* the court first affirmed that section 7(a)(1) creates an "affirmative duty on each federal agency to conserve each of the species listed

9. *See* Ruhl, *supra* note 3, at 1125.

10. Sarah Krakoff et al., to Martha Williams, U.S. Fish and Wildlife Service, Memorandum, Federal Agency Obligations under Section 7(a)(1) of the Endangered Species Act (Feb. 6, 2024) [hereinafter Krakoff Mem.].

11. *See, e.g.,* Tenn. Valley Auth. v. Hill, 437 U.S. 153, 180–85 (1978) (discussing the general conservation mandate of the ESA); Friends of the Wild Swan, Inc. v. U.S. Fish and Wildlife Serv., 945 F. Supp. 1388, 1399 (D. Or. 1996) (suggesting "comprehensive" duty to conserve species); Defs. of Wildlife v. Andrus, 428 F. Supp. 167, 170 (D.D.C. 1977) (FWS's duck-hunting regulation did not adequately address the agency's "affirmative duty" at least to minimize inadvertent killing of listed waterfowl); Pyramid Lake Paiute Tribe of Indians v. U.S. Dep't of Navy, 898 F.2d 1410, 1416–17 (9th Cir. 1990) (recognizing that agencies have "affirmative obligations" under section 7(a)(1)); Connor v. Andrus, 453 F. Supp. 1037, 1041 (W.D. Tex. 1978) (FWS has an "affirmative duty" under section 7(a)(1) to bring listed species to the point where they may be removed from the list).

12. *See generally* Ruhl, *supra* note 3, at 1135.

13. Carson-Truckee Water Conservancy Dist. v. Clark, 741 F.2d 257, 260–61 (9th Cir. 1984) (upholding Bureau of Reclamation decision to refuse a request for a new water contract, even though bureau possessed the discretion to execute such a contract).

14. *Pyramid Lake,* 898 F.2d at 1417.

15. *Defs. of Wildlife,* 428 F. Supp. at 170.

16. Fla. Key Deer v. Stickney, 864 F. Supp. 1222 (S.D. Fla. 1994).

pursuant to [the ESA]."[17] The court then went further than prior decisions by requiring that the U.S. Department of Agriculture (USDA) "develop" or "adopt" conservation programs for listed species.[18]

Subsequent lower court opinions reflect a slightly different view of section 7(a)(1) than *Glickman.* In *Strahan v. Linnon*[19] and *Hawksbill Sea Turtle v. FEMA,*[20] the district courts of Massachusetts and the Virgin Islands, respectively, held that ESA section 7(a)(1) conservation plans are "voluntary measures."[21] Unlike the situation in *Glickman,* however, the defendant agency in each case had taken at least some active steps to fulfill its section 7(a)(1) obligations. The dispositive issue, therefore, was not whether an agency must do something to conserve species, but rather whether what it had done was sufficient. In both cases, the courts concluded that in light of the plaintiffs' failure to specify particular alternative conservation measures that the agency should have implemented, the court would not intrude upon the agency's discretion as to the choice of measures.[22]

Both *Strahan* and *Hawksbill Sea Turtle* suggest that some courts may be reluctant to set aside an agency's affirmative efforts to implement section 7(a)(1). Instead, it appears that courts are inclined to emphasize that federal agencies enjoy considerable discretion under section 7(a)(1) and are reluctant to require that federal agencies develop species-specific conservation programs under section 7(a)(1).[23] Even in *Glickman,* had the USDA implemented measures specifically designed to address species dependent upon the Edwards Aquifer, the result might have been different. As a general rule, as long as an agency's choice

17. 156 F.3d 606, 616 (5th Cir. 1998) (USDA ordered to consult with FWS to develop programs for the conservation of species dependent upon the Edwards Aquifer in central Texas).

18. *Id.* at 618 (noting that mere "incidental benefits" to listed species, arising from other agency programs, are insufficient to fulfill an agency's section 7(a)(1) obligation).

19. 967 F. Supp. 581 (D. Mass. 1997).

20. 11 F. Supp. 2d 529 (D.V.I. 1998).

21. *Strahan,* 967 F. Supp. at 596; *Hawksbill Sea Turtle,* 11 F. Supp. 2d at 542–43.

22. *Strahan,* 967 F. Supp. at 595–96; *Hawksbill Sea Turtle,* 11 F. Supp. 2d at 543.

23. Defs. of Wildlife v. U.S. Fish & Wildlife Serv., 797 F. Supp. 2d 949 (D. Ariz. 2011); Defs. of Wildlife v. U.S. Fish & Wildlife Serv., 354 F. Supp. 2d 1156, 1174 (Or. 2005); Defs. of Wildlife v. Babbitt, 130 F. Supp. 2d 121, 135 (D.C. 2001).

of conservation measures is rational[24] and within the agency's authority to implement,[25] and arguably nothing suggests that some other alternative would provide greater conservation benefits while equally satisfying the agency's primary mission and objectives,[26] then the cases allow agencies considerable discretion when deciding how to fulfill their section 7(a)(1) obligations.

The ambiguity surrounding the nature of the section 7(a)(1) obligation prompted the Fish and Wildlife Service (FWS) to request guidance from the Solicitor's Office. And on February 6, 2024, the Solicitor's Office responded with a memorandum titled "Federal Agency Obligations Under Section 7(a)(1) of the Endangered Species Act." The memorandum explains that the section 7(a)(1) obligation begins when the species is listed, and it does not require an agency action such as with the trigger for section 7(a)(2). But its implementation occurs within an agency's relevant jurisdiction or authority. While the details for implementation are discretionary, the obligation for some conservation program is nondiscretionary and it must be meaningful (not merely have "insignificant effects"). The memorandum provides that section 7(a)(1) "requires Federal agencies to develop programs for the conservation of specific species, and to exercise their authorities broadly to achieve the conservation goals of the ESA," although "[w]ithin that clear mandate . . . [they] have discretion about what actions and measures to take."[27]

3.3 Recovery Plans

Although recovery plan development was slow in maturing during the ESA's formative years, many now believe that the recovery planning process is critical for the success of the Act and the

---

24. Connor v. Andrus, 453 F. Supp. 1037, 1041 (W.D. Tex. 1978) (FWS regulation designed to conserve Mexican duck was rejected because record did not support FWS's determination that the regulation would benefit the duck).

25. Platte River Whooping Crane Critical Habitat Maint. Trust v. FERC, 962 F.2d 27, 34 (D.C. Cir. 1992) (holding that section 7(a)(1) "does not expand the powers conferred on an agency by its enabling act").

26. *See, e.g.*, Pyramid Lake Paiute Tribe of Indians v. U.S. Dep't of Navy, 898 F.2d 1410, 1417 (9th Cir. 1990).

27. *See* Krakoff Mem., *supra* note 10, at 6.

ability to achieve the ESA's objective.[28] ESA section 4(f) requires the Secretary to develop and implement "recovery plans" for the conservation and survival of each listed species, unless the Secretary finds that a recovery plan will not promote species conservation.[29] To the maximum extent practicable, the Secretary must give priority to the listed species most likely to benefit from recovery plans, such as those in immediate conflict with construction projects or other economic activity.[30] The Secretary is expressly forbidden from prioritizing recovery plans based upon the taxonomic classification of a species.[31] Although no timetable is required for development of recovery plans,[32] the ESA requires the Secretary to report back to Congress every two years on the status of efforts to develop and implement recovery plans for all listed species.[33]

Recovery plans must be developed and implemented through a public process,[34] and they usually are prepared by a recovery team that includes representatives of state, Tribal, or federal agencies; academic institutions; private individuals; and private

28. *See generally* William L. Andreen, *Separating Fact from Fiction in Evaluating the Endangered Species Act: Recognizing the Need for Ongoing Conservation Management and Regulation*, 56 IDAHO L. REV. 39 (2020); Federico Cheever, *The Road to Recovery: A New Way of Thinking About the Endangered Species Act,* 23 ECOLOGY L.Q. 1 (1996); Jennifer Jeffers, *Reversing the Trend Towards Species Extinction or Merely Halting It?: Incorporating the Recovery Standard into ESA Section 7 Jeopardy Analyses,* 35 ECOLOGY L.Q. 455 (2008); Daniel J. Rohlf, *Section 4 of the Endangered Species Act: Top Ten Issues for the Next Thirty Years,* 34 ENV'T L. 483, 550 (2004); Jason C. Rylander, *Recovering Endangered Species in Difficult Times: Can the ESA Go Beyond Mere Salvage?*, 42 ENV'T L. REP. 10017 (2012). *See also* Ya-Wei Li, *Recovery, in* ENDANGERED SPECIES ACT: LAW, POLICY, AND PERSPECTIVES 77 (Donald C. Baur & Ya-Wei Li eds., 3d ed. 2021); PROP. & ENV'T RSCH. CTR., A FIELD GUIDE FOR WILDLIFE RECOVERY: THE ENDANGERED SPECIES ACT'S ELUSIVE SEARCH TO RECOVER SPECIES—AND WHAT TO DO ABOUT IT 10–13 (2023), https://www.perc.org/wp-content/uploads/2023/09/PERC_Field-Guide-for-Wildlife-Recovery.pdf.

29. 16 U.S.C. § 1533(f)(1).

30. *Id.* § 1533(f)(1)(A). *See* 48 Fed. Reg. 43,098 (1983) (FWS listing and recovery priority guidelines).

31. 16 U.S.C. § 1533(f)(1)(A). Congress expressed concern that about 5 percent of listed species had received up to 45 percent of the available funding for recovery planning and noted that preferential treatment of "higher life forms" has no basis in the Act. S. REP. NO. 100-240, at 9 (1988), *reprinted in* 1988 U.S.C.C.A.N. 2700, 2708.

32. NMFS and FWS policy contemplate finalizing recovery plans within two and a half years of a species listing. 50 Fed. Reg. 34,272 (1994).

33. 16 U.S.C. § 1533(f)(3).

34. *Id.* § 1533(f)(4) (providing for public notice and opportunity for review and comment). In *Friends of Blackwater v. Salazar,* 2012 WL 3538236 (D.C. Cir. Aug. 17, 2012), the court held that recovery plans are nonbinding documents and need not dictate whether a species can be delisted.

organizations.[35] Whenever possible, recovery plans will be developed for multiple species, and the Services will seek to minimize the social and economic impacts of recovery activities. To the maximum extent practicable, each recovery plan should include

- a description of site-specific management actions as may be necessary to achieve conservation and survival of the species;
- objective measurable criteria that, if met, would result in the delisting of the species; and
- time and cost estimates to carry out the plan measures, and to achieve intermediate steps toward the goal of recovery.[36]

3.3.1 Discretion of FWS and NMFS in Recovery Plan Preparation and Content

Once the Secretary determines that a recovery plan would promote the conservation of a species, the ESA provides no statutory time limit governing when the Secretary must develop and publish the plan.[37] Unless, therefore, either FWS or the National Marine Fisheries Service (NMFS) has "unreasonably" delayed the development of a recovery plan, courts appear unlikely to order recovery plan preparation.[38] And, similarly, the contents of a

35. 50 Fed. Reg. 34,272 (1994).

36. 16 U.S.C. § 1533(f)(1)(B)(i)–(iii). The Services generally follow guidance on the recovery plan process and development, which they update, *e.g.*, NOAA Fisheries, Recovery Planning Handbook, Vers. 1.0 (Oct. 2020); NOAA, Listing and Recovery Priority Guidelines, 84 Fed. Reg. 18243 (Apr. 20, 2019). NOAA describes how, while "recovery plans are often developed for a single species, plans are also developed for the simultaneous recovery of several listed species when they occur together." NOAA Fisheries, Recovery Plans (2025), https://www.fisheries.noaa.gov/national/endangered-species-conservation/recovery-species-under-endangered-species-act. For the Fish and Wildlife Service, a notable multi-species plan is the South Florida-Species Recovery Plan. The Fish and Wildlife Service employs species status assessments (SSAs) to inform the development of recovery plans. For policies, see https://www.fws.gov/library/collections/recovery-policies-and-regulations.

37. Or. Nat. Res. Council v. Turner, 863 F. Supp. 1277, 1282 (D. Or. 1994).

38. *Id.* at 1284 (delay attributable to prioritization of recovery planning efforts was reasonable). For a discussion about the ability to require the agency to implement aspects of the plan, see *Conservation Northwest v. Kempthorne,* 2007 WL 1847143 (W.D. Wash. 2007) (unreported).

recovery plan are discretionary.[39] Although some courts suggest that the recovery plan requirement "breathes discretion at every pore,"[40] at least one court has held that the Secretary's discretion might be circumscribed by an obligation on the agency to fulfill its statutory commands to the fullest extent feasible or possible.[41] But courts seem unlikely to set aside any reasonable, good-faith effort to prepare recovery plans that contain measurable criteria.[42]

3.3.2 Federal Agency Discretion in Implementing Recovery Plans

Consistent with the discretion afforded the Secretary when developing recovery plans, these plans are not documents carrying the "force of law."[43] As one court noted, a recovery plan "presents a guideline for future goals, but does not mandate any actions,"[44]

39. Morrill v. Lujan, 802 F. Supp. 424, 433 (S.D. Ala. 1992) ("the contents of the plan are discretionary, as evidenced by the language 'to the maximum extent practicable'"); Strahan v. Linnon, 967 F. Supp. 581, 597 (D. Mass. 1997) ("Case law instructs that the . . . content of recovery plans is discretionary[.]"), *aff'd,* 187 F.3d 623 (1st Cir. 1998) (per curiam).

40. *See, e.g.,* Fund for Animals, Inc. v. Rice, 85 F.3d 535, 547 (11th Cir. 1996) (quoting Strickland v. Morton, 519 F.2d 467, 469 (9th Cir. 1975)).

41. Fund for Animals v. Babbitt, 903 F. Supp. 96, 107, 110–12 (D.D.C. 1995) (holding that FWS had not met its ESA section 4(1)(B)(ii) obligation to provide objective, measurable criteria for recovery). *See also* Defs. of Wildlife v. Babbitt, 130 F. Supp. 2d 121, 131–35 (D.D.C. 2001), *later opinion,* Defs. of Wildlife v. Norton, 2003 WL 24122459 (D.D.C. 2003) (reviewing revised BOs following remand). In *Homebuilders Ass'n of Northern California v. U.S. Fish & Wildlife Service,* 616 F.3d 983, 989 (9th Cir. 2010), the Ninth Circuit observed that the "ESA does require a determination of criteria for measuring when a species will be conserved, but that requirement applies to the preparation of a recovery plan."

42. In *Center for Biological Diversity v. Haaland,* 562 F. Supp. 3d 68 (D. Ariz. 2021), involving a challenge to the recovery plan for the Mexican gray wolf, the court explained how plans need not be "exhaustively detailed," but they must have at least a sufficient explanation and for what corrective actions are being proposed or rejected. The court remanded the case to the Service to develop a compliant recovery plan. *See also* Save Bull Trout v. Williams, 544 F. Supp. 3d 1047 (D. Mont. 2021) (reviewing whether plan contained objective, measurable criteria), *but cf.* Save Bull Trout v. Williams, 51 F.4th 1101 (9th Cir. 2022) (dismissed and explaining lack of jurisdiction).

43. *Fund for Animals v. Rice,* 85 F.3d at 548. The Service has stated that such plans are not regulatory documents but rather guidance. *E.g.,* Friends of Blackwater v. Salazar, 2012 WL 3538236 (D.C. Cir. Aug. 17, 2012).

44. Or. Nat. Res. Council v. Turner, 863 F. Supp. 1277, 1284 (D. Or. 1994). The court also stated that "the development and publication of a recovery plan in and of itself would not have afforded the endangered species any additional protection." *Id.*

and courts normally will not "second guess" the Secretary's motives for not following the recovery plan.[45] But an agency's deviation from a recovery plan, unless explained, can amount to arbitrary and capricious behavior, otherwise impermissible under the Administrative Procedure Act.[46]

Despite the discretionary nature of recovery planning generally, recovery plans are viewed as an integral component of species conservation, and while early development of recovery plans was slow, the development of such plans has been much more robust during the last two decades. Today, most of the listed wildlife species have recovery plans.[47] FWS maintains a searchable database of its existing plans,[48] and NMFS, too, operates a recovery plan web page.

ESA's Conservation Directives

ESA Provision	Conservation Directive
Section 2(b) Purposes	"The purposes of this chapter are to provide a means whereby the ecosystems upon which endangered species and threatened species depend may be conserved." (16 U.S.C. § 1531(b))
Section 2(c) Policy	"[A]ll federal departments and agencies shall seek to conserve endangered species and threatened species and shall utilize their authorities in furtherance of the purposes of this chapter." (16 U.S.C. § 1531(c))

(continued)

45. Nat'l Wildlife Fed'n v. Nat'l Park Serv., 669 F. Supp. 384, 389 (D. Wyo. 1987).

46. *See* Defs. of Wildlife v. Hall, 565 F. Supp. 2d 1160, 1170 (D. Mont. 2008). *Cf.* Ctr. for Biological Diversity v. Bernhardt, 480 F. Supp. 3d 69 (D.D.C. 2020) (allowing case to proceed involving recovery plan); Friends of Blackwater v. Salazar, 691 F.3d 428 (D.C. Cir. 2012) (deviation from plan upheld). In *Center for Biological Diversity v. Haaland*, 58 F.4th 412 (9th Cir. 2023), involving a petition to amend the recovery plan for the grizzly bear, the court (one judge dissenting) reviewed a lower court's judgment that recovery plans are not final, reviewable agency actions, suggesting that they may not be, and that consequently a decision not to modify a plan would not be a final agency action.

47. FWS maintains a box score web page for, inter alia, recovery plans. *See* U.S. Fish & Wildlife Serv., *Listed Species Reports*, https://ecos.fws.gov/ecp/species-reports (last visited July 15, 2025).

48. *See* U.S. Fish & Wildlife Serv., *Species with Recovery Plans*, https://ecos.fws.gov/ecp/report/species-with-recovery-plans (last visited July 15, 2025).

ESA's Conservation Directives *(continued)*

ESA Provision	Conservation Directive
Section 3(3) Definitions	"The terms 'conserve,' 'conserving,' and 'conservation' mean to use and the use of all methods and procedures which are necessary to bring any [listed] species to the point at which the measures provided pursuant to the Act are no longer necessary." (16 U.S.C. § 1532(3))
Section 4(f) Recovery Plans	Recovery plans are developed and implemented expressly for the "conservation and survival" of the listed species. (16 U.S.C. §§ 1533(f)(1), (1)(B)(I))
Section 5 Implementation of Conservation Programs	The Secretaries of the Interior and Commerce, and the Secretary of Agriculture (with respect to national forest land), shall establish and implement a program to conserve all species, and shall use land acquisition authority as appropriate. (16 U.S.C. § 1534)
Section 6 Cooperation with States	Provides for management agreements and cooperative agreements with states for the establishment of areas and programs for conservation of listed species. (16 U.S.C. § §1535(b), (c))
Section 7(a)(1) Federal Agency Conservation Obligations	Federal agencies shall use their authorities in carrying out programs for the conservation of listed species. (16 U.S.C. § 1536(a)(1))
Section 8 International Cooperation	The Secretary may provide financial and personnel assistance to, and may encourage bilateral and multilateral agreements with, foreign countries in order to develop, promote, and encourage conservation of fish, wildlife, or plants. (16 U.S.C. § 1537(a), (c))
Section 10 Permits	No permit may be granted under Section 10 that contravenes the purposes and policies of ESA section 2 (which includes conservation). (16 U.S.C. § 1539(d))
Section 10(j) Reintroductions	The Secretary may authorize the release of experimental populations if the Secretary determines that such releases will further the conservation of such species. (16 U.S.C. § 1539(j)(2)(A))

4 Prohibited Acts and Penalties: Sections 9 and 11

4.1 Overview

Section 9 of the Endangered Species Act (ESA) reflects Congress's effort to address threats to species comprehensively.[1] It is, in short, a suite of prohibitions that, as noted by J.B. Ruhl, serves as "the central prohibitory ESA provision."[2] Section 9 outlines the ESA's prohibited acts and accompanying consequences that apply to individuals and entities, private as well as public.

Any "person" subject to the jurisdiction of the United States is subject to the prohibitions of section 9.[3] Through a 1988 amendment, Congress clarified that, in addition to individuals, a governmental, business, or private entity is subject to section 9; thus, the Act defines *person* broadly to include an individual, corporation, partnership, trust, association, or any other private entity; any officer, employee, agent, department, or instrumentality of the federal government, of any state, municipality, or political subdivision of a state, or of any foreign government; any state, municipality, or

---

1. 16 U.S.C. § 1538.

2. J.B. Ruhl, *Regional Habitat Planning Under the Endangered Species Act: Pushing the Legal and Practical Limits of Species Protection,* 44 Sw. L.J. 1393, 1397 (1991). *See also* Federico Cheever, *An Introduction to the Prohibition Against Takings in Section 9 of the Endangered Species Act of 1973: Learning to Live with a Powerful Species Preservation Law,* 62 U. Colo. L. Rev. 109 (1991); George Cameron Coggins & Irma S. Russell, *Beyond Shooting Snail Darters in Pork Barrels: Endangered Species and Land Use in America,* 70 Geo. L.J. 1433, 1460 (1982) (characterizing ESA as creating "a cocoon of legal protection" for listed species). *See generally* Steven P. Quarles, Paul S. Weiland & Brian Ferrasci-O'Malley, *Another Take on "Take": The Section 9 Prohibition, in* Endangered Species Act: Law, Policy, and Perspectives 141 (Donald C. Baur & Ya-Wei Li eds., 3d ed. 2021).

3. 16 U.S.C. § 1538.

political subdivision of a state; or any other entity subject to the jurisdiction of the United States.[4]

With the exception of the occasional, unsuccessful state claim that the Tenth Amendment prohibits application of section 9 to state governmental entities,[5] the definition of *person* is sufficiently broad to preclude substantial litigation on the issue. The principal issue, therefore, is not "who" section 9 covers, but rather what conduct it prohibits.

4.2 Conduct Prohibited

Section 9's prohibition applies to a wide range of human activities; in limited circumstances, certain inactivity and some omissions are prohibited. Except as explicitly allowed through operation of other ESA provisions,[6] section 9 prohibits the following activities with respect to endangered, and in many instances threatened,[7] fish and wildlife:

- Importing or exporting endangered species;[8]

---

4. *Id.* § 1532(12). The definition owes its breadth in part to the congressional response to a 1988 Ninth Circuit Court of Appeals decision, which held that municipalities were not "persons" under the ESA. United States v. Rancho Palos Verde, 841 F.2d 329 (9th Cir. 1988).

5. *See, e.g.,* Strahan v. Coxe, 127 F.3d 155, 163 (1st Cir. 1997) (holding that "a governmental third party pursuant to whose authority an actor directly exacts a taking of an endangered species may be deemed to have violated the provision of the ESA"); Loggerhead Turtle v. Cnty. Council of Volusia Cnty., 148 F.3d 1231 (11th Cir. 1998) (holding that county could potentially be in violation of section 9 by harming listed turtles through inadequate regulation of beachfront lighting); United States v. Town of Plymouth, 6 F. Supp. 2d 81, 90–91 (D. Mass. 1998) (preliminary injunction was issued enjoining town's permitting of off-road vehicles, based on findings that operation of the vehicles was causing take of endangered piping plovers).

6. See Sections 4.8 and Chapters 6, 7, and 10 for a thorough discussion of the exceptions to takings provided in various provisions of the ESA.

7. *See* Section 4.3.

8. 16 U.S.C. § 1538(a)(1)(A). Section 3(10) of the ESA defines *import* as follows:

> The term "import" means to land on, bring into, or introduce into, any place subject to the jurisdiction of the United States, whether or not such landing, bringing, or introduction constitutes an importation within the meaning of the customs laws of the United States.

16 U.S.C. § 1532(10).

- "Taking" any endangered species within the United States, its territorial sea, or upon the high seas;[9]
- Possessing, selling, delivering, carrying, transporting, or shipping any endangered species unlawfully taken, in the course of any commercial activity;[10]
- Engaging in any activity involving interstate or foreign commerce in endangered species;[11] and
- Violating any regulation of the Secretary pertaining to endangered or threatened species.[12]

As discussed more fully later, in Section 4.4, ESA section 9(a)(2)[13] extends limited protection to listed plants, while ESA section 9(c) makes unlawful the trade of wildlife in violation of the Convention on International Trade in Endangered Species of Wild Fauna and Flora (CITES).[14] And the ESA further provides that it is unlawful even to *attempt* to commit a violation of section 9, or to solicit another to commit such a violation or cause such an offense to be committed.[15]

4.3 Threatened Species and Section 4(d) Rules

Congress did not mandate applying the section 9(a)(1) prohibitions to threatened species, but rather left it to the discretion of the Secretaries of the Interior and Commerce to promulgate regulations deemed "necessary and advisable" to conserve threatened

---

9. *Id.* § 1538(a)(1)(B), (C).

10. *Id.* § 1538(a)(1)(D). Section 3(2) of the ESA defines *commercial activity* as follows:

> The term "commercial activity" means all activities of industry and trade, including, but not limited to, the buying or selling of commodities and activities conducted for the purpose of facilitating such buying and selling: *provided, however,* that it does not include exhibitions of commodities by museums or similar cultural or historical organizations.

16 U.S.C. § 1532(2). By regulation, the phrase "industry and trade" encompasses only those activities "in the pursuit of gain or profit." 50 C.F.R. § 17.3.

11. 16 U.S.C. § 1538(a)(1)(E), (F).

12. *Id.* § 1538(a)(1)(G).

13. *Id.* § 1538(a)(2).

14. See Chapter 9, Section 9.5 for a discussion of CITES.

15. 16 U.S.C. § 1538(g).

species of fish and wildlife.[16] For a threatened species of fish and wildlife, "the Secretary may by regulation prohibit . . . any act prohibited under Section [9]."[17] The Secretaries of the Interior and Commerce generally have treated threatened species differently.

For many years, the Secretary of the Interior exercised his discretion under section 4(d) to extend the full range of section 9 prohibitions to all threatened species under the jurisdiction of the Department of the Interior, unless the Service decided affirmatively to promulgate an individual "4(d) rule" for a particular species.[18] Because section 9 provides the maximum protection available to threatened species, any species-specific section 4(d) rule promulgated by the Fish and Wildlife Service (FWS) generally decreases the protections afforded to the particular threatened species at issue.[19] The Secretary of the Interior's blanket application of section 9 prohibitions to all threatened species, except those subject to an individual section 4(d) rule, was upheld by the D.C. Circuit in 1993.[20] Though the court held the ESA and its legislative history to be ambiguous with respect to whether the Secretary could protect all threatened species in a blanket rule, the court concluded that the regulation was a "reasonable and permissible construction of the ESA."[21] As of 2021, the Service reported that it had issued over 100 species-specific section 4(d) rules.[22] The first Trump administration's Interior Department amended the regulation to apply the take prohibition to threatened species only when the Service affirmatively promulgated a section 4(d) rule.[23] When challenged, and at the request of the Biden administration, a court vacated and remanded the regulation.[24] FWS responded by proposing and then adopting a slight

---

16. *Id.* § 1533(d).
17. *Id.*
18. 50 C.F.R. § 17.31(a).
19. *See id.* §§ 17.40–17.48 (§ 4(d) rules promulgated by FWS), 17.84 (§ 4(d) rules promulgated by FWS to address "experimental populations"). See Chapter 10 for a discussion of experimental populations.
20. Sweet Home Chapter of Cmtys. for a Great Or. v. Babbitt, 1 F.3d 1, 5–8 (D. C. Cir. 1993), *rev'd on other grounds,* 515 U.S. 687, 692 n.5 (1995).
21. 1 F.3d at 8.
22. For the North American Wolverine, recently listed as threatened, the Service issued an "interim" 4(d) rule identifying specific conservation measures and exceptions. 88 Fed. Reg. 83,726 (Nov. 30, 2023).
23. Fish & Wildlife Serv., Regulations for Prohibitions to Threatened Wildlife and Plants, 84 Fed. Reg. 44,753 (Aug. 27, 2019).
24. Center for Biological Diversity v. Haaland, 609 F. Supp. 3d 1058 (N.D. Cal. 2022), *amended and voluntary remand,* 641 F. Supp. 3d 835 (N.D. Cal. 2022).

modification of its historic approach toward section 4(d), with a blanket rule and possibility of a specific section 4(d) rule.[25]

The Secretary of Commerce implements section 4(d) differently from the Secretary of the Interior, extending section 9 prohibitions/protections to threatened species on a case-by-case basis. As a result, the prohibitions outlined in ESA section 9 do not apply to threatened species listed by the National Marine Fisheries Service (NMFS) unless and until NMFS promulgates a section 4(d) rule governing a particular threatened species.[26] Section 4(d) emerged in the 1990s as a mechanism for implementing the ESA in a more flexible manner, and while a section 4(d) rule generally decreases the protections applicable to threatened species under FWS jurisdiction, a NMFS section 4(d) rule conversely is necessary to afford section 9 protection to such species.[27]

4.4 Plants

Although the ESA provides for listing and protection of endangered or threatened plants, listed plants are not protected to the same extent as listed animals, because the section 9(a)(1)(C) prohibition against "take" applies only to listed wildlife. Endangered plants are subject to the protection of a separate prohibition in section 9(a)(2) making it unlawful to remove and reduce to possession any such species from areas under federal jurisdiction; maliciously damage or destroy any such species on any such area; or remove, cut, dig up, or damage or destroy any such species on any other area in knowing violation of any law or regulation of any state or in the course of any violation of a state criminal trespass law.[28]

The phrase "areas under Federal jurisdiction" generated litigation, with the Ninth Circuit concluding that it does not include

25. Fish & Wildlife Serv., Regulations Pertaining to Endangered and Threatened Wildlife and Plants, 88 Fed. Reg. 40,742 (June 22, 2023) (proposed rule); 89 Fed. Reg. 23,919, 23,939 (April 5, 2024) (final rule) (codified at 50 C.F.R. § 17.31). Along with some other clarifications, the Service "extend[ed] to federally recognized Tribes the exceptions to prohibitions for threatened species that the regulations currently provide to the employees or agents of the Service and other Federal and State agencies to aid, salvage, or dispose of threatened species." 89 Fed. Reg. at 23,919.

26. *See* 50 C.F.R. pt. 223 (§ 4(d) rules promulgated by NMFS).

27. *See, e.g.*, 65 Fed. Reg. 42,481 (2000) (NMFS § 4(d) rule extending certain ESA § 9 protections to several threatened species of salmon and steelhead).

28. 16 U.S.C. § 1538(a)(2)(B).

areas over which Congress has the ability to exercise federal jurisdiction, such as over "waters of the United States" under the Clean Water Act.[29]

Similar to the prohibitions affecting endangered wildlife, endangered plants are subject to a full panoply of protections prohibiting their import, export, and other activities involving interstate or foreign commerce in protected plants.[30] Yet, while section 9 prohibits "possession" of endangered wildlife taken in violation of the ESA, one may possess an illegally obtained plant without violating section 9.[31] Just as threatened wildlife may be afforded the same protection as endangered wildlife, threatened plants also may be afforded the same protections afforded to endangered plants.[32] FWS, however, has not extended the same blanket protection to threatened plants as it has to threatened wildlife.[33] Rather, the prohibitions against "maliciously" (a term undefined by the ESA and implementing regulations) damaging plants, or damaging or destroying plants in violation of state law or in the course of criminal trespass,[34] remain applicable only to endangered plants, unless provided for in a special regulation regarding a particular threatened plant species.

4.5 Prohibited "Take": What Constitutes Harm

By many accounts, a far-reaching aspect of section 9 is its prohibition against "take" of protected species of fish and wildlife.[35] *Take* is defined broadly in the ESA as "to *harass, harm,* pursue, hunt, shoot, wound, kill, trap, capture, or collect, or to attempt to engage in any such conduct."[36] An oft-quoted statement from the ESA's legislative

29. N. Cal. River Watch v. Wilcox, 633 F.3d 766 (9th Cir. 2011).
30. 16 U.S.C. § 1538(a)(2)(A), (C), (D), (E).
31. *Compare* 16 U.S.C. § 1538(a)(1)(D) *with* 16 U.S.C. § 1538(a)(2)(C).
32. 16 U.S.C. §§ 1534(d), 1538(a)(2)(E).
33. *See* 50 C.F.R. § 17.71(a) (1998) (extending the protections outlined in 50 C.F.R. § 17.61 to threatened plants; however, the ESA's statutory (§ 9(a)(2)) prohibition against malicious damage or destruction is curiously absent from 50 C.F.R. § 17.6.).
34. The prohibition against taking plants while in the course of violating state trespass law was added to section 9 in a 1988 amendment. S. Rep. No. 100-240, at 12–13 (1988), *reprinted in* 1988 U.S.C.C.A.N. 2700, 2711–12.
35. 16 U.S.C. § 1538(a)(1)(B).
36. *Id.* § 1532(18) (emphasis added).

history expresses Congress's intent with regard to the extent of the "take" prohibition; the term *take* is "defined in the broadest possible manner to include every conceivable way in which a person can 'take' or attempt to 'take' any fish or wildlife."[37]

The regulations further define two elements of the "take" definition, the terms *harass* and *harm:*

> *Harass* in the definition of "take" in the Act means an intentional or negligent act or omission which creates the likelihood of injury to wildlife by annoying it to such an extent as to significantly disrupt normal behavioral patterns which include, but are not limited to, breeding, feeding, or sheltering.[38]
>
> *Harm* in the definition of "take" in the Act means an act which actually kills or injures wildlife. Such act may include significant habitat modification or degradation where it actually kills or injures wildlife by significantly impairing essential behavioral patterns, including breeding, feeding, or sheltering.[39]

These definitions, particularly the definition of *harm,* have produced a significant body of case law, including the 1995 Supreme Court decision in *Babbitt v. Sweet Home*.[40] However, even the most superficial understanding of section 9 jurisprudence requires some familiarity with two earlier opinions from the Ninth Circuit, known as *Palila I* and *Palila II.*

4.5.1 *Palila I* and *II*: Habitat Modification May Result in Prohibited Harm

In 1981, the Ninth Circuit affirmed a lower court determination that feral goats and sheep, maintained by the state of Hawaii,

37. S. REP. NO. 93-307 (1973), *reprinted in* 1973 U.S.S.C.A.N. 2995. See Cheever, *supra* note 2, at 128–30 for a good overview of the legislative history of § 9.

38. 50 C.F.R. § 17.3. *See, e.g.,* Ctr. for Biological Diversity v. Marina Point Dev. Co., 535 F.3d 1026, 1036–37 (9th Cir. 2008) (alleged harassment of eagles from construction but issue rendered moot by delisting of species); Cold Mountain v. Garber, 375 F.3d 884, 889–90 (9th Cir. 2004) (alleged harassment of bald eagles from helicopters); Fund for Animals v. Fla. Game & Fresh Water Comm'n, 550 F. Supp. 1206 (S.D. Fla. 1982) (alleged harassment from boats).

39. 50 C.F.R. § 17.3. NMFS has promulgated its own "harm" definition, substantially mirroring the FWS definition. 50 C.F.R. § 222.102. *See also* 64 Fed. Reg. 60,727 (1999).

40. 515 U.S. 687 (1995).

were harming the endangered palila bird.[41] The goats and sheep browsed on seedlings of the mumane tree, thereby denying the palila the benefit of the mature mumane trees that would have grown from the seedlings. Because the palila depended on the mumane trees for its survival (food, shelter, and nest sites), the court held that elimination of the goats and sheep was necessary to the bird's survival; thus, the state's maintenance of the goat and sheep herd was a violation of section 9.[42] Commentators agree that the Ninth Circuit's opinion in *Palila I* was a watershed event in section 9 jurisprudence, because habitat modification alone was determined to amount to a prohibited "take."[43] FWS took the *Palila I* opinion seriously and amended the regulatory definition of *harm* to clarify that "habitat modification alone without any attendant death or injury of the protected wildlife" is not a section 9 violation.[44] It is perhaps fitting, then, that another dispute involving the palila bird provided the factual background for application of the new "harm" regulation.

In 1985, the original plaintiffs in *Palila I* again brought suit to allege that the palila bird was being harmed by damage to the critical mumane tree. In this new case, evidence showed that another animal, the mouflon sheep, was also eating mumane tree shoots. Applying the new 1981 definition of *harm,*[45] the Ninth Circuit held that Hawaii's maintenance of the sheep herd violated section 9. Specifically, the court held that the 1981 rule change "did not embody a substantial change" in the definition of *harm,* and that activities that significantly degraded the palila's habitat, and caused actual injury to the palila, remained prohibited.[46]

41. Palila v. Haw. Dep't of Land & Nat. Res. (*Palila I*), 639 F.2d 495 (9th Cir. 1981), *aff'g* 471 F. Supp. 985 (D. Haw. 1979). *But see* N. Slope Borough v. Andrus, 486 F. Supp. 332, 362 (D.D.C. 1980) (refusing to enjoin offshore oil leasing to protect endangered whale species on the ground that no injunction should issue unless "danger to the protected species is sufficiently imminent or certain"), *aff'd in part, rev'd in part,* 642 F.2d 589 (D.C. Cir. 1980); California v. Watt, 520 F. Supp. 1359 (C.D. Cal. 1981) (mere "threat" to survival of listed species held insufficient to amount to a section 9 violation, without more "immediate injury"), *aff'd in part, rev'd in part,* 683 F.2d 1254 (9th Cir. 1982), *rev'd on other grounds sub nom.* Sec'y of the Interior v. California, 464 U.S. 312 (1984).

42. *Palila I,* 639 F.2d at 497.

43. *See, e.g.,* Daniel J. Rohlf, The Endangered Species Act: A Guide to Its Protections and Implementation 63 (1989); Cheever, *supra* note 2, at 143.

44. 46 Fed. Reg. 54,748 (1981).

45. *Id.* The 1981 rule remains unaltered. 50 C.F.R. § 17.3.

46. Palila v. Haw. Dep't of Land & Nat. Res. (*Palila II*), 649 F. Supp. 1070, 1075 (D. Haw. 1986), *aff'd,* 852 F.2d 1106 (9th Cir. 1988).

Likewise, the court rejected the notion that "potential" harm to listed species was not "actual harm" as contemplated by the new definition.[47]

Though *Palila II* was by no means the only opinion of its era holding habitat modification to be a prohibited harm of listed species,[48] the scope and clarity of the opinion was such that it could not be ignored by other circuits.

4.5.2 *Sweet Home*: "Harm" Definition Upheld

In 1994, the D.C. Circuit decided a case in direct conflict with *Palila II*. The plaintiffs in *Sweet Home* were landowners and logging industry representatives who claimed economic injury due to application of the "harm" regulation to protect red-cockaded woodpeckers and the northern spotted owl.[49] In response to the plaintiffs' facial challenge to the FWS's 1981 regulation defining *harm* (the same regulation considered in *Palila II*), the D.C. Circuit held that the ESA prohibition on take prohibited only those activities amounting to "a direct application of force against the animal taken";[50] thus, the "harm" regulation was held invalid. The Supreme Court granted certiorari to resolve the "square conflict"[51] between the D.C. Circuit's *Sweet Home* decision and the Ninth Circuit's *Palila II* decision. Adding to the palila bird's legacy, on April 14, 1995, the Court reversed the D.C. Circuit and reaffirmed the application of the "harm" prohibition to habitat modification.[52]

The *Sweet Home* plaintiffs framed their case as a facial challenge to the "harm" regulation, as opposed to an as-applied challenge. The Court, therefore, assumed arguendo that the plaintiffs'

47. *Palila II,* 852 F.2d at 1108. As discussed in Section 4.6, courts continue to struggle to determine when potential harm to a listed species is sufficiently imminent or causally related to the habitat-modifying behavior as to constitute a take.

48. *See, e.g.,* Sierra Club v. Lyng, 694 F. Supp. 1260 (E.D. Tex. 1988), *aff'd in part, vacated in part sub nom.* Sierra Club v. Yeuter, 926 F.2d 437 (5th Cir. 1991) (holding that U.S. Forest Service logging practices harmed red-cockaded woodpeckers); Defs. of Wildlife v. Adm'r of EPA, 688 F. Supp. 1334 (D. Minn. 1988), *rev'd on other grounds,* 882 F.2d 1294 (8th Cir. 1989).

49. Sweet Home Chapter of Cmtys. for a Great Or. v. Babbitt, 17 F.3d 1463 (D.C. Cir. 1994), *rev'd,* 515 U.S. 687 (1995).

50. 17 F.3d at 1465.

51. *Sweet Home,* 515 U.S. at 695.

52. *Id.* at 707.

logging activities would have the effect, though unintended, "of detrimentally changing the natural habitat of both listed species and that, as a consequence, members of those species will be killed or injured."[53] The only question then before the Court was whether the "harm" regulation was a permissible construction of the ESA. The Court ultimately concluded that "the Secretary reasonably construed the intent of Congress when he defined 'harm' to include 'significant habitat modification or degradation that actually kills or injures wildlife.'"[54]

Writing for the majority, Justice Stevens found support for the Secretary's definition of the word *harm* in the dictionary definition of the term. Webster's defines *harm* as "to cause hurt or damage to: injure."[55] Habitat modification that results in actual injury to members of listed species meets the dictionary definition of *harm*. Likewise, the dictionary definition is devoid of any reference to "direct" application of force, as opposed to indirect injury.[56] Moreover, the majority held that if harm were limited to direct injuries, the term would have no meaning that did not duplicate the meaning of the other words included in the statutory definition of *take*.[57] Simply put, the ordinary meaning of the word *harm* was held to support the Secretary's definition.

The majority also concluded that the comprehensive nature of the ESA, combined with Congress's explicit reference in the ESA to conservation of "the *ecosystems* upon which endangered and threatened species depend," supported the Secretary's broad definition of *harm*.[58] Referencing its 1978 decision in *Tennessee Valley Authority v. Hill*, where the Court elaborated on the comprehensive nature of the ESA, the *Sweet Home* Court noted that the Secretary's inclusion of habitat modification in the "harm" definition had added weight to the Court's conclusion that the Tellico Dam would "harm" the snail darter.[59]

The Court similarly suggested that the Secretary's "harm" definition comported with the ESA's legislative history, particularly

53. *Id.* at 696.
54. *Id.* at 708.
55. *Id.* at 697 (quoting Webster's Third New International Dictionary 1034 (1966)).
56. *Id.*
57. *Id.* at 697–98.
58. *Id.* at 698–99 (emphasis added) (quoting 16 U.S.C. § 1531(b)) (citing Tenn. Valley Auth. v. Hill, 437 U.S. 153 (1978)).
59. *Id.* at 697–99 (citing *Hill,* 437 U.S. at 184 n.30).

the 1982 ESA amendments authorizing limited takings, when such takings are "incidental to, and not the purpose of, the carrying out of an otherwise lawful activity."[60] Recognizing that incidental take permits under section 10 provide an exception to the section 9 takings prohibition, and that such permits are available only when the taking is unintended or indirect (i.e., "incidental to, and not the purpose of" the proposed activity), the Court concluded that Congress must have intended to apply the "harm" prohibition to unintended takings, such as habitat modification, or the section 10 permit provision would be meaningless.[61] In response to the dissent's suggestion that the section 9 take prohibition is limited to the deliberate actions of hunters and trappers, the majority cited instances in the ESA's legislative history where Congress expressed its intent to define take broadly, and where Congress even gave examples of prohibited, indirect harm or harassment of listed species.[62] The majority found nothing in the ESA's legislative history that weighed against the Secretary's application of the "harm" prohibition to habitat modification.

Applying *Chevron*[63] deference, the Court concluded that Congress delegated broad administrative and interpretive power to the Secretary under the ESA, and that, based on the text, structure, and legislative history of the ESA, the Secretary reasonably construed the intent of Congress when defining *harm* to include habitat modification or degradation that actually kills or injures wildlife. With respect to whether the current definition of *harm* is facially valid, therefore, the issue was largely settled in *Sweet Home*.[64] Yet, as discussed next, the Court's majority recognized

60. *Id.* at 700 (quoting 16 U.S.C. § 1539(a)(1)(B)). Incidental take permits are discussed in Chapter 6, Section 6.2.

61. *Id.* at 700–01. The Court was also persuaded that the legislative history of the 1982 amendments illustrates that Congress clearly had habitat modification in mind when crafting the section 10 incidental take permit provision. *Id.* at 707 (citing S. Rep. No. 97-418, at 10 (1982); H. R. Conf. Rep. No. 97-835, at 30–32 (1982)).

62. *Id.* at 704–06.

63. Chevron U.S.A., Inc. v. NRDC, Inc., 467 U.S. 837, 865–66 (1984); *but see* Loper Bright Enters. v. Raimondo, 603 U.S. 369 (2024) (overruling *Chevron*). See Chapter 2, note 9 for a discussion of *Loper Bright* and its implications in the ESA context. The *Loper Bright* court made clear that "[b]y overruling *Chevron* . . . the Court does not call into question prior cases," like *Sweet Home*, "that relied on the *Chevron* framework." 603 U.S. at 376.

64. The Supreme Court's *Sweet Home* decision, however, does not preclude further regulatory developments and any resulting implications from them. For instance, the second Trump administration has proposed to rescind both the FWS and NMFS regulatory definitions of harm. 90 Fed. Reg. 16,102 (Apr. 17, 2025).

that much uncertainty remains with respect to actual application of the "harm" prohibition to individual fact patterns.[65]

4.6 Causation: Reasonable Certainty and the New Era of Section 9 Litigation

Although the *Sweet Home* Court validated the broad regulatory definition of *harm,* the Court also noted that actual application of the "harm" standard could prove difficult. The Court's discussion of causation touched on issues that have permeated section 9 litigation since its inception; until *Sweet Home,* though, they were rarely articulated in terms of causation. Words such as *certain, imminent, proximate, foreseeable, speculative,* and *conjectural* likely will remain part of the ESA section 9 lexicon for years to come.

The *Sweet Home* majority held that the "harm" regulation incorporates "ordinary requirements of proximate causation and foreseeability."[66] In addition, the Court apparently adopted "but-

---

The proposal is for the Services to rely instead on the ESA's statutory definition of "take" rather than providing a regulatory definition for one subcomponent of take, i.e., "harm." *Id.* at 16,103. If finalized, this regulatory proposal could have implications for both ESA section 7(a)(2) consultations and section 10 incidental take permitting and habitat conservation planning. Without the regulatory harm definition, the Services may consider that impacts to listed species' habitat alone are not sufficient to implicate the section 7(a)(2) consultation or section 10 permitting processes, although adverse effects to designated critical habitat alone may still be a sufficient section 7(a)(2) consultation and avoidance of jeopardy/adverse modification trigger. The regulatory proposal suggests that in relying on the ESA's statutory definition of "take," FWS or NMFS may not find take to occur as a result of indirect "injury to a population of animals," but instead may require an "affirmative act[ ] . . . directed immediately and intentionally against a particular animal." 90 Fed. Reg. at 16,103 (quoting *Sweet Home*, 515 U.S. at 719–20 (Scalia, J., dissenting)) (alteration in *Federal Register* quote). At the same time, even without a regulatory definition of harm, a reviewing court may still consider that the term, or the definition of take generally, applies to significant habitat altering activities that result in injury or death to a member of an ESA-protected species. These issues await resolution in further regulatory or judicial developments.

65. *Sweet Home,* 515 U.S. at 708. In spite of this uncertainty, however, section 9 litigants cannot invoke the "rule of lenity" with respect to the "harm" definition; the *Sweet Home* Court rejected the notion, concluding that the "harm" regulation provided fair notice and fair warning of its consequence. *Id.* at 704 n.18.

66. *Id.* at 700 n.13. *See* Lawrence R. Liebesman & Steven G. Davison, *Takings of Wildlife Under the Endangered Species Act after* Babbitt v. Sweet Home

for" causation as the proper means of establishing whether a particular activity is, or will be, the cause of a prohibited harm to listed species.[67] With the exception of some interesting discussion by Justice O'Connor in her concurring opinion, the Court did not attempt to precisely define proximate cause, foreseeability, or but-for causation, but the majority suggested that under some circumstances, "minimal or unforeseeable harm" may not violate the ESA.[68]

Justice O'Connor captured the state of the law for proximate cause by noting that "proximate causation is not a concept susceptible of precise definition," and the Justice further opined that the concept "normally eliminates the bizarre."[69] Justice O'Connor also observed that proximate cause injects "a foreseeability element into the [ESA]" and the "harm" regulation.[70] But Justice O'Connor parted company with the majority when she stated that she would have overturned *Palila II,*[71] and that she did not believe the mouflon sheep consumption of mumane seeds proximately caused "actual death or injury to identifiable [palila] birds."[72] Yet the majority and Justice O'Connor agreed in acknowledging that application of the harm prohibition to individual fact patterns will have to be resolved on a case-by-case basis.[73]

Lower court opinions predating and following *Sweet Home* provide guidance—albeit limited—on instances when harm might occur, or not. For example, in what one commentator termed "the extreme end of the spectrum,"[74] the Eighth Circuit held that EPA's

---

Chapter of Communities for a Great Oregon, 5 U. Balt. J. Env't L. 137, 155–58 (1997) (providing a detailed discussion of section 9 causation). For Professor Davison's follow-up article, see Steven G. Davison, *The Aftermath of Sweet Home Chapter: Modification of Wildlife Habitat as a Prohibited Taking in Violation of the Endangered Species Act,* 27 Wm. & Mary Env't L. & Pol'y Rev. 541 (2003).

67. *Sweet Home,* 515 U.S. at 700 n.13.

68. *Id.* at 699.

69. *Id.* at 713 (O'Connor, J., concurring) (quoting Jerome B. Grubart, Inc. v. Great Lakes Dredge & Dock Co., 513 U.S. 527, 536 (1995)).

70. *Id.*

71. The majority specifically noted the conflict between *Palila II* and the D.C. Circuit's *Sweet Home* decision and chose to reverse the D.C. Circuit; *Palila II* survives.

72. 515 U.S. at 714.

73. *Id.* at 713. The majority had noted that "all persons who must comply with the [ESA] will confront difficult questions of proximity and degree . . . [which must be addressed] through case-by-case resolution and adjudication." *Id.* at 708.

74. James C. Kilbourne, *The Endangered Species Act Under the Microscope: A Closeup Look from a Litigator's Perspective,* 21 Env't L. 499, 583 (1991).

decision to register strychnine as a pesticide "was critical to the resulting poisonings" of listed species.[75] Courts also have held a causal link to exist between

- state licensing of fishing and lobstering equipment and subsequent whale entanglement in the equipment;[76]
- Forest Service timber management practices and woodpecker abandonment of nesting cavities;[77]
- town permitting of vehicles on beaches and crushing deaths of plovers;[78]
- county permitting of beachfront lighting and disorientation of turtles;[79]
- logging and the impairment of breeding by marbled murrelets.[80]

Conversely, several courts have dismissed section 9 claims when causation was found lacking or too attenuated. For example, the Ninth Circuit (in a post–*Palila II* opinion) held that one year's diversion of water to lands leased by the U.S. Navy did not cause harm to the endangered cui-ui fish.[81] Likewise, the First Circuit held that causation was not sufficient to find that the U.S. Coast Guard had violated section 9 by issuing certificates of documentation (analogous to drivers' licenses) for non-Coast Guard vessels, when those vessels struck endangered whales.[82] In an earlier First Circuit case, the court declined a request to hold that a "one in a million" risk of harm is sufficient to find a section 9 violation.[83] The court refused to enjoin a deer hunt that allegedly

---

75. Defs. of Wildlife v. EPA, 882 F.2d 1294, 1301 (8th Cir. 1989).
76. Strahan v. Coxe, 127 F.3d 155, 159 (1st Cir. 1997).
77. Sierra Club v. Yeutter, 926 F.2d 437 (5th Cir. 1991).
78. United States v. Town of Plymouth, 6 F. Supp. 2d 81, 90–91 (D. Mass. 1998) (memorandum and order).
79. Loggerhead Turtle v. Cnty. Council of Volusia Cnty., 148 F.3d 1231 (11th Cir. 1998) (for standing purposes, the court determined that a causal link existed between county permitting of beachfront lighting and the resulting disorientation of turtle hatchlings).
80. Marbled Murrelet v. Babbitt, 83 F.3d 1060, 1067–68 (9th Cir. 1996) (court also determined that the proposed logging would increase the likelihood of attack by predators).
81. Pyramid Lake Paiute Tribe v. U.S. Dep't of Navy, 898 F.2d 1410, 1420 (9th Cir. 1990).
82. Strahan v. Coxe, 127 F.3d 155 (1st Cir. 1997).
83. Am. Bald Eagle v. Bhatti, 9 F.3d 163, 165 (1st Cir. 1993).

created a risk to eagles because the eagles might ingest carrion containing lead slugs; the court considered the low likelihood of lead ingestion by eagles, as well as the fact that the plaintiffs had not introduced any evidence that any eagle had ever ingested lead in such a fashion.[84]

One of the principal issues that surfaces in cases involving section 9 is the standard of proof necessary for a court to enjoin potential take before evidence exists that the defendant's conduct actually has resulted in the loss of an individual member of the species.[85] Although the *Sweet Home* majority may have left room for some argument on the issue of future versus past injury,[86] lower courts confronted with the issue consistently find liability when the defendant's conduct is reasonably certain to cause a take of the species.

The Ninth Circuit explicitly rejects any need for "historic injury," holding that liability can arise when a "reasonably certain" and "imminent" threat of harm to listed species can be established.[87] Likewise, the First Circuit recognized that "actual injury" may be shown when the activity "actually harmed the species *or* if continued *will* actually, as opposed to potentially, cause harm to the species."[88] The court also limited application of section 9 to future harm by requiring the threat of harm to be greater than

84. *Id.* at 166.

85. An incidental take statement in a biological opinion might provide evidence of take liability, to the extent the activity is not shielded by that statement. *See* Wishtoyo Found. v. United Water Conserv. Dist., 2018 WL 6265099 (C.D. Cal. Sept. 23, 2018), *aff'd*, 795 Fed. App'x 541 (9th Cir. 2020).

86. Babbitt v. Sweet Home Chapter of Cmtys. for a Great Or., 515 U.S. 687, 700 n.13 (1995) ("the Government cannot enforce the section 9 prohibition until an animal has actually been killed or harmed"). Language accompanying the 1981 FWS regulation redefining *harm* arguably lends credence to the notion that historic death or injury is required for harm. *See* 46 Fed. Reg. 54,749, 54,749–50 (1981).

87. Forest Conservation Council v. Rosboro Lumber Co., 50 F.3d 781, 784–87 (9th Cir. 1995). *See also* Defs. of Wildlife v. Bernal, 204 F.3d 920 (9th Cir. 2005); Env't Prot. Info. Ctr. v. Simpson Timber Co., 255 F.3d 1073 (9th Cir. 2001); *Marbled Murrelet*, 83 F.3d at 1064–65 (holding that language in *Sweet Home*, which apparently precludes application of section 9 to future harm, is "dictum"); Greenpeace v. NMFS, 106 F. Supp. 2d 1066 (W.D. Wash. 2000). *Cf.* Protect Our Waters v. Flowers, 377 F. Supp. 2d 844, 879–81 (E.D. Cal. 2004) (take of kit fox and red-legged frogs).

88. *Am. Bald Eagle*, 9 F.3d at 165–66 (emphasis added). *See also* Strahan v. Coxe, 127 F.3d 155, 164 (1st Cir. 1997) (discussing activity in terms of whether it "is likely to result" in a violation of section 9).

"substantial."[89] In another high profile district court opinion in Maryland, the court held that the Ninth Circuit standard applied to a wind power project that the court determined was reasonably certain to produce take of the protected Indiana bat.[90]

Little doubt exists that injury to a particular animal can result in a section 9 violation. It remains unclear, however, to what extent injury to a species or population as a whole can be said to be a prohibited act. The *Sweet Home* majority apparently would have limited the application of the "harm" prohibition to injury to "particular animals."[91] Likewise, Justice O'Connor stated in her concurring opinion that "the [harm] regulation is limited by its terms to actions that actually kill or injure individual animals."[92] But the Court's discussion of this issue is inconclusive, and most of the cases appear to avoid the issue because they involve plaintiffs' efforts to address reasonably certain harms to individual members of species.

This raises the apparent tension between the *Sweet Home* majority opinion and *Palila II*—the very case it relied upon (and implicitly upheld) as one-half of the circuit split justifying certiorari. The *Palila II* court held that death or injury to individual members of a species is not required to show harm.[93] *Sierra Club v. Lyng* illustrates that, like the Ninth Circuit, the Fifth Circuit (at least prior to *Sweet Home*) would not have required proof "of the death of specific or individual members of the species."[94] Given that the Supreme Court's discussion of this issue may be dictum, that the Court did not single out *Palila II* or *Lyng*[95] for reversal on the issue, and that the Court in fact implicitly affirmed *Palila II* with respect to its application of the "harm" regulation, the issue legitimately remains unresolved.

---

89. *Am. Bald Eagle,* 9 F.3d at 166 n.5.

90. Animal Welfare Inst. v. Beech Ridge Energy, LLC, 675 F. Supp. 2d 540 (D. Md. 2009), *amended by stipulation of parties,* 2010 WL 11484179 (D. Md. Jan. 26, 2010).

91. *Sweet Home,* 515 U.S. at 700 n.13.

92. *Id.* at 709 (O'Connor, J., concurring).

93. Palila v. Haw. Dep't of Land & Nat. Res. (*Palila II*), 649 F. Supp. 1070, 1075 (D. Haw. 1986) (noting that an act that "prevents the recovery of the species" is prohibited).

94. Sierra Club v. Lyng, 694 F. Supp. 1260, 1270 (E.D. Tex. 1988).

95. *See* Liebesman & Davison, *supra* note 66, at 168–69 (suggesting that *Sweet Home* modifies *Lyng*'s determination that death or injury to individual animals is not required to find a prohibited harm).

4.7 Section 11 Penalties: Overview

Section 11 of the ESA[96] establishes the penalties that may be levied against one who violates section 9. These penalties collectively present a comprehensive and severe suite of preventative and punitive measures, including civil penalties, criminal fines, injunctions,[97] forfeiture, attorneys' fees, and license/permit revocation.

4.7.1 Monetary Penalties, Imprisonment, Forfeiture

Any person who "knowingly"[98] violates any section 9 prohibition or implementing regulation (with the exception of limited record-keeping requirements), with respect to any *endangered* animal or plant, is subject to a civil penalty[99] of up to $25,000 (as otherwise adjusted)[100] and a criminal penalty of up to $100,000 (as otherwise adjusted) and up to one year of imprisonment.[101] Any person who knowingly violates any regulation with respect to *threatened* animals or plants is subject to as much as a $12,000 (as otherwise adjusted)[102] civil penalty and a criminal penalty of up to $25,000 (as otherwise adjusted) and up to six months of imprisonment.[103] Any person who "otherwise violates any provision" of the ESA is subject to a civil penalty of up to $500 (as otherwise adjusted).[104] Finally, any equipment or vehicles used to aid in any ESA violation may be seized and are subject to permanent forfeiture.[105]

---

96. 16 U.S.C. § 1540.

97. *Id.* § 1540(e)(6) (providing that the U.S. attorney general may seek to enjoin any person who is alleged to be in violation of any provision of the ESA or its implementing regulations). See Chapter 11 for a discussion of section 11's "citizen suit" provision.

98. *See infra* notes 106–115 and accompanying text.

99. Civil penalties may be assessed only after proper notice and opportunity for hearing. 16 U.S.C. § 1540(a)(1). See 5 U.S.C. § 554 and 50 C.F.R. pt. 11 for hearing procedures.

100. 16 U.S.C. § 1540(a)(1).

101. *Id.* § 1540(b)(1). Because a criminal violation of the ESA relating to endangered species is a class A misdemeanor as defined by 18 U.S.C. § 3559(a)(6), ESA section 11's fine is supplanted by 18 U.S.C. § 3571(b)(5).

102. 16 U.S.C. § 1540(a)(1). Interestingly, persons "engaged in business" as importers of fish, wildlife, or plants may be subject to the same civil penalty levied by this subsection, for knowing *or unknowing* violations.

103. *Id.* § 1540(b)(1).

104. *Id.*

105. 16 U.S.C. § 1540(e)(4)(B). Likewise, all fish, wildlife, and plants "taken, possessed, sold, purchased, offered for sale or purchase, transported, delivered,

4.7.2 Scienter

Criminal or civil violations of the ESA may be proven only upon a showing that the defendant "knowingly" violated the ESA.[106] In 1978, Congress changed the ESA's intent requirement to "reduce" the standard for violations of the ESA "from 'willfully' to 'knowingly,'" and to clarify that "criminal violations of the Act [are] a general rather than a specific intent crime."[107] In spite of this seemingly clear statement of the degree of intent required for an ESA civil or criminal violation,[108] enough ambiguity remains that defendants continue to plead that their state of mind precludes conviction on ESA criminal counts.[109]

In 1990, the Fifth Circuit upheld the conviction of defendant Oanh Vu Nguyen on charges that he violated the ESA by possessing a threatened loggerhead sea turtle.[110] Although some facts in evidence indicated that the defendant knew it was illegal to keep the turtle, the court held these facts irrelevant,[111] concluding that "it is sufficient that Nguyen knew that he was in possession of *a* turtle," and that "the government was not required to prove that Nguyen knew that this turtle is a threatened species or that it is illegal to transport or import it."[112] In another Fifth Circuit opinion rendered only one year after *Nguyen,* the court opined that requiring a showing of specific intent would render the ESA "ineffective because it would be nearly impossible to show that an accused intended to violate the Act."[113]

---

received, carried, shipped, exported or imported" in violation of the ESA are subject to forfeiture.

106. 16 U.S.C. § 1540(a)(1).

107. H.R. Rep. No. 95-1625, at 26 (1978), *reprinted in* 1978 U.S.C.C.A.N. 9453, 9476.

108. Neither civil nor criminal penalties require a showing of specific intent. *See* H.R. Conf. Rep. No. 95-1804, at 26, *reprinted in* 1978 U.S.C.C.A.N. 9484, 9493 (noting that "the Conferees do not intend to make knowledge of the law an element of *either civil penalty or criminal violations* of the [Endangered Species] Act") (emphasis added).

109. *See, e.g.,* Babbitt v. Sweet Home Chapter of Cmtys. for a Great Or., 515 U.S. 687, 696 n.9 (1995) (speculating that the court might impute a scienter requirement to the section 11(a)(1) civil penalty applicable when one "otherwise violates" the ESA, but stating that the instant case was not a challenge to enforcement of that provision).

110. United States v. Nguyen, 916 F.2d 1016 (5th Cir. 1990).

111. *Id.* at 1018.

112. *Id.* (emphasis added).

113. United States v. Ivey, 949 F.2d 759, 766 (5th Cir. 1991).

Likewise, in 1998, the Ninth Circuit was unmoved by defendant Chad McKittrick's argument that he thought he was shooting a wild dog, when in fact the animal turned out to be an endangered gray wolf.[114] The important fact, in the court's view, was that McKittrick knew he "was shooting an animal."[115] As in situations involving less direct means of "take" than shooting, the lack of a specific intent to take a member of a listed species is generally no defense.

4.8 Bodily Harm Defense

Among the several exceptions to liability in the ESA, section 11 explicitly provides that no civil or criminal liability will attach for any ESA offense when the otherwise illegal act was committed "based on a good faith belief that [the actor] was acting to protect himself or herself, a member of his or her family, or any other individual, from bodily harm from any endangered or threatened species."[116] This defense does not extend to actions taken to protect property of any kind, including livestock and pets.[117]

---

114. United States v. McKittrick, 142 F.3d 1170, 1177 (9th Cir. 1998).

115. *Id.* The same rationale was applied in two other cases involving shooting of listed wildlife. *See* United States v. Billie, 667 F. Supp. 1485, 1492–93 (S.D. Fla. 1987) (rejecting argument that government must prove that defendant knew the animal he shot was an endangered Florida panther); United States v. St. Onge, 676 F. Supp. 1044, 1045 (D. Mont. 1988) (holding that government only had to prove that the defendant knew he was shooting an animal, which subsequently turned out to be a threatened grizzly bear; defendant's claim that he thought he was shooting an elk was irrelevant).

116. 16 U.S.C. § 1540(a)(3), (b)(3).

117. *See* Christy v. Hodel, 857 F.2d 1324 (9th Cir. 1988) (upholding fine imposed against rancher who shot a listed grizzly bear that was killing the rancher's sheep).

5 Consultation: Section 7(a)(2)

5.1 Overview

When a federal action triggers section 7, the federal agency must comply by consulting with the National Marine Fisheries Service (NMFS) or Fish and Wildlife Service (FWS) and by avoiding activities that are likely to jeopardize listed species or adversely modify those species' critical habitat. Courts and legal commentators often quote the Supreme Court's admonition in *Tennessee Valley Authority v. Hill* that "one would be hard pressed to find a statutory provision whose terms were any plainer" than section 7 of the Endangered Species Act (ESA).[1] The volume of legal commentary, regulation, and litigation arising from section 7 attests to its seemingly unambiguous far-reaching language.[2]

ESA section 7(a)(2) applies exclusively to federal agencies (and indirectly to private applicants for federal permits, approvals, or funding), and it imposes both a procedural and substantive obligations on federal agencies when they authorize, fund, or carry out any discretionary action.[3] It requires that each federal agency

> shall, *in consultation with* and with the assistance of [NMFS or FWS], insure that any action authorized, funded, or carried out by such agency . . . is *not likely to jeopardize* the continued existence of any endangered species or threatened species

1. Tenn. Valley Auth. v. Hill, 437 U.S. 153, 173 (1978).
2. *See* James C. Kilbourne, *The Endangered Species Act Under the Microscope: A Closeup Look from a Litigator's Perspective,* 21 Env't L. 499, 525 (1991) (noting that ESA section 7(a)(2) is "undoubtedly the most well known, and certainly the most frequently litigated, obligation pertaining to federal agencies").
3. 16 U.S.C. § 1536(a)(2).

> or result in the *destruction or adverse modification* of [critical habitat].[4]

The procedural and substantive mandates are designed to ensure that agencies (1) engage in appropriate consultation with FWS or NMFS when a proposed action may affect listed species or designated critical habitat, and (2) avoid jeopardizing listed species or destroying or adversely modifying designated critical habitat.

The section 7 consultation process is guided generally by what are called the 402 Joint Section 7 Consultation Regulations, which are at 50 C.F.R. 402, and the Services' *Consultation Handbook*.[5] The 402 regulations further contemplate that the federal agencies can develop "counterpart" regulations to supplement the 402 regulations,[6] and agencies also can enter into memoranda of agreement or other similar documents to assist in the consultation process.[7] Generally, the consultation process is divided into an informal consultation and a formal consultation process, with the former occasionally obviating the need for the latter. The charts

---

4. *Id.* (emphases added); 50 C.F.R. § 402.01. *See* 16 U.S.C. § 1532(7) (defining "federal agency" as "any department, agency, or instrumentality of the United States").

5. U.S. Fish & Wildlife Serv. & Nat'l Marine Fisheries Serv., Endangered Species Consultation Handbook (Mar. 1998) [hereinafter Consultation Handbook]. *See* 64 Fed. Reg. 31,285 (1999) (announcing availability of handbook). This handbook predates the Services' latest changes to the 402 regulations, at 89 Fed. Reg. 24,268 (Apr. 5, 2024), and possibly any subsequently issued changes made by a new administration.

6. The history of counterpart regulations has not necessarily been promising. Counterpart regulations, for instance, were developed for the national fire plan, 68 Fed. Reg. 68,254 (Dec. 8, 2003) (50 C.F.R. § 402.30), but in December 2011, BLM indicated that the alternative consultation process had not proved effective. Assistant Director, Renewable Resources, Bureau of Land Management, Instruction Memorandum No. 2012-049 (Dec. 11, 2011). *See* Defs. of Wildlife v. Salazar, 842 F. Supp. 2d 181 (D.D.C. 2012) (reviewing national fire plan consultation regulations); *see also* Joint Counterpart Regulations re Actions Under the Federal Insecticide, Fungicide, and Rodenticide Act, 69 Fed. Reg. 47,732 (Aug. 5, 2004). *But cf.* Wash. Toxics Coal. v. U.S. Fish & Wildlife Serv., 457 F. Supp. 2d 1158 (W. D. Wash. 2006) (reviewing counterpart regulations).

7. *E.g.*, Memorandum of Agreement Between the Environmental Protection Agency, Fish and Wildlife Service, and National Marine Fisheries Service Regarding Enhanced Coordination Under the Clean Water Act and Endangered Species Act, 66 Fed. Reg. 11,201 (2001). Specific consultation issues might be addressed through a memorandum as well. The U.S. Army Corps of Engineers and NMFS, for instance, entered into an agreement for how to assess the effects of existing structures during a consultation process. Memorandum Between the Department of the Army (Civil Works) and the National Oceanic and Atmospheric Administration, Jan. 5, 2022.

at the end of this chapter, from the *Consultation Handbook,* illustrate the process for each of these consultations.

5.2 Agency Action

Because section 7(a)(2) of the ESA applies only to discretionary federal agency actions, the first inquiry is whether any "federal agency" is engaging in any "action." Although the ESA does not define the word *action*, the Services define the term in their Joint Section 7 Consultation Regulations:

> *Action* means all activities or programs of any kind authorized, funded, or carried out, in whole or in part, by federal agencies in the United States or upon the high seas. Examples include, but are not limited to:
>
> (a) actions intended to conserve listed species or their habitat;
> (b) the promulgation of regulations;
> (c) the granting of licenses, contracts, leases, easements, rights-of-way permits, or grants-in-aid; or
> (d) actions directly or indirectly causing modifications to the land, water, or air.[8]

As the succeeding discussion notes, clearly identifying a "federal agency . . . action" is essential; it informs the consultation process. And courts generally construe the term *action* broadly.[9]

Examples of when courts have determined that federal agency activities satisfy the ESA definition of *agency action* include federal program activities as well as federal permitting and licensing activities. Federal program activities triggering section 7 are quite varied, and they include agency development of management plans for public lands,[10] timber sales,[11] operation of federal dams,[12] and providing funding for programs that are not

8. 50 C.F.R. § 402.02.

9. *See, e.g.,* Tenn. Valley Auth. v. Hill, 437 U.S. 153 (1978) (rejecting notion that section 7 applies only to projects in planning stage); Conner v. Burford, 848 F.2d 1441, 1453 (9th Cir. 1982).

10. *E.g.,* Ctr. for Biological Diversity v. BLM, 422 F. Supp. 2d 1115 (N.D. Cal. 2006).

11. Lane Cnty. Audubon Soc'y v. Jamison, 958 F.2d 290, 294–95 (9th Cir. 1992) (BLM timber sales enjoined pending consultation on interim strategy).

12. Bennett v. Spear, 520 U.S. 154 (1997).

federally operated.[13] A similarly broad approach toward *agency action* applies to private activities requiring some form of federal agency approval, whether in issuing a license or permit, granting a right-of-way, or entering into a contract. Section 7, therefore, has applied to the U.S. Army Corps of Engineers' issuance of Clean Water Act section 404 dredge and fill material (wetlands) permits,[14] licenses and permits issued by the Federal Energy Regulatory Commission,[15] and the Bureau of Reclamation's renewal of existing water service contracts[16] and annual delivery of water under existing water service contracts.[17] But conversely, merely giving advice to a private entity does not necessarily rise to the level of an agency action,[18] nor would generic funding of state programs "federalize" state agency actions, requiring the state agency to engage in a section 7(a)(2) consultation.[19]

Identifying an agency action can become controversial or difficult when one of three interrelated circumstances exists: when an agency fails to act, when an agency previously acted but the action is ongoing, or when the agency lacks sufficient discretion

---

13. *E.g.*, Fla. Key Deer v. Paulison, 522 F.3d 1133 (11th Cir. 2008) (FEMA's implementation of the National Flood Insurance Program); Nat'l Wildlife Fed'n v. FEMA, 345 F. Supp. 2d 1151 (W.D. Wash. 2004) (same); Fla. Key Deer v. Stickney, 864 F. Supp. 1222 (S.D. Fla. 1994) (same).

14. Nat'l Wildlife Fed'n v. Norton, 332 F. Supp. 2d 170 (D.D.C. 2004).

15. *See* Cal. Sportfishing Prot. All. v. FERC, 472 F.3d 593, 599 (9th Cir. 2006) (issuance of hydroelectric license triggers section 7(a)(2)).

16. NRDC v. Jewell, 749 F.3d 776 (9th Cir. 2014); NRDC v. Houston, 146 F.3d 1118, 1125 (9th Cir. 1998); NRDC v. Norton, 236 F. Supp. 3d 1198 (E.D. Cal. 2017).

17. O'Neil v. United States, 50 F.3d 677, 680–81 (9th Cir. 1995) (consultation requirement triggered because Bureau of Reclamation must act annually to deliver water pursuant to existing contracts). *But cf.* NRDC v. Salazar, 686 F.3d 1092 (9th Cir. 2012) (settlement contracts not subject to section 7(a)(2)).

18. Marbled Murrelet v. Babbitt, 83 F.3d 1068, 1073–75 (9th Cir. 1996) (FWS advice to lumber company, as to how to avoid take of listed species during logging operation, did not represent discretionary involvement or control for purposes of ESA section 7). When the agency's action has little or no effect on the activity and does not operate as any form of an approval for the activity, section 7(a)(2) might not apply. *E.g.*, Ark Initiative v. U.S. Forest Serv., 2010 WL 3323661 (D. Colo. 2010) (agency acceptance of a vision document), *aff'd on other grounds*, 660 F.3d 1256 (10th Cir. 2011); Tex. Indep. Producers & Royalty Owners Ass'n v. EPA, 410 F.3d 964, 979 (7th Cir. 2005) (section 7 not triggered by ministerial acceptance of a notice); Ctr. for Biological Diversity v. Chertoff, 2009 WL 839042 (N.D. Cal. 2009) (unpublished) (Coast Guard's issuance of advisory notices did not trigger section 7(a)(2)). *Cf.* Turtle Island Restoration Network v. NMFS, 340 F.3d 969 (9th Cir. 2003) (agency action existed when NMFS exercised discretion and conditioning authority).

19. *See* Or. Nat. Res. Council v. Hallock (D. Or. 2006) (unpublished). Federal funding often creates a difficult question under section 7. *See* Ctr. for Biological Diversity v. HUD, 541 F. Supp. 2d 1091 (D. Ariz. 2008) (consultation not required), *aff'd unpublished opinion*, 359 F. App'x 781 (9th Cir. 2009).

when undertaking an action. When, for instance, an agency fails to act to address alleged ongoing threats to a species, it is essential to distinguish the agency's failure to act from the agency's ongoing actions. The Ninth Circuit has indicated that the failure to act does not itself trigger section 7(a)(2).[20] But when the agency retains sufficient discretion to alter its ongoing actions, that same court has held that section 7(a)(2) applies.[21] In *Tennessee Valley Authority v. Hill,* for instance, the Court emphasized that section 7 still applied even though the project was almost completed, because the agency still had an activity left to carry out.[22] The 402 regulations expressly note that section 7(a)(2) applies only to discretionary agency actions.[23] And when an agency lacks discretion over an action, including an ongoing agency action, section 7(a)(2) does not apply. The issue for ongoing agency actions, therefore, generally becomes whether the agency has retained sufficient discretion to alter or control the activity presenting a threat to listed species or their designated critical habitat.[24] In

20. *See* W. Watershed Project v. Matejko, 468 F.3d 1099, 1108 (9th Cir. 2006).

21. *See* Karuk Tribe of Cal. v. U.S. Forest Serv., 681 F.3d 1006 (9th Cir. 2012) (ESA applied to notice of intent to conduct mining activities on national forest lands); *Turtle Island Restoration Network v. NMFS*, 340 F.3d at 976–77 (section 7 applied to ongoing actions); Klamath Water Users Protective Ass'n v. Patterson, 191 F.3d 1115 (9th Cir. 1999) (Bureau of Reclamation ownership and retention of management discretion at a dam were held to trigger consultation on operation of the dam); Pac. Rivers Council v. Thomas, 30 F.3d 1050, 1053–56 (9th Cir. 1994) (Forest Service is required to consult on its existing land and resource management plans whenever a species is listed that may be affected by ongoing and future forest management projects).

22. Tenn. Valley Auth. v. Hill, 437 U.S. 153, 173 (1978) ("It has not been shown . . . how TVA can close the gates of the Tellico Dam without 'carrying out' an action that has been 'authorized' and 'funded' by a federal agency. Nor can we understand how such action will '*insure*' that the snail darter's habitat is not disrupted."). *Cf. id.* at 196 (Powell, J., dissenting) (arguing that the ESA should not apply to a project that was completed or substantially completed when its threat to an endangered species was discovered).

23. 50 C.F.R. § 402.03 ("Section 7 and the requirements of this Part apply to all actions in which there is discretionary federal involvement and control.").

24. *See, e.g.,* Grand Canyon Trust v. U.S. Bureau of Reclamation, 691 F.3d 1008, 1019 (9th Cir. Aug. 13, 2012) (annual operating plans did not trigger section 7); NRDC v. Salazar, 686 F.3d 1092 (9th Cir. 2012) (renewal of settlement contracts did not trigger section 7); Cal. Sportfishing Prot. All. v. FERC, 472 F.3d 593 (9th Cir. 2006) (ongoing hydroelectric operation is not an agency action when agency lacks authority to control); W. Watershed Project v. Matejko, 468 F.3d 1099, 1108, 1110 (9th Cir. 2006) (agency did not retain discretion); Wash. Toxics Coal. v. EPA, 413 F.3d 1024 (9th Cir. 2005) (pesticide program requires ESA compliance); Ground Zero Ctr. for Non-Violent Action v. Dep't of Navy, 383 F.3d 1082 (9th Cir. 2004) (consultation not required); Env't Prot. Info. Ctr. v. Simpson Timber Co., 255 F.3d 1073, 1083 (9th Cir. 2001) (no retained discretion); Platte River Whooping Crane Trust v. FERC, 962 F.2d 27, 32–33 (D.C. Cir. 1992) (no "action" existed when FERC was required to issue an annual operation license

National Association of Homebuilders v. Defenders of Wildlife,[25] the Supreme Court upheld the regulation, and concluded that the Environmental Protection Agency's delegation of Clean Water Act permitting authority under section 402 of that act did not trigger section 7(a)(2), because the agency lacked sufficient discretion under the Clean Water Act to apply ESA criteria to its decision. A slightly different issue surfaced with the delegation of the section 404 program to the State of Florida.[26]

5.3 Effects of the Action

Once an agency determines that a particular activity is an "action," the agency must then assess the action's effects on listed species or critical habitat. And when doing so, the agencies employ "the best scientific and commercial data available."[27] The "effects of an action" include "all consequences to listed species or critical habitat that are caused by the proposed action, including the consequences of other activities that are caused by the proposed action but that are not part of the action."[28] Notably, a "consequence is caused by the proposed action if it would not occur but for the proposed action and it is reasonably certain to occur," even if the effects of the action might "occur later in time" and "outside the immediate area involved in the action."[29] During

"under the terms and conditions of the existing license"); Sierra Club v. Babbitt, 65 F.3d 1502 (9th Cir. 1995) (no action exists when reciprocal right-of-way agreement did not give Bureau of Land Management authority to affect road construction by private parties).

25. 551 U.S. 644 (2007).

26. Office of Water, David P. Ross, Memorandum on Endangered Species Act Section 7(a)(2) Consultation for State and Tribal Clean Water Act Section 404 Program Approvals EPA (Aug. 27, 2020); Request for Comment on Whether EPA's Approval of a Clean Water Act Section 404 Program is Non-Discretionary for Purposes of Endangered Species Act Section 7 Consultation, 85 Fed. Reg. 30,953 (May 21, 2020). Florida sought a programmatic consultation where future state permittees would be shielded from section 9 liability (a programmatic incidental take statement). Ctr. for Biological Diversity v. Regan, 734 F. Supp. 3d 1 (D.D.C. 2024), *appeal pending in* Ctr. for Biological Diversity v. Regan, No. 24-5101 (D.C. Cir.). EPA discussed the relationship of the ESA and the delegation of the section 404 permitting program in its 2024 rulemaking on delegations. EPA, Clean Water Act Section 404 Tribal and State Assumption Program, 89 Fed. Reg. 103,454, 103,463 (Dec. 18, 2024).

27. 16 U.S.C. § 1536(a)(2).

28. 50 C.F.R. § 402.02; 89 Fed. Reg. 24,268, 24,274, 24,297 (Apr. 5, 2024).

29. *Id.*

the first Trump administration, the Services concluded that too much emphasis was being placed on categorizing effects, such as "direct" or "indirect," and amended the regulations to remove the regulatory definition for "indirect" effect. The Biden administration's 2024 regulations agreed that such categorization is unnecessary, and the regulations now focus on merely the "effects of the action."[30] The Services explain that the "definition and the 'but for' and 'reasonably certain to occur' causation provide a clear test of what constitutes an effect of the action."[31] This "but for" test reflects, according to the Services, their "longstanding practices and has not changed the scope of" their analyses.[32] The Services also noted that additional information about "effects of the action" will be included in a new *Consultation Handbook*.

A determination of the effects of a proposed action will dictate whether, and to what extent, consultation is required for a particular action and will ultimately determine whether the proposed action may proceed.[33] In many respects, then, section 7 compliance begins and ends with a critical focus on the effects of a proposed action.

In one example of an effect that would occur later in time, in *National Wildlife Federation v. Coleman*, the Fifth Circuit held that the Department of Transportation had failed to consider the effects on sandhill cranes of future private development that would result from highway construction.[34] In another case, the Tenth Circuit held that the Army Corps of Engineers, in considering whether to grant the Clean Water Act permit necessary for construction of a dam, must consider the future effects of the increased consumptive use of water that will result from the dam and affect whooping cranes 150 miles away.[35] The court explained that ignoring

30. 89 Fed. Reg. at 24,271.

31. *Id.*

32. *Id.* at 24,272.

33. Consultation is not required for federal actions that are "environmentally neutral" and thus have no effect on a listed species. Marin Audubon Soc'y v. Seidman, Civ. No. 91-2029 (N.D. Cal. Nov. 21, 1991), *aff'd*, 999 F.2d 543 (9th Cir. July 13, 1993) (unpublished) (FDIC sale of note, secured by property that was habitat for listed species, was not an action affecting the species).

34. Nat'l Wildlife Fed'n v. Coleman, 529 F.2d 359, 373 (5th Cir. 1976) (holding that residential and commercial development "that can be expected to result from the construction of the highway" must be considered as an indirect effect of highway construction).

35. Riverside Irr. Dist. v. Andrews, 758 F.2d 508, 512 (10th Cir. 1985), *cited with approval in* Consultation Handbook, *supra* note 5, at 4-28.

such effects would allow the agency to "wear blinders that Congress has not chosen to impose."[36]

The 1998 *Consultation Handbook* discusses indirect effects in some detail,[37] and includes the following example of a federal action with indirect effects:

> A very complex example of indirect effects arose in determining effects of renewing water service contracts from a large reclamation project (Friant Unit of the Central Valley Project) in the San Joaquin Basin of California. Upon checking with other Federal and State agencies, the FWS determined that the distribution of water for agricultural use on the higher east side of the Valley provided a hydrologic head maintaining the groundwater table on the west side of the Valley at a level making it economical to pump. As a result, occupied habitats for several species on the west side of the Valley were being destroyed because the pumped water could be used to convert this land to agriculture.[38]

Future groundwater development, for instance, was considered an indirect effect of water service contract renewal. Although purely speculative actions do not meet the definition of a "reasonably certain to occur" action, the phrase does not require a guarantee that the action will occur.[39]

One issue that joins considering the *effects of an action* with an identification of the *action* is how to treat existing infrastructure. This issue has surfaced in connection with the operation of hydroelectric projects, and whether the existence of a dam is part of the action whose effects ought to be considered under section 7.[40]

5.3.1 The Environmental Baseline

The logical first question for an analysis of a project's likely effects is, "Effects on what?" Determining the likely effects of an action on a species or its critical habitat requires an evaluation of the

36. *Id.*
37. Consultation Handbook, *supra* note 5, at 4-27–31.
38. *Id.* at 4-28.
39. *Id.* at 4-30.
40. *E.g.*, Friends of the River v. NMFS, 786 Fed. App'x 666 (9th Cir. 2019) (court held it was arbitrary and capricious for agency to change its position without a reasoned explanation).

"status of the species or critical habitat at issue," including the status of the "present environment in which the species or critical habitat exist."[41] This snapshot in time,[42] referred to as the "environmental baseline," directs agencies to identify and understand existing conditions before considering the effects of a proposed action on those conditions. After all, an inadequate baseline analysis can tarnish an effects analysis.[43]

The *environmental baseline* for section 7 consultation purposes is defined as:

> [t]he condition of the listed species or its designated critical habitat in the action area, without the consequences to the listed species or designated critical habitat caused by the proposed action. The environmental baseline includes the past and present impacts of all Federal, State, or private actions and other human activities in the action area, the anticipated impacts of all proposed Federal projects in the action area that have already undergone formal or early section 7 consultation, and the impact of State or private actions which are contemporaneous with the consultation in process. The impacts to listed species or designated critical habitat from Federal agency activities or existing Federal agency facilities that are not within the agency's discretion to modify are part of the environmental baseline.[44]

Of particular note is the inclusion in the baseline of the impacts of federal actions that already have undergone consultation. Agencies are well advised to meet their consultation obligations sooner rather than later, before the baseline becomes further degraded as other federal actions complete consultation. This approach arguably creates a veritable "race to the baseline," with the last-in-time agency action running a higher risk that the environmental baseline can handle no further degradation without

41. Proposed Joint Consultation Regulations, Supplementary Information, 48 Fed. Reg. 29,990, 29,994 (1983).

42. Consultation Handbook, *supra* note 5, at 4-22, describes the environmental baseline as "a snapshot of a species' health at a specific point in time."

43. *See* Appalachian Voices v. U.S. Dep't of the Interior, 25 F.4th 259, 272–73 (4th Cir. 2022).

44. 50 C.F.R. § 402.02; 89 Fed. Reg. 24,268, 24,274 (Apr. 5, 2024). This seemingly structured approach toward identifying the likely effects of an action is not necessarily completely congruent with modern ecological principles. *See* Fred Bosselman, *What Lawmakers Can Learn from Large-Scale Ecology,* 17 J. Land Use & Env't L. 207 (2002); J. B. Ruhl & James Salzman, *Gaming the Past: The Theory and Practice of Historic Baselines in the Administrative State,* 64 Vand. L. Rev. 1 (2011).

jeopardizing a listed species or resulting in adverse modification of critical habitat. The Ninth Circuit, after all, suggests that "the proper baseline analysis is not the proportional share of responsibility the federal agency bears for the decline in the species, but what jeopardy might result from the agency's proposed actions in the present and future human and natural contexts."[45]

But often identifying an environmental baseline is difficult, particularly when the proposed action involves the continuation of prior activities or an extension or modification of those ongoing prior activities. This has become particularly evident in the struggle over defining the environmental baseline for the operation of the federal hydroelectric dams that constitute the Federal Columbia River Power System.[46] It also has surfaced elsewhere, when parties engage in debates over natural conditions or the period for those conditions that are said to preexist the prior activity.[47] In addition, rising greenhouse gas emissions and the resulting effect on climate makes the process even more difficult because of the influence on any baseline analysis.

---

45. Nat'l Wildlife Fed'n v. NMFS, 524 F.3d 917, 930 (9th Cir. 2008). Nor may an agency exclude from its baseline past effects from nondiscretionary actions that continue to the present and possibly the future; *see id.* at 926, 928; *see also* Ctr. for Biological Diversity v. BLM, 746 F. Supp. 2d 1055, 1106 (N.D. Cal. 2009); Pac. Coast Fed'n of Fishermen's Ass'n v. Gutierrez, 606 F. Supp. 2d 1122, 1176 (E.D. Cal. 2008) ("The approach enunciated by the court in *NWF v. NMFS* does not require NMFS to include the entire environmental baseline in the agency action subject to review. It simply requires that NMFS appropriately consider the effects of its actions within the context of other existing human activities that impact the listed species. [T]he proper baseline analysis is not the proportional share of responsibility the federal agency bears for the decline in the species, but what jeopardy might result from the agency's proposed actions *in the present and future human and natural contexts.*" (emphasis in original) (citations and internal quotation marks omitted)).

46. *See* Michael C. Blumm et al., *Practiced in the Art of Deception: The Failure of Columbia Basin Salmon Recovery Under the Endangered Species Act,* 36 Env't L. 709, 736 (2006). In one relicensing of a hydroelectric project involving an instance of an already degraded baseline, a court chided the agency for failing to assess the impact of continued operations. Am. Rivers v. FERC, 895 F.3d 32, 47 (D.C. Cir. 2018).

47. *E.g., In re* Operation of the Mo. River Sys. Litig., 421 F.3d 618, 632–33 (8th Cir. 2005); Klamath Water Users Protective Ass'n v. Patterson, 191 F.3d 1115 (9th Cir. 1999). *See* A. Dan Tarlock, *Ecosystem Services in the Klamath Basin: Battlefield Casualties or the Future,* 22 J. Land Use & Env't L. 207, 240 (2007); *see also* San Luis & Delta-Mendota Water Auth. v. Salazar, 760 F. Supp. 2d 855 (E.D. Cal. 2010).

5.3.2 Cumulative Effects

When a particular agency action leads to formal consultation,[48] FWS or NMFS must evaluate both the effects of the action and the cumulative effects on the listed species or critical habitat.[49] Unlike direct, indirect, interdependent, or interrelated effects, which are all part of an agency's initial determination of the "effects of the action," cumulative effects are not initially considered by an action agency to determine the extent of its consultation obligations.[50] Rather, once an agency has determined that the effects of a proposed action warrant formal consultation, cumulative effects are added to the effects of the action to determine whether the proposed action will result in jeopardy to a listed species or adverse modification or destruction of critical habitat.

Cumulative effects are defined in the 402 regulations as "those effects of future State or private activities, not involving Federal activities, that are reasonably certain to occur within the action area of the Federal action subject to consultation."[51] To meet the "reasonably certain to occur" standard, there must be more than a "mere possibility that the action may proceed . . . bearing in mind the economic, administrative, or legal hurdles which remain to be cleared."[52] The Services recently cautioned that this *reasonably certain to occur* language "adds an element of foreseeability and a limitation to [its] causation standard for determining 'effects of the action.'"[53] And it should "prevent[] the Services from engaging in speculative analyses."[54]

If a biological assessment (BA) is prepared,[55] the 402 regulations recommend that it contain a "consideration" of cumulative effects.[56] Likewise, if an agency initiates formal consultation,

48. See Section 5.4.4 for a discussion of formal consultation.
49. 50 C.F.R. § 402.14(g)(3).
50. *See, e.g.*, Sierra Club v. Marsh, 816 F.2d 1376, 1387 (9th Cir. 1987) (cumulative effects not relevant for determining whether agency must reinitiate consultation).
51. 50 C.F.R. § 402.02. *See also* CONSULTATION HANDBOOK, *supra* note 5, at 4-30–31 (discussing cumulative effects).
52. Preamble to Final Joint Consultation Rules, 51 Fed. Reg. 19,926, 19,933 (1986).
53. 89 Fed. Reg. 24,268, 24,270 (Apr. 5, 2024).
54. *Id.*
55. See Section 5.4.3 for a discussion of the BA requirement.
56. 50 C.F.R. § 402.12(f)(4).

the 402 regulations require the action agency to include, in its request to initiate formal consultation, an "analysis of any cumulative effects."[57]

5.3.3 Phased Consultations

Many federal agency actions or processes employ multilayered decision-making, often raising the question of when section 7 consultation is appropriate and what the scope of that consultation should cover. Should, for instance, the consultation process apply to the leasing of public lands to a private entity or, instead, only to when the private entity eventually develops and submits for approval an actual plan for the use of those lands? Potentially, however, an agency could segregate a possibly harmful proposed action into a series of small steps, each of which would, when examined separately, appear environmentally benign.

The Services address this issue in a few ways.[58] An agency might engage in a programmatic consultation, which would "allow the Services to consult on the effects of programmatic actions such as—

1. Multiple similar, frequently occurring, or routine actions expected to be implemented in particular geographic areas; and
2. A proposed program, plan, policy, or regulation proving a framework for future proposed actions."[59]

Programmatic consultations contemplate that the agency will use a tiered approach toward a review of specific agency actions, first examining the impacts broadly in the programmatic document and then using that information in subsequent biological opinions (BO) for decisions involving specific activities contemplated by and consistent with that broader programmatic document.[60] For such programmatic consultations where there is a framework in place for the review of future specific actions that might be

57. *Id.* § 402.14(c)(1)(iv).

58. A faster consultation process can also be developed with expedited timelines under the 402 regulations. *Id.* § 402.14(l).

59. 50 C.F.R. § 402.02.

60. *See* Melinda E. Taylor & Richard E. Sayers, Jr., *Interagency Consultation and Conservation Duties Under Section 7*, *in* Endangered Species Act: Law, Policy, and Perspectives 111, 134 (Donald C. Baur & Ya-Wei Li, eds., 3d ed. 2021).

authorized, funded, or carried out, "and any take of a listed species would not occur unless and until those future action(s) are authorized, funded, or carried out" and are themselves "subject to further section 7 consultation," the agency may avoid having to develop an incidental take statement during consultation and rely on the "[f]ramework programmatic action."[61] The 402 regulations attempt to address this issue and allow "incremental step" consultations when the action is authorized by a statute that allows the agency to take incremental steps toward completion of the action.[62] The Services then may issue a biological opinion on the incremental step being considered.[63] And the action agency may proceed with the incremental step if

- the BO does not conclude that the incremental step would violate section 7(a)(2);
- the action agency continues consulting with respect to the entire action;
- the action agency fulfills its obligation to obtain data upon which to base a final decision on the entire action;
- the incremental step does not violate section 7(d) of the ESA;[64] and
- there is a reasonable likelihood that the entire action will not violate section 7(a)(2) of the ESA.[65]

These criteria, when considered along with an agency's obligation to consider the indirect effects ("reasonably certain to occur") of any action,[66] have made it difficult for some agencies to engage in an incremental consultation process that segments the consultation process into phases based on the agency's processes or decisions. One prominent instance where an incremental approach has received judicial endorsement is in the leasing of oil and gas on the Outer Continental Shelf.[67]

61. *Id.; see* 50 C.F.R. § 402.02.

62. 50 C.F.R. § 402.14(k). See Preamble to Joint Consultation Regulations, 51 Fed. Reg. 19,926, 19,954 (1986) (noting the intended consistency of the regulations with N. Slope Borough v. Andrus, 642 F.2d 589 (D.C. Cir. 1980)).

63. 50 C.F.R. § 402.14(k). In doing so, the Service also will include "its views on the entire action." *Id.*

64. See Section 5.6 for a discussion of ESA section 7(d).

65. 50 C.F.R. § 402.14(k)(1)–(5).

66. See Section 5.3.2 for a discussion of indirect effects.

67. Ctr. for Biological Diversity v. Dep't of the Interior, 563 F.3d 466, 482–83 (D.C. Cir. 2009) (ESA claim not ripe at leasing stage); *see also N. Slope Borough*, 642 F.2d at 608 (holding that segmented consultation was appropriate for offshore

5.4 The Consultation Process

If a federal agency determines that it is proposing to take an "action" that triggers section 7(a)(2), the 402 regulations and *Consultation Handbook* contemplate that the agency should then determine whether that action "may affect" a listed species or its critical habitat; if so the agency must then "consult" with NMFS or FWS[68] (depending on the particular species affected[69]) to ensure that the action does not jeopardize the listed species or adversely modify or destroy its critical habitat.[70] In satisfying the section 7 consultation requirements, agencies must utilize the best scientific and commercial data available,[71] and agencies that fail to consult properly risk that a court might enjoin their activity.[72]

The consultation process unfolds depending upon how the agency and the Secretary answer a sequence of questions regarding the nature of the proposed agency action and its potential effects on listed species or critical habitat. The following discussion generally mirrors the chronological sequence of the ESA section 7 process.

---

leasing activities, in light of "checks and balances" provided by Outer Continental Shelf Land Act (OCSLA)); Vill. of False Pass v. Watt, 565 F. Supp. 1123, 1156 (D. Alaska 1983), *aff'd sub nom.* Vill. of False Pass v. Clark, 733 F.2d 605 (9th Cir. 1984) (following rationale of *North Slope,* allowed incremental-step consultation under OCSLA). *But cf.* Conner v. Burford, 848 F.2d 1441, 1453 (9th Cir. 1988) (holding that the Mineral Leasing Act, unlike the OCSLA, did not contemplate incremental-step activities); Ksanka Kupaqa Xa'lcin v. U.S. Fish & Wildlife Serv., 534 F. Supp. 3d 1261, 1270 (D. Mont. 2021) (discussing Conner and searching into the scope of action and resulting activities), *appeal dismissed* 2021 WL 420503 (9th Cir. July 19, 2021).

68. For purposes of this chapter, NMFS and FWS are alternatively referred to as "the Services," "the Secretary," "the Director," or "the consulting agencies." Other federal agencies are the "action agencies" for purposes of section 7 consultation.

69. See 50 C.F.R. §§ 223.102 and 224.101 for lists of endangered and threatened species under NMFS jurisdiction, and 50 C.F.R. §§ 17.11 (wildlife) and 17.12 (plants) for lists of endangered and threatened species under FWS jurisdiction.

70. 16 U.S.C. § 1536(a)(2).

71. *Id.*

72. *See, e.g.,* Pac. Rivers Council v. Robertson, 854 F. Supp. 713, 724 (D. Or. 1993) (holding that procedural violations of the ESA, such as not initiating section 7 consultation when required, mandate that the underlying action be enjoined), *aff'd in part, rev'd in part sub nom.* Pac. Rivers Council v. Thomas, 30 F.3d 1050 (9th Cir. 1994).

5.4.1 Presence of Listed Species or Critical Habitat in the Action Area

To evaluate the effects of a proposed project on listed species or critical habitat, agencies initially determine what species or critical habitat is present in the "action area." The *action area* for any proposed project is defined quite broadly to include all areas directly or indirectly affected by the action, not merely those in "the immediate area involved in the action."[73] For "major construction activities,"[74] the ESA and 402 regulations require the action agency to communicate with the Services in writing to identify listed species or designated critical habitat that may be present in the action area.[75] And for "major construction activities" occurring in the presence of listed species or critical habitat, the action agency must prepare a BA. For other actions, the regulations provide that an action agency may (and often does) solicit assistance from the Secretary when determining what species and critical habitat might be present in the action area.[76] Once a species or its habitat is identified, the action agency and the Secretary must then determine if and to what degree that species or habitat will be affected.

5.4.2 "May Affect" Determination

Upon determining that a listed species or designated critical habitat may be present in the action area, the action agency should then determine whether the proposed action "may affect" a listed species.[77] The 402 regulations contemplate that, if a BA is

---

73. 50 C.F.R § 402.02.

74. 16 U.S.C. § 1536(c)(1). These are "construction projects" or "other undertaking[s] having similar physical impacts" that are major federal actions that would otherwise trigger an environmental impact statement (EIS) under the National Environmental Policy Act. 50 C.F.R. § 402.02.

75. 50 C.F.R. § 402.12(c). The Service must respond to the action agency's request for a list of species affected within 30 days. *Id.* § 402.12(d).

76. Agencies often seek the expertise of the Services in developing species and critical habitat lists for nonconstruction activities, and the Services will meet the same 30-day response time when possible. Consultation Handbook, *supra* note 5, at 3-2.

77. 50 C.F.R. § 402.14(a) (providing that agencies should review their actions at the "earliest possible time to determine whether any action may affect listed species or critical habitat").

required, this determination may be made in the BA itself. For other activities, the "may affect" determination need not be contained in a formal document, although a detailed written record is advisable.

The term *may affect* is not defined in the ESA or the 402 regulations, but the *Consultation Handbook* defines it as "the appropriate conclusion when a proposed action may pose *any* effects on listed species or designated critical habitat."[78] This definition, combined with the breadth of the previously discussed "effects of the action,"[79] sets the "may affect" threshold quite low.[80]

Agencies may conclude the informal consultation process if they determine that the action will have "no effect" on listed species or critical habitat.[81] Although not required, an agency may voluntarily request from the Services a written concurrence with the "no effect" determination; this concurrence might be "useful for the Administrative Record"[82] should the agency's determination be challenged.

5.4.3 Biological Assessment Preparation or Informal Consultation

If the action agency determines, in consultation with the appropriate Service and possibly state and Tribal resource agencies, that listed species or their critical habitat may be present in the action area and affected, the next question is whether any such species or habitat is "likely to be adversely affected." Section 7(c) of the ESA generally contemplates that the action agency can answer this question through the preparation of a BA, and possibly in combination with the development of an environmental document under NEPA.[83] Even if not required, many agencies, in prac-

---

78. Consultation Handbook, *supra* note 5, at xvi.

79. See Section 5.3 for a discussion of "effects of the action."

80. In a case involving a challenge to the sufficiency of consultation or alternatively the necessity for reinitiation of consultation, one court observed how the standard is "very low." Ctr. for Biological Diversity v. U.S. Army Corps of Eng'rs, 2020 WL 9073339 (S.D. Fla. Aug. 28, 2020).

81. *See* Newton Cnty. Wildlife Ass'n v. Rogers, 141 F.3d 803, 810 (8th Cir. 1998) ("A finding of no effect obviates the need for consultation.").

82. Consultation Handbook, *supra* note 5, at 3-12.

83. 16 U.S.C. § 1736(c); 50 C.F.R. § 402.14(b) (formal consultation is not required for actions that are not likely to adversely affect listed species or critical habitat). Also, where appropriate, a state, or local agency, private organization, or

tice, prepare BAs, particularly for proposed actions that arguably might impact species or their habitat. Failure to prepare a necessary BA could constitute a "substantial" violation of the ESA.[84] The Act requires that, in particular, an agency must complete its BA prior to executing any contract for construction (for "major construction activities"), and before any construction is begun.[85]

Determining whether any listed species or critical habitat might be adversely affected occurs during the process often referred to as informal consultation. Informal consultation generally means the internal communications between the Service and the federal agency designed to assist the action agency in determining whether formal consultation will be necessary.[86] During this process, the Service may suggest modifications to the action that the federal agencies could implement to avoid the likelihood of adverse effects to listed species or critical habitat.[87]

The contents of the BA are "at the discretion" of the action agency; the 402 regulations advise that the following types of information be considered for inclusion:

- The results of an on-site inspection of the area affected by the action;
- The views of recognized experts on the species at issue;
- A review of the literature and other information;
- An analysis of the effects of the action on the species and habitat, including consideration of cumulative effects;
- An analysis of alternate actions considered by the federal agency for the proposed action.[88]

At a minimum, the BA, by definition, should evaluate "potential effects" of the action on listed species and designated critical habitat.[89] Regardless of the information included in the BA, the agency must use the "best scientific and commercial data

---

individual may voluntarily prepare a biological assessment. *See* Preamble to Final Joint Consultation Rules, 51 Fed. Reg. 19,926, 19,945 (1986).

84. Thomas v. Peterson, 841 F.2d 332 (9th Cir. 1988) (Forest Service road construction enjoined because of failure to prepare BA).

85. 16 U.S.C. § 1536(c); 50 C.F.R. § 402.12(b)(2).

86. 50 C.F.R. § 402.13(a).

87. *Id.* § 402.13(b).

88. *Id.* § 402.12(f). *See* Strahan v. Linnon, 967 F. Supp. 581, 594 (D. Mass. 1997) ("the contents of the BA are discretionary").

89. 50 C.F.R. § 402.02 (definition of "biological assessment").

available."[90] And the regulations contemplate that the BA should be completed within 180 days of the agency's receipt of a list of species present in the action area, unless the Secretary and action agency agree to a longer time period.[91]

The goal of the BA, as with the informal consultation period itself, is to determine whether the proposed action is, or is not, likely to adversely affect listed species or critical habitat.[92] If the action agency concludes that its proposed action is not likely to cause either of these results, and the Service concurs in writing,[93] no further consultation is required. It is imperative, however, that to avoid engaging in formal consultation, the Service issue a *written concurrence* before the action agency can proceed with its proposed action; otherwise, formal consultation is required.[94] The determination that a species may be affected but is not likely to be adversely affected is subject to judicial scrutiny.[95] And, conversely, if the action agency or the BA indicates that the action is likely to adversely affect a listed species or critical habitat, formal consultation must occur.

When the consultation process involves a private applicant seeking some form of federal authorization, that private applicant has the ability to suggest that the action agency designate the applicant as a "designated nonfederal representative."[96] Often this option is attractive for the private applicant, because it allows the applicant to engage with the Service early in the process.

---

90. 16 U.S.C. § 1536(a)(2).

91. 50 C.F.R. § 402.12(i). If an applicant is involved, the 180-day period may not be extended without first notifying the applicant of the estimated length of the proposed extension and the reasons why the extension is necessary. *Id.*

92. *Id.* § 402.12(k).

93. *Id.* § 402.12(j). The Service must respond to the action agency within 30 days of receipt of the BA, stating whether it concurs with the action agency's conclusions. *Id.*

94. *E.g.*, Pac. Rivers Council v. Thomas, 30 F.3d 1050 (9th Cir. 1994). In *Western Watersheds Project v. Kraayenbrink*, 630 F.3d 1187, 1208–12 (9th Cir. 2010), the court held that the Bureau of Land Management acted arbitrarily and capriciously in concluding that 18 amendments to grazing regulations did not adversely affect listed species and, consequently, improperly failed to consult.

95. *E.g.*, Sierra Club v. Van Antwerp, 661 F.3d 1147 (D.C. Cir. 2011) (remanded for more reasoned explanation as to why action was not likely to adversely affect eastern Indigo Snake); Pres. Our Island v. U.S. Army Corps of Eng'rs, 2009 WL 2511953 (W.D. Wash. 2009) (unpublished).

96. *See* 50 C.F.R. § 402.02. A federal agency may, usually upon request of the private applicant, designate the applicant as its nonfederal representative by giving the Secretary notice in writing of the designation. *Id.* § 402.08. See Section 5.9 for a discussion of the role of the applicant.

5.4.4 Formal Consultation and the Biological Opinion

If the action agency determines (through its own analysis, informal consultation, or preparation of a BA) that its proposed action is likely to adversely affect[97] listed species or critical habitat, formal consultation is required.[98] The formal consultation process begins with a written request from the action agency to the Service, and ends with issuance by the Service of a BO.[99] The 402 regulations require that any written request to initiate formal consultation include

- a description of the proposed action, the purpose of the proposed action, any measures to avoid, minimize, or offset the action's effects;
- the duration, timing, and location of the action;
- the components and proposed method of carrying out the action;
- maps and other such materials depicting the proposed action;
- any other available relevant information on the effects to listed species or designated critical habitat;
- a description of the specific area that may be affected by the action;
- a description of any listed species or any critical habitat that may be affected by the action, along with a description of the manner in which the action may impact the species or designated critical habitat, including any cumulative effects; and
- relevant reports, including any environmental impact statement (EIS), environmental assessment (EA), or BA.[100]

These criteria may inform agencies' preparation of BAs, as formal consultation is often initiated by transmitting the BA to the Service.

97. *See* Consultation Handbook, *supra* note 5, at 3-13 (defining "is likely to adversely affect" as the appropriate conclusion when "any" adverse effect may occur that is not insignificant, discountable, or beneficial).
98. 50 C.F.R. § 402.14(a), (b).
99. *Id.* § 402.02 (definition of "formal consultation").
100. *Id.* § 402.14(c).

5.4.5 Biological Opinion

The term *biological opinion* is a regulatory creation not specifically identified in the ESA. Rather, section 7(b) of the Act requires that, promptly after conclusion of consultation,[101] the Secretary provide to the action agency (and any applicant) a "written statement setting forth the Secretary's opinion, and a summary of the information on which the opinion is based, detailing how the agency action affects the species or its critical habitat."[102] Through regulation, these "written statements" are referred to as "biological opinions,"[103] and the Services employ the best available scientific evidence when preparing these opinions and are generally afforded deference in assessing the relevant data.[104] According to a 2023 D.C. Circuit decision, however, the lack of sufficient information may not justify erring on the side of species protection under the "best scientific and commercial data available" requirement.[105] The Services have incorporated into the standard the reasonably certain to occur test employed when examining the effects of the action, and as such that test is now part of a BO.[106]

---

101. Consultation must conclude within 90 days of its initiation, or within such other time mutually agreed to by the Service and the agency. 16 U.S.C. § 1536(b).

102. 16 U.S.C. § 1536(b)(3)(A).

103. 50 C.F.R. § 402.02 (defining "biological opinion").

104. *See, e.g.*, Nantucket Residents Against Turbines v. U.S. Bureau of Ocean Energy, 100 F.4th 1, 12 (1st Cir. 2024); Defs. of Wildlife v. U.S. Forest Serv., 94 F.4th 1201, 1234 (10th Cir. 2024); Ctr. for Biological Diversity v. Haaland, 87 F.4th 980 (9th Cir. 2023); Appalachian Voices v. U.S. Dep't of the Interior, 25 F.4th 259, 268–69 (4th Cir. 2022). The action agency is charged with furnishing the relevant Service the "best scientific and commercial data available." 50 C.F.R. § 402.14(d). *See* Bennett v. Spear, 520 U.S. 154, 176–77 (1997) (discussing the purposes of the requirement to use the best available scientific and commercial data); Greenpeace Action v. Franklin, 14 F.3d 1324 (9th Cir. 1992) (discussing "uncertainty" with regard to scientific data); DANIEL J. ROHLF, THE ENDANGERED SPECIES ACT: A GUIDE TO ITS PROTECTIONS AND IMPLEMENTATION 125–33 (1989) (discussing earlier cases interpreting the "best scientific and commercial data available" requirement). The purpose of this requirement has been said to be ensuring that the agency does not ignore available scientific evidence. *See* Am. Wildlands v. Kempthorne, 530 F.3d 991, 998 (D.C. Cir. 2008). *Cf.* Kern Cnty. Farm Bureau v. Allen, 450 F.3d 1072, 1080 (9th Cir. 2006) (agency cannot ignore available evidence that appears better than evidence relied upon); Rock Creek All. v. U.S. Fish & Wildlife Serv., 390 F. Supp. 2d 993 (D. Mont. 2005) (agency cannot rely upon disputed report that expressly indicated it was not applicable to situation).

105. Me. Lobstermen's Ass'n v. Nat'l Marine Fisheries Serv., 70 F.4th 582, 595–96 (D.C. Cir. 2023).

106. *See* 89 Fed. Reg. 24,268, 24,280–82 (Apr. 5, 2024) (noting relationship of BO to effects of the action and reasonable certainty standard).

The contents of a BO are prescribed by the 402 regulations. Every BO must include a summary of the information on which the opinion is based, a detailed discussion of the effects of the action on listed species or critical habitat, and the Service's opinion as to whether the action is likely to jeopardize the continued existence of a listed species or result in destruction or adverse modification of critical habitat.[107] Any BO finding jeopardy or adverse modification of critical habitat must also include "reasonable and prudent alternatives" (RPAs) to the proposed action, if any.[108] Consequently, there are three types of biological opinions: a "no jeopardy" opinion, a jeopardy opinion with RPAs, and a jeopardy opinion with no RPAs.

After receipt of a BO, it is the action agency's responsibility—not the Service's—to decide how to proceed.[109] Although technically BOs serve only an "advisory function,"[110] in practice they carry considerable weight, and action agencies are hesitant to act contrary to a BO's conclusions. Action agencies generally recognize that a court is not likely to afford the agency's scientific expertise greater deference than the expertise of the Services, to whom Congress has entrusted the administration of the Act; as such, an action agency must "articulate its reasons for disagreement" with the BO, and the agency "runs a substantial risk if its (inexpert) reasons turn out to be wrong."[111] By the same token, however, even when a BO concludes that the proposed action will not jeopardize a listed species or adversely modify or destroy critical habitat, an action agency may not simply rubber-stamp the Service's analysis.[112] Nonetheless, an action agency need not undertake a separate, independent analysis in the absence of new information not already considered by the Service.[113]

107. 50 C.F.R. § 402.14(h).

108. *Id.* See Section 5.4.5.3 for a discussion of RPAs in more detail.

109. 50 C.F.R. § 402.15(a); Aluminum Co. of Am. v. Adm'r of EPA, 175 F.3d 1156, 1160–61 (9th Cir. 1999). *See* Tribal Vill. of Akutan v. Hodel, 869 F.2d 1185, 1193 (9th Cir. 1988) (action agency's deviations from BO do not constitute violation of the ESA if agency implements adequate alternative measures).

110. Preamble to Final Joint Consultation Regulations, 51 Fed. Reg. 19,926, 19,928 (1986).

111. Bennett v. Spear, 520 U.S. 154, 169 (1997).

112. *Aluminum Co. of Am.*, 175 F.3d at 1161 (citing Res. Ltd., Inc. v. Robertson, 35 F.3d 1300, 1304 (9th Cir. 1994)). *See also* Ctr. for Biological Diversity v. Regan, 2024 WL 1602457 (D.D.C. Apr. 12, 2024) (EPA violated the ESA when it relied on a flawed BO).

113. *Aluminum Co. of Am.*, 175 F.3d at 1161 (citing Stop H-3 Ass'n v. Dole, 740 F.2d 1441, 1460 (9th Cir. 1984)).

5.4.5.1 Jeopardy

The substantive objective of the section 7 consultation process is to ensure that agencies do not jeopardize listed species or adversely modify or destroy those species' critical habitats.[114] The Supreme Court deems this an affirmative "command," and concluded in 1978 that the then-existing language of section 7 "admits of no exception."[115] Though Congress responded to *Tennessee Valley Authority v. Hill* by creating certain limited exceptions to section 7's substantive mandates,[116] the mandatory nature of section 7 remains intact. Agencies must avoid "jeopardy" and "adverse modification" and "destruction of" critical habitat.

A BO must contain a determination of whether the effects of the action, taken together with cumulative effects,[117] are likely to jeopardize the species as a whole or destroy or adversely modify critical habitat.[118] The 402 regulations contemplate that, to *jeopardize the continued existence* of a listed species, means "engag[ing] in an action that reasonably would be expected, directly or indirectly, to reduce appreciably the likelihood of both the survival and recovery of a listed species in the wild by reducing the reproduction, numbers, or distribution of that species."[119] In *National Wildlife Federation v. NMFS,*[120] the Ninth Circuit interpreted the jeopardy analysis as requiring the consideration of both the likely effect on survival of the species as well as the likely effect on recovery.

When a BO addresses jeopardy to a DPS, the Service may need to consider how an action affects a subpopulation of a species "to give a reasoned jeopardy opinion."[121]

---

114. 16 U.S.C. § 1536(a)(2).

115. Tenn. Valley Auth. v. Hill, 437 U.S. 153, 173 (1978).

116. See Section 5.4.5.4 for a discussion of incidental take associated with federal actions, and see Chapter 7 for a discussion of the section 7 exemption process.

117. 50 C.F.R. § 402.14(g)(4).

118. *See* Consultation Handbook, *supra* note 5, at 4-34; *see also* Butte Env't Council v. U.S. Army Corps of Eng'rs, 620 F.3d 936, 948 (9th Cir. 2010) (citing same).

119. 50 C.F.R. § 402.02.

120. 481 F.3d 1224 (9th Cir. 2007), *amended and superseded by* 524 F.3d 917 (9th Cir. 2008).

121. Defs. of Wildlife v. U.S. Forest Serv., 94 F.4th 1210, 1225 (10th Cir. 2024).

5.4.5.2 Adverse Modification or Destruction

Section 7(a)(2) not only prohibits actions that are likely to jeopardize listed species but also independently prohibits any *adverse modification* or *destruction* of *critical habitat*—regardless of the action's likely effect on the species itself. The phrase *destruction or adverse modification* of critical habitat is defined in the 402 regulations as "a direct or indirect alteration that appreciably diminishes the value of critical habitat as a whole for the conservation of a listed species."[122] Such alterations include, but are not limited to, alterations adversely modifying any of those physical or biological features that were the basis for determining the habitat to be critical.

The interpretation of the statutory standard for adverse modification has become problematic, triggering the question of whether appreciably reducing the recovery of the species is sufficient to establish adverse modification or destruction, or whether, as the 402 regulations suggest, there must be an impact on both survival and recovery. A standard that can look only at recovery would be a broader inquiry.[123] In *Gifford Pinchot Task Force v. U.S. Fish & Wildlife Service,*[124] the Ninth Circuit reviewed the regulation in light of the statutory mandate and held that the Services erred in concluding that the proposed action had to impact both the survival *and* the recovery of the species. Instead, adverse modification or destruction can occur when the proposed action appreciably reduces the likelihood of species recovery. And section 7(a)(2) does not per se bar the mere loss of some critical habitat, unless the amount of lost habitat satisfies the threshold.[125]

122. 50 C.F.R. § 402.02.

123. *See* Ctr. for Biological Diversity v. BLM, 746 F. Supp. 2d 1055, 1100–04 (N.D. Cal. 2009), *vacated in part by* 2011 WL 337364 (N.D. Cal. Jan. 29, 2011).

124. 378 F.3d 1059 (9th Cir. 2004), *amended by* 387 F.3d 968 (9th Cir. 2004). *See also* Miccosukee Tribe of Indians v. United States, 566 F.3d 1257 (11th Cir. 2009); N.M. Cattle Growers Ass'n v. U.S. Fish & Wildlife Serv., 248 F.3d 1277 (10th Cir. 2001); Sierra Club v. U.S. Fish & Wildlife Serv., 245 F.3d 434, 441–42 (5th Cir. 2001).

125. *See* Butte Env't Council v. U.S. Army Corps of Eng'rs, 620 F.3d 936 (9th Cir. 2010); *see also* 77 Fed. Reg. 51,503, 51,507 (Aug. 24, 2012) (discussing adverse modification or destruction standard). For an analysis of the adverse modification and destruction language, see Dave Owen, *Critical Habitat and the Challenge of Regulating Small Harms,* 64 Fla. L. Rev. 141 (2012) (providing an empirical analysis).

5.4.5.3 Reasonable and Prudent Alternatives

When a BO concludes that the prohibited jeopardy or adverse modification is likely, the opinion must also contain RPAs to the proposed action, if any exist.[126] By definition, a *reasonable and prudent alternative* is one that

- can be implemented in a manner consistent with the purposes of the action;
- can be implemented consistent with the scope of the action agency's legal authority and jurisdiction;
- is economically and technologically feasible; and
- would avoid jeopardy or adverse modification of critical habitat.[127]

When developing RPAs, the Services may propose alternatives that "permeate the full range of discretionary authority held by [the action] agency" and may specify an RPA that "involves the maximum exercise of federal agency authority" when necessary to avoid jeopardy.[128] Often, recovery plans for species can inform the development of RPAs.

The final determination of whether a proposed alternative is in fact reasonable and prudent lies with the action agency. The action agency is not required to select the first RPA developed, nor must the action agency select an RPA that might be the "best" alternative.[129] Rather, the agency may select an RPA that otherwise meets the section 7 mandate to avoid jeopardy to listed species, or destruction or adverse modification of critical habitat. Often the action agency and the Service engage in discussions about reasonableness, appropriateness, or ability to implement a possible RPA. If a private applicant is involved, it is often prudent for that applicant to engage in the dialogue about whether a particular RPA is technologically or economically feasible, as well as whether the legal authority exists to implement the RPA.[130] However, once an RPA is selected, the agency must ensure implementation of the

126. 50 C.F.R. § 402.14(h)(3).
127. *Id.* § 402.02.
128. Preamble to Joint Consultation Regulations, 51 Fed. Reg. 19,926, 19,937 (1986).
129. Sw. Ctr. for Biological Diversity v. Bureau of Reclamation, 143 F.3d 515, 522–23 (9th Cir. 1998).
130. *See* 50 C.F.R. § 402.02.

RPA provisions prior to engaging in activities that adversely affect the species or critical habitat.[131]

In addition to RPAs, the Service can include in its BO "conservation recommendations." *Conservation recommendations* are purely discretionary recommendations made by the Service to the action agency and are intended to serve as nonbinding measures that will help minimize or avoid adverse effects on listed species or their habitats.[132] These conservation recommendations also can serve as part of an agency's conservation program under section 7(a)(1) of the Act.[133]

5.4.5.4 Incidental Take Statements

Federal agencies often confront scenarios where their particular action may result in some "take" of individual members of a listed species, without causing prohibited jeopardy or adverse modification of critical habitat. Without some authorization allowing such take, an agency or private party acting pursuant to a federal permit would be violating section 9 of the Act.[134] Congress remedied this "dilemma"[135] in 1982, when it amended the ESA to allow for the "incidental" taking of listed species in connection with otherwise lawful federal actions.[136]

As long as an action may proceed (whether as originally proposed or in accordance with an RPA) without violating section 7(a)(2)'s substantive prohibitions, any BO issued with respect to that action must include an incidental take statement (ITS), which permits take of listed species incidental to the agency actions.[137]

131. Sierra Club v. Marsh, 816 F.2d 1376, 1389 (9th Cir. 1987) (Corps of Engineers failed to ensure implementation of mitigation plans prior to constructing highway and flood control devices).

132. 50 C.F.R. § 402.02.

133. See Chapter 3, Section 3.2 for a discussion of section 7(a)(1).

134. See Chapter 4 for a discussion of section 9's take prohibition.

135. *See* H.R. Rep. No. 567, at 26 (1982), reprinted in 1982 U.S.C.C.A.N. 2807, 2826 (describing the purpose behind Congress's 1982 amendment of ESA section 7).

136. *Id.*

137. 16 U.S.C. § 1536(b)(4); 50 C.F.R. § 402.14(i). "The FWS must issue an Incidental Take Statement if the BiOp concludes no jeopardy to listed species or adverse modification of critical habitat will result from the proposed action, but the action is likely to result in incidental taking." Or. Nat. Res. Council v. Allen, 476 F.3d 1031, 1036 (9th Cir. 2007). The absence of an ITS may render a biological opinion arbitrary and capricious, unless the Service can justify that no take is reasonably likely to occur. *See* Ctr. for Biological Diversity v. NOAA Fisheries, 644 F. Supp. 3d 574, 588 (N.D. Cal. 2022); Ctr. for Biological Diversity v.

Incidental take refers to "takings that result from, but are not the purpose of, carrying out an otherwise lawful activity conducted by the federal agency or applicant."[138] Any taking that is in compliance with an ITS is exempt from the Act's prohibitions and penalties.[139] The Supreme Court summarized the import of an ITS as follows: "[T]he biological opinion's incidental take statement constitutes a permit authorizing the action agency to 'take' the endangered or threatened species as long as it respects the Service's 'terms and conditions.'"[140]

The contents of an ITS are prescribed by statute. Each ITS must

- specify the impact of the take on the species;
- specify those "reasonable and prudent measures" (RPMs) that the Secretary considers necessary or appropriate to minimize such impact; and
- set forth terms and conditions to implement those reasonable and prudent measures.[141]

Defining the level or degree of allowable take often is problematic. "Congress has clearly declared a preference for expressing take in numerical form, and an [ITS] that utilizes a surrogate instead of a numerical cap on take must explain why it was impracticable to express a numerical measure of take."[142] A specified take level serves as a trigger that, when that level is exceeded, removes the ITS safe harbor and necessitates that the parties

---

Ross, 613 F. Supp. 3d 336, 340, 345–46 (D.D.C. 2020); *see also* Ctr. for Biological Diversity v. Regan, 734 F. Supp. 3d 1 (D.D.C. 2024) (for the delegation of the Clean Water Act section 404 program to Florida, invalidating BO for, in part, how it addressed the ITS), *appeal pending in* Ctr. for Biological Diversity v. Regan, No. 24-5101 (D.C. Cir.); Ctr. for Biological Diversity v. Salazar, 695 F.3d 893 (9th Cir. 2012) (ITS required even if no section 9 take liability).

138. 50 C.F.R. § 402.02 (defining "incidental take").

139. 16 U.S.C. § 1536(o). *See, e.g.*, Ramsey v. Kantor, 96 F.3d 434 (9th Cir. 1996) (holding that anyone, not just agencies or applicants, may take listed species in a manner contemplated by an ITS).

140. Bennett v. Spear, 520 U.S. 154, 170 (1997).

141. 16 U.S.C. § 1536(b)(4)(C). *See also* 50 C.F.R. § 402.14(i) (setting forth additional detail for ITSs).

142. Or. Nat. Res. Council, 476 F.3d at 1037 (invalidating ITS, concluding no rational connection between take authorization and scope of the underlying proposed action).

reinitiate consultation.[143] Yet establishing a precise level may not always work, and the Services have employed "surrogates" when identifying a level would be impractical.[144] A "surrogate" can be appropriate when it

- describes the causal link between the surrogate and take of the listed species;
- explains why it is not practical to express the amount or extent of anticipated take or to monitor take-related impacts in terms of individuals of the listed species; and
- sets a clear standard for determining when the level of anticipated take has been exceeded.[145]

The RPMs may not serve a general mitigation purpose, but instead must be designed to actually minimize the amount or extent of the anticipated take.[146] RPMs, and the terms and conditions implementing them, cannot alter the basic design, location, scope, duration, or timing of the action and may involve only "minor changes."[147] Ultimately, the real import of RPMs and terms and conditions is that they must be implemented, or any incidental take occurring pursuant to the action is unlawful.[148] One recent change to RPMs is that the Services included offsets ("measures implemented inside or outside of the action area") as a possible form of an RPM.[149]

143. Ariz. Cattle Growers Ass'n v. U.S. Fish & Wildlife Serv., 273 F.3d 1229, 1249 (9th Cir. 2001).

144. The Ninth Circuit has posited that a permissible level of take ought to be expressed in the form of a specific number. *See id.* Yet the court further notes that it has "never held that a numerical limit is required. Indeed, we have upheld Incidental Take Statements that used a combination of numbers and estimates." *Id.* But when a numerical limit is not specified, the Service must "establish that no such numerical value could be practically obtained." *Id.* at 1250. *See also* Ctr. for Biological Diversity v. Salazar, 695 F.3d 893 (9th Cir. 2012) (discussing numerical or surrogate take in an ITS). The ITSs are reviewed under an arbitrary and capricious standard and should include enough specificity to ensure that there is some measurable enforceable trigger that might prompt the need to reinitiate consultation. *See* Sierra Club v. U.S. Dep't of the Interior, 990 F.3d 898, 905 (9th Cir. 2021) (upholding challenge to ITS).

145. 50 C.F.R. § 402.14(i)(1)(i); *see* Sierra Club v. U.S. Dep't of the Interior, 899 F.3d 260, 271 (4th Cir. 2018).

146. Consultation Handbook, *supra* note 5, at 4-50.

147. 50 C.F.R. § 402.14(i)(2).

148. 16 U.S.C. § 1536(o) (exempting from the ESA's takings prohibitions only takings that are "in compliance" with the ITS).

149. 50 C.F.R. § 402.14(i)(2); 89 Fed. Reg. 24,268, 24,283–90 (Apr. 5, 2024).

5.4.5.5 Challenges to Biological Opinions

Once issued, BOs can be challenged in federal court for consistency with the Act as well as for a decision whether the judgments rendered in the BO are arbitrary or capricious.[150] In *Bennett v. Spear,*[151] the Supreme Court held that a BO containing an ITS could be challenged under the Administrative Procedure Act (APA) in a district court. Although the ESA contains a citizen suit provision, the Court held that the provision and its accompanying 60-day-notice requirement applies to federal agencies only when they are engaging in nondiscretionary agency actions, and that the issues involved in a challenge to a BO are not nondiscretionary. While in practice many citizen plaintiffs continue to file 60-day-notice letters pursuant to the citizen suit provision, such notice is not required, and parties may initiate a lawsuit challenging a BO in federal district court, invoking the court's jurisdiction under 28 U.S.C. § 1331 and the sovereign immunity waiver and cause of action under the APA. In some circumstances, challenges to a BO must be brought in conjunction with a challenge to the underlying agency action and in the court in which that challenge occurs.[152]

5.5 Reinitiation of Consultation

When a federal agency has retained any discretionary involvement in or control over a particular action, the agency remains under a continuing obligation to reinitiate consultation if conditions so warrant.[153] This might need to be a degree of discretion that would allow the agency to benefit the species.[154] Pursuant to

150. *E.g.,* Miccosukee Tribe of Indians of Fla. v. United States, 566 F.3d 1257 (11th Cir. 2009); Ctr. for Biological Diversity v. U.S. Fish & Wildlife Serv., 450 F.3d 930 (9th Cir. 2006). In *Dow AgroSciences v. NMFS,* 637 F.3d 259 (4th Cir. 2011), for instance, the court held that the BO was reviewable under APA section 704, because the underlying EPA program for registration of insecticides did not provide an adequate forum for challenging the BO.

151. 520 U.S. 154 (1997).

152. *Cf.* City of Tacoma v. FERC, 460 F.2d 53, 75 (D.C. Cir. 2006).

153. *See* NRDC v. Haaland, 102 F.4th 1045, 1074 (9th Cir. 2024); Ctr. for Biological Diversity v. U.S. Forest Serv., 522 F. Supp. 3d 611, 616 (D. Ariz. 2021). In response to cases where the duty of reinitiation was litigated, in 2024, the Services clarified that the obligation to reinitiate consultation stems from the action agency, and the Services may alert the action agency of the possible need for reinitiation. 89 Fed. Reg. 24279–80 (Apr. 5, 2024).

154. *NRDC v. Haaland,* 102 F.4th at 1074 (citing Turtle Island Restoration Network v. NMFS, 340 F.3d 969 (9th Cir. 2003)).

the 402 regulations, consultation must be reinitiated if any of the following four circumstances arises:

1. The amount or extent of taking specified in the ITS is exceeded;
2. New information reveals effects of the action that may affect listed species or critical habitat in a manner or to an extent not previously considered;
3. The identified action is subsequently modified in a manner that causes an effect to the listed species or critical habitat that was not considered in the biological opinion or written concurrence;
4. A new species is listed or critical habitat designated that may be affected by the identified action.[155]

Certain agency actions, such as ongoing programmatic land use planning, may require regular reinitiation, particularly when the action area is broad and could encompass many new species' listings.[156] And a reinitiation of consultation may, according to the Ninth Circuit, moot out any claim seeking reinitiation.[157]

5.6 Irreversible/Irretrievable Commitments of Resources

Once initiated,[158] until formal consultation is properly concluded no action may proceed if that action may affect listed species or critical habitat. Section 7(d) of the ESA prohibits any agency or

155. 50 C.F.R. § 402.16.

156. *Id.* § 402.16(b); *see* Pac. Rivers Council v. Thomas, 30 F.3d 1050 (9th Cir. 1994) (enjoining Forest Service activities because consultation had not been initiated on the Forest Service's land and resource management plans after subsequent listing of chinook salmon). In *Cottonwood Environmental Law Center v. U.S. Forest Service*, 789 F.3d 1075, 1085 (9th Cir. 2015), the court held that the Forest Service had to reinitiate consultation on its land use plan after the designation of critical habitat.

157. *See* All. for Wild Rockies v. Forest Serv., 907 F.3d 1105, 1121 (9th Cir. 2018); All. for Wild Rockies v. Savage, 897 F.3d 1025, 1031 (9th Cir. 2018); *but cf.* White v. U.S. Army Corps of Eng'rs, 659 F.3d (N.D. Cal. 2023) (suggesting live controversy for both section 7 and section 9 claims remains as long as reinitiation not complete).

158. Initiation of formal consultation occurs upon acceptance of a written request. *See* 50 C.F.R. § 402.14(c).

applicant, after initiation of consultation, from making any irreversible or irretrievable commitments of resources that would foreclose the formulation or implementation of any RPA.[159] "Section 7(d) was enacted to ensure that the status quo would be maintained during the consultation process to prevent agencies from sinking resources into a project in order to ensure its completion regardless of its impacts on endangered or threatened species."[160] The section 7(d) bar, therefore, joins with the separate section 7(a)(2) procedural requirements to ensure that the consultation process is completed prior to proceeding with any action that may affect a listed species or critical habitat.[161] By regulation, the Services have extended the scope of section 7(d) to "re-initiation" of consultation and have determined that the prohibition is in effect "until the requirements of section 7(a)(2) are satisfied."[162]

Neither the ESA nor its implementing regulations define what constitutes an "irreversible or irretrievable commitment" subject to the section 7(d) prohibition. The *Consultation Handbook* provides limited guidance regarding the application of section 7(d) during the consultation process other than to state that the section 7(d) restriction is triggered by the determination of "may affect."[163] The *Consultation Handbook* also states that

> [n]ot all irreversible and irretrievable commitments of resources are prohibited. The formulation or implementation of any

159. 16 U.S.C. § 1536(d).

160. Wash. Toxics Coal. v. EPA, 413 F.3d 1024, 1034–35 (9th Cir. 2005); N. Slope Borough v. Andrus, 486 F. Supp. 332, 356 (D.D.C.), *aff'd in part and rev'd in part on other grounds*, 642 F.2d 589 (D.C. Cir. 1980).

161. Pac. Rivers Council v. Thomas, 30 F.3d 1050, 1056–67 (9th Cir. 1994) (enjoining Forest Service timber sales, range management activities, grazing permits, and road-building projects because the Forest Service had not properly completed consultation). A court also might avoid any section 7(d) claim by instead enjoining any commitment of resources. *E.g.*, Ctr. for Biological Diversity v. Haaland, No. 23-CV-20495-PAS, 2024 WL 81309 (S.D. Fla. Jan. 8, 2024). Other barriers to a section 7(d) claim might be raising the claim before consultation or failing to provide a 60-day notice. *E.g.*, Orr v. U.S. Env't Prot. Agency, 641 F. Supp. 3d 258, 272 (W.D.N.C. 2022), *modified on appeal* 2024 WL 2874280 (4th Cir. 2024).

162. 50 C.F.R. § 402. 09. The preamble to the Joint Consultation Regulations explains that the "requirements of section 7(a)(2) are satisfied" when the agency either receives a no-jeopardy opinion or chooses a valid reasonable and prudent alternative. 51 Fed. Reg. 19,926, 19,940 (1986). A section 7(d) violation can occur if the agency reinitiates consultation and is likely to exceed any allowable take permitted in an existing BO's ITS. *See* Ctr. for Biological Diversity v. U.S. Forest Serv., 820 F. Supp. 2d 1029 (D. Ariz. 2011). *But cf.* Defs. of Wildlife v. Bureau of Ocean Mgmt., 684 F.3d 1242 (11th Cir. 2012) (section 7(d) not necessarily applicable when an existing BO still applicable during a reinitiation of consultation).

163. Consultation Handbook, *supra* note 5, at 2-7.

> reasonable and prudent alternatives must be foreclosed by the resource commitment to violate section 7(d). Thus, resource commitments may occur as long as the action agency retains sufficient discretion and flexibility to modify its action to allow formulation and implementation of an appropriate reasonable and prudent alternative. Destroying potential alternative habitat within the project area, for example, could violate section 7(d).[164]

Courts applying section 7(d) have struggled somewhat to provide a measure of consistency. On the one hand, the Ninth Circuit has observed that the purpose of the provision is to "maintain the status quo,"[165] and at least one district court noted that the legislative history of the provision indicates a congressional desire to prevent agencies from "steamrolling" a project by investing resources during the early stages of the project.[166] Several courts have treated actions taken during the consultation process as a violation of section 7(d). In *Natural Resources Defense Council v. Houston,*[167] environmental groups sought to enjoin the Bureau of Reclamation from entering into renewal contracts to supply water from a dam unit based on the Bureau's alleged violation of various statutes, including the ESA. The court found that the 40-year water contracts were a prohibited irreversible and irretrievable commitment of resources.[168] The court reasoned that, because the contracts did not allow for a reduction in the amount of water delivered under the contract, the reasonable and prudent alternative of reallocating contracted water from irrigation to conservation was foreclosed.[169] Therefore, the contracts that were entered into before the completion of the consultation process were subject to rescission.[170] In analyzing a timber company's commitment of resources in *Environmental Protection Information Center v. Pacific Lumber Co.,* the court looked to the fact that

164. *Id.*

165. Lane Cnty. Audubon Soc'y v. Jamison, 958 F.2d 290, 294 (9th Cir. 1992). *See also* Wash. Toxics Coal. v. EPA, 413 F.3d 1024, 1034–35 (9th Cir. 2005), *cert denied sub nom.* CropLife of Am. v. Wash. Toxics Coal., 546 U.S. 1090 (2006).

166. N. Slope Borough v. Andrus, 486 F. Supp. 332, 356 (D.D.C.), *aff'd in part, rev'd in part,* 642 F.2d 589 (D. C. Cir. 1980).

167. 146 F.3d 1118, 1124 (9th Cir. 1998).

168. *Id.* at 1128.

169. *Id.*

170. *Id. See also* Lane Cnty. Audubon Soc'y v. Jamison, 958 F.2d 290 (9th Cir. 1992) (enjoining all timber sales until the timber sale selection criteria and guidelines relied on by the BLM were subject to the consultation process under section 7(a)(2)).

the logging operations at issue in the case could cause the erosion and mass wasting of steeply sloped hillsides that contribute to the severe degradation of streams and coho salmon habitat.[171] The court found that those effects would foreclose the formulation and implementation of alternative measures.[172] Therefore, the plaintiffs were entitled to a preliminary injunction to stop the logging operations.[173]

Yet other decisions suggest that sunk costs alone might not violate section 7(d). For example, in *Bays' Legal Fund v. Brown,*[174] the district court determined that an investment of more than $100 million prior to the completion of consultation did not violate section 7(d) because the project proponents retained sufficient flexibility to alter the project's design if necessary to protect endangered whales.[175] Even when courts have enjoined activities found to be in violation of section 7(d), they have implicitly recognized that not all activities are precluded during consultation.[176] In the seminal *Pacific Rivers* case, the Ninth Circuit concluded that timber sales, for instance, are per se violations of ESA section 7(d), when the action agency has not completed the consultation process.[177]

Action agencies, therefore, should be cautioned that, along with any potential standard for awarding preliminary injunctions, section 7(d) is of limited use in many circumstances where an activity may affect a listed species or potentially jeopardize the species or adversely modify or destroy its critical habitat. Section 7(d) does not sanction activities that might take a listed species pending the completion of consultation. On balance, the cases suggest that an underlying consideration in determining whether particular activities constitute an irreversible and irretrievable commitment of resources is whether the actions taken foreclose

---

171. 67 F. Supp. 2d 1113, 1122 (N.D. Cal.), *vacated by* 257 F.3d 1071 (9th Cir. 1999) (after case became moot).

172. 67 F. Supp. 2d at 1126.

173. *Id.*

174. 828 F. Supp. 102 (D. Mass. 1993).

175. *Id.* at 112.

176. *See* Pac. Rivers Council v. Thomas, 30 F.3d 1050, 1057 (9th Cir. 1994) (stating that because consultation had not been initiated at the time of hearing, "we need not address . . . whether the various commitments of resources were irreversible and irretrievable"); NRDC v. Houston, 146 F.3d 1118, 1128 (9th Cir. 1998) (Bureau of Reclamation contracts, executed prior to conclusion of consultation, were not adequately conditioned to allow for future needs of endangered species).

177. *Pac. Rivers Council,* 30 F.3d at 1057 (*citing Lane Cnty.,* 958 F.2d at 295).

the possibility to implement reasonable and prudent alternatives. If the resources committed to the project can be used in a manner that does not affect the existence of listed species, and the actions taken do not effectively tie the agencies' hands in identifying any reasonable and prudent alternatives that might be required to avoid jeopardy from the project as proposed, the section 7(d) prohibition should not apply.

5.7 Conferencing

Section 7(a)(4) of the ESA is one of the few provisions addressing species that are not yet listed as endangered or threatened.[178] Section 7(a)(4) requires each federal agency to "confer" with the Secretary with respect to any agency action that is "likely to jeopardize the continued existence" of any species proposed to be listed, or that is likely to result in destruction or adverse modification of proposed critical habitat.[179] A finding of likely jeopardy or adverse modification triggers conferencing. But conferencing does not impose the same substantive obligations on agencies as a consultation (the recommendations are nonbinding), and the section 7(d) limitation on commitment of resources is not applicable to conferencing.

Like consultation, conferencing may be informal or formal, and the process requires significant interaction between the action agency and the Service. The procedural value of conferencing is that the opinion issued at the conclusion of the conference may ultimately be adopted as the BO if and when the species is listed or critical habitat is designated.[180]

With respect to continuing or ongoing agency actions, the conferencing procedures are useful. If, for instance, a federal agency does not conference on a proposed species, and the particular ongoing action will cause some incidental take of the species, the ongoing action would have to cease upon listing of the species, until the action agency reinitiates and completes

---

178. 16 U.S.C. § 1536(a)(4).

179. *Id. See* James C. Kilbourne, *The Endangered Species Act Under the Microscope: A Closeup Look from a Litigator's Perspective,* 21 Env't L. 499, 556–58 (1991) (detailed discussion of the ESA conferencing requirement).

180. 50 C.F.R. § 402.10(d).

consultation and receives an ITS. In contrast, an agency that has conferenced with respect to its ongoing action and the proposed species may find itself with a BO, with any necessary protection through an incidental take statement, upon the effective date of the listing of the species.[181]

5.8 The Role of Tribes

As explained in more detail in Chapter 8, Tribal interests can play an important role in the administration of the Act. The Secretaries, when administering natural resource programs, appreciate that Native American Tribal lands in the lower 48 states comprise many millions of acres of land, and the same is true for traditional Native lands in Alaska. And when administering programs in the lower 48, the Secretaries exercise a federal trust responsibility and must respect Tribal rights and the obligations of the United States toward the tribes. As part of the unique status of tribes, therefore, the Secretaries must ensure a meaningful government-to-government relationship with the tribes when a consultation process might affect Tribal interests.[182]

5.9 The Role of Private Applicants

Section 7 of the ESA affords certain procedural rights to persons who qualify as "applicants." The ESA itself defines the term *applicant* somewhat narrowly:

> The term "permit or license applicant" means, when used with respect to an action of a federal agency for which exemption is

---

181. During the 30-day period between publication of a final rule listing a species and the effective date of the rule, the Service may convert the conference opinion into a biological opinion, pursuant to 50 C.F.R. § 402.10(d).

182. *E.g.*, Exec. Order No. 13,175, Consultation and Coordination with Indian Tribal Governments (Nov. 6, 2000); Secretarial Order No. 3206, Working with Tribes, American Indian Tribal Rights, Federal Trust Responsibilities, and the Endangered Species Act (June 5, 1997). *See* Chapter 8, Section 8.5. This book only addresses the ESA, while other statutes and policies outline further responsibilities involving consultations with Tribal Nations and indigenous peoples.

> sought under section 1536 of this title, any person whose application to such agency for a permit or a license has been denied primarily because of the application of section 1536(a) of this title to such agency action.[183]

The consulting agencies have determined that the statutory definition of *applicant* is "of limited use in the consultation context because it focuses on the exemption process."[184] The 402 regulations define *applicant* more broadly to include "any person, as defined in section 3(13) of the Act, who requires formal approval or authorization from a Federal agency as a prerequisite to conducting the action."[185] For section 7 consultation purposes, applicants include a wide array of individuals seeking permits, licenses, leases, letters of authorization, or "any other form of authorization or approval"[186] from a federal agency as a prerequisite for carrying out an action. But conversely, the consulting agencies have indicated that those merely seeking funding from a federal agency are not applicants, unless the request for funding is coupled with a requirement for separate federal agency authorization or approval prior to carrying out the action for which the funding is sought.[187] Likewise, a "prospective permit applicant" is not an applicant.[188]

Examples of instances where federal agencies have approved a request for applicant status include a mine operator seeking plan of operations and permit approvals on national forest land; floatboat outfitters seeking renewal of a Forest Service special-use permit; a regional water authority seeking a Bureau of Land Management right-of-way; and a permit applicant for a railroad right-of-way across federal land.

The *Consultation Handbook* provides further guidance for determining whether one is an applicant. Specifically, the handbook notes that the type, or scope, of a particular section 7 consultation affects the determination of whether applicants exist; the more discrete and narrowly focused the action being consulted

183. 16 U.S.C. § 1532(12).

184. Supplementary Information Accompanying Final Section 7 Consultation Rules, 51 Fed. Reg. 19,926, 19,930 (1986).

185. 50 C.F.R. § 402.02.

186. *See* Supplementary Information Accompanying Final Section 7 Consultation Rules, 51 Fed. Reg. at 19,930.

187. *Id.*

188. *Id.*

on, the more likely it is that persons exist who qualify as applicants.[189] The specific example given in the handbook is worthy of examination:

> Users of public resources (e.g., timber companies harvesting on national forests) are not parties to programmatic section 7 consultations dealing with an agency's overall management operations, including land management planning and other program level consultations. However, users who are party to a discrete action (i.e., where they are already the successful bidder on a timber sale that becomes the subject of later consultation or re-initiation when a new species is listed or new critical habitat is designated) may participate as applicants in the section 7 process.[190]

This example apparently recognizes a consultation continuum; on one end of the continuum are broad, programmatic consultations unlikely to confer applicant status on anyone, and on the other end of the continuum are the very narrow, "discrete" consultations involving specific actions.

Any person determined by an action agency to qualify as an applicant is entitled to[191]

- submit information for consideration during consultation;[192]
- be informed by the action agency, in writing, of the estimated length of any delay in preparing a BA, and the reasons for the delay;[193]
- refuse to consent to more than a 60-day extension by FWS or NMFS of the 90-day time limit for the duration of formal consultation;[194]
- review the draft BO and provide comments on the draft through the action agency;[195]

---

189. Consultation Handbook, *supra* note 5, at 2-12.
190. *Id.*
191. *Id.* at 2-13.
192. 50 C.F.R. § 402.14(d).
193. 16 U.S.C. § 1536(c)(1); 50 C.F.R. § 402.12(i).
194. 16 U.S.C. § 1536(b)(1)(B); 50 C.F.R. § 402.14(e).
195. 50 C.F.R. § 402.14(g)(5). The applicant obtains a copy of the draft BO by requesting one from the action agency; all comments "must be submitted to the Service through the Federal agency, although the applicant may send a copy of its comments directly to the Service." *Id.*

- discuss with NMFS or FWS the basis of the biological determinations in the draft BO, and assist in the development of reasonable and prudent alternatives (in the case of a draft "jeopardy opinion");[196]
- receive a copy of the final BO;[197]
- initiate the exemption process if the BO concludes that the proposed action is likely to jeopardize the continued existence of a listed species, and that there are no reasonable and prudent alternatives to the proposed action;[198] and
- request "early consultation" prior to actually applying for a federal license or permit.[199]

In addition, applicants may serve as the designated nonfederal representative of the federal action agency for the purposes of conducting informal consultation and preparing a BA.[200] In fact, the action agency may not designate any other nonfederal representative for these purposes without the agreement of the applicant.[201] From a project applicant's perspective, it can be advantageous to seek applicant status in the consultation and make use of these opportunities for input and review in the consultation process. In that way, the applicant can contribute its expertise, information, and input while its project's future and potential management constraints based on ESA factors are being addressed in the interagency consultation process. The ultimate responsibility for compliance with section 7, however, always remains with the federal action agency.[202]

196. *Id.*

197. 16 U.S.C. § 1536(b)(3)(A) (providing that the Service must "promptly," after the conclusion of consultation, provide the action agency and the applicant a copy of the BO); 50 C.F.R. § 402.14(e)(3) (providing that the action agency and the applicant will receive a copy of the BO within 45 days of the conclusion of formal consultation).

198. 16 U.S.C. § 1536(g)(1); 50 C.F.R. § 451.02(c).

199. 50 C.F.R. § 402.11.

200. *Id.* § 402.08.

201. *Id.*

202. *Id.*

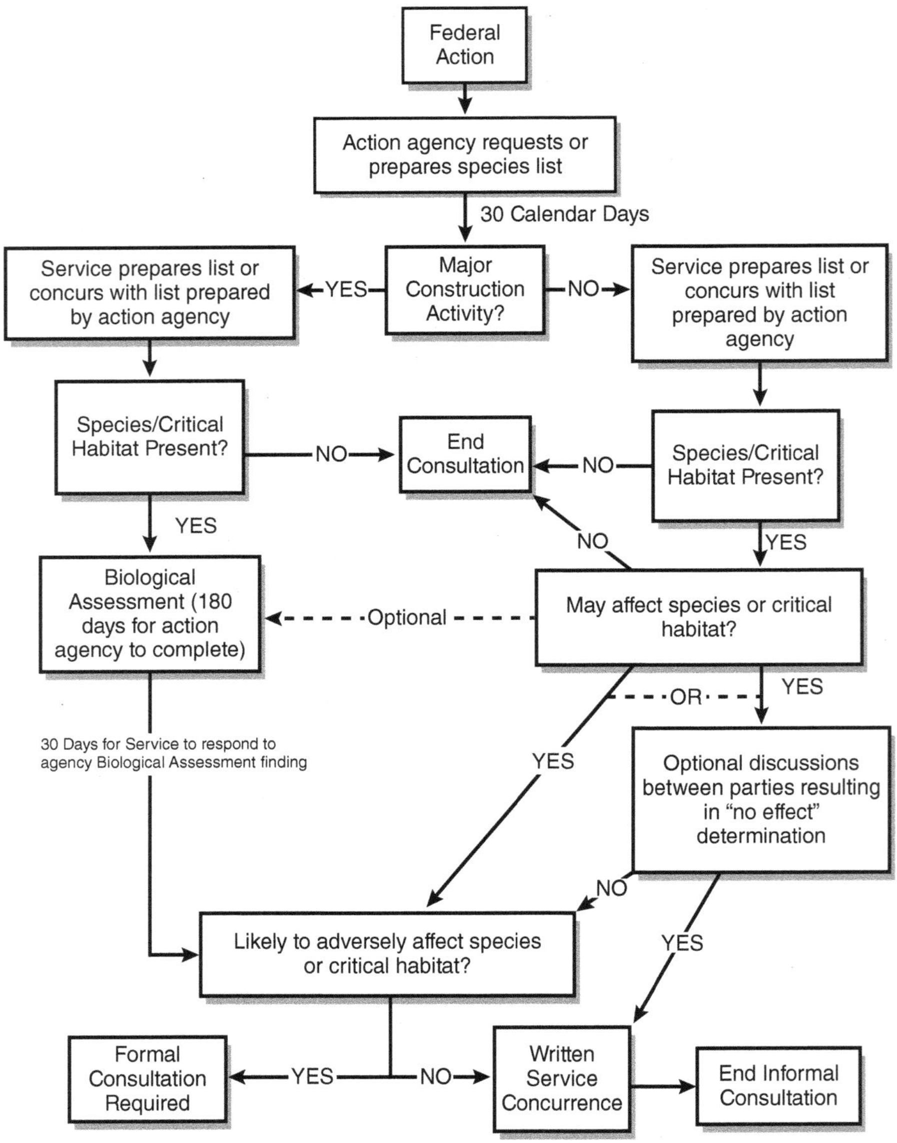

Informal Consultation Process

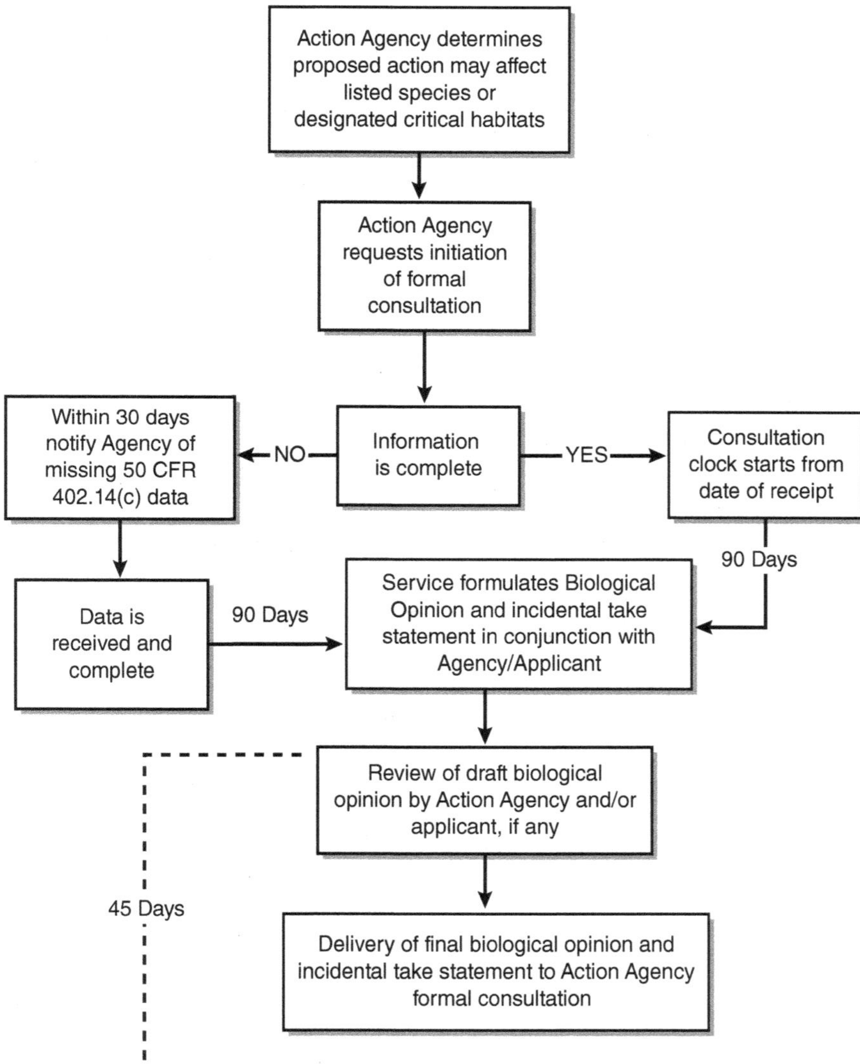

Formal Consultation Process

6 Incidental Take Permits and Other Allowable Take

6.1 Overview

The ESA includes various mechanisms for allowing parties to engage in otherwise prohibited activities. In some circumstances, even an otherwise illegal "knowing take"[1] of a listed species may be allowed. This chapter provides an overview of the exceptions contained in ESA section 10.[2] Other authorized takings, such as those (1) under an incidental take statement associated in a section 7 biological opinion for actions authorized, funded, or carried out by federal agencies;[3] (2) consistent with any rule promulgated under section 4(d) for threatened species;[4] or (3) for activities that may affect members of "experimental populations"[5] are discussed elsewhere. The section 10 program for permitting the take of species is a robust aspect of the ESA, particularly because the Services crafted creative mechanisms (such as the "no surprises" and "safe harbor" policies discussed later in this chapter) to facilitate making section 10 permits a more attractive option for addressing conflicts between private activities and the needs of endangered and threatened species.[6]

---

1. See Chapter 4 for a detailed discussion of section 9 prohibited take of listed species.

2. 16 U.S.C. § 1539.

3. Incidental take of listed species in connection with federal actions is discussed in Section 5.4; taking of species under the Act's exemption process (the so-called God Squad proceeding) is discussed in Chapter 7.

4. See Section 4.3 for a detailed discussion of 4(d) rules.

5. See Chapter 10 for a detailed discussion of experimental populations.

6. *See generally* J.B. Ruhl, *How to Kill Endangered Species, Legally: The Nuts and Bolts of Endangered Species Act "HCP" Permits for Real Estate Development*, 5 ENV'T L. 345 (1999); J.B. Ruhl, *Endangered Species Act Innovations in the Post-Babbittonian Era—Are There Any?*, 14 DUKE EVN'T L. & POL'Y F. 419–40 (Spring

6.2 Incidental Take Permits

In 1982, Congress amended the ESA to resolve the "concerns of private landowners who are faced with having otherwise lawful activities . . . prevented by [ESA] Section 9 prohibitions against takings."[7] By creating ESA section 10(a)(1)(B),[8] Congress authorized an otherwise prohibited taking of listed species "if such taking is incidental to, and not the purpose of, the carrying out of an otherwise lawful activity."[9] Congress specifically intended for these section 10 incidental take permits (hereinafter section 10 permits or ITPs) to encourage "unique partnerships" between the public and private sectors and serve the dual purposes of conserving species while providing desirable long-term assurances to participating landowners.[10] Section 10 permits have since become a popular device for resolving conflicts between the needs of listed species and proposed land-use activities. This has occurred, in part, because the Services developed creative policies, promulgated extensive section 10 permit regulations,[11] and published comprehensive handbooks containing "detailed but flexible guidelines" to guide section 10 permit applicants through the process.[12] Indeed, during the first decade of the program, only 14 ITPs had been issued.[13] Today, the Fish and Wildlife Service (FWS) maintains a database of issued permits, with the total number of Habitat Conservation Plans, Safe Harbor Agreements, Candidate

---

2004); Robert Meltz, RL31796, *The Endangered Species Act (ESA) and Claims of Property Rights Takings* (2013); Jessica Owley, *Keeping Track of Conservation*, 42 Ecology L.Q. 79 (2015).

7. H.R. Conf. Rep. No. 97-835, at 29 (1982), *reprinted in* 1982 U.S.C.C.A.N. 2860, 2870.

8. 16 U.S.C. § 1539(a)(1)(B).

9. *Id.*

10. H.R. Rep. No. 97-567, at 30–31 (1982), *reprinted in* 1982 U.S.C.C.A.N. 2830–31.

11. FWS regulations governing all Service permits are published at 50 C.F.R. pt. 13. In addition, FWS has published specific rules governing section 10 permits. 50 C.F.R. §§ 17.22(b), 17.32(b). Permitting rules for species under NMFS jurisdiction are published at 50 C.F.R. pt. 222.

12. *See* FWS & NMFS, Joint Endangered Species Habitat Conservation Planning Handbook (Nov. 1996). The Services released an addendum to the 1996 Handbook in 2000, incorporating a five-point policy emphasizing (1) biological goals and objectives, (2) adaptive management, (3) monitoring, (4) permit duration, and (5) public participation. 65 Fed. Reg. 35,242 (June 1, 2000). In 2016, the Services published a revised *Habitat Conservation Planning Handbook* incorporating the 2000 addendum [hereinafter HCP Handbook]. 81 Fed. Reg. 93702 (Dec. 21, 2016).

13. Spirit of the Sage Council v. Norton, 411 F.3d 225, 227 (D.C. Cir. 2005).

Conservation Agreements, and Candidate Conservation Agreements with Assurances as of May 2025 exceeding 1,700.[14]

6.3 Habitat Conservation Plans

The essential element of any section 10 permit is the applicant's proposed "conservation plan."[15] This conservation plan, called a "habitat conservation plan"[16] (HCP), must specify

- the impact that will likely result from the taking;
- the steps the applicant will take to "minimize and mitigate" such impacts, and the funding that will be available to implement such steps;
- alternative actions to the taking that the applicant has considered, and the reasons why the alternatives are not being used; and
- such other measures as the Secretary may require as necessary or appropriate for purposes of the plan.[17]

---

14. *See* U.S. Fish & Wildlife Serv., Conservation Plans and Agreements Database, https://ecos.fws.gov/ecp/report/conservation-plans-type-region (last visited July 15, 2025).

15. 16 U.S.C. § 1539(a)(2)(A). Congress modeled the section 10 permit program on a plan developed by private parties to address the impacts of development on endangered butterflies near the San Bruno Mountains in California. The San Bruno Plan was viewed by Congress as the "model for the incidental take permit" and the standard against which the "adequacy of other plans should be measured." H.R. Conf. Rep. No. 97-835, at 31 (1982), *reprinted in* 1982 U.S.C.C.A.N. 2807, 2872. *See* Friends of Endangered Species v. Jantzen, 760 F.2d 976, 982–83 (9th Cir. 1985) (upholding the San Bruno plan largely due to Congress's reliance on that plan). A potential applicant should appreciate that take associated with research or development of the habitat conservation plan itself is not allowed unless carried out pursuant to a valid permit. *See* Hamilton v. City of Austin, 8 F. Supp. 2d 886 (W.D. Tex. 1998) (pre-HCP activities designed to determine the parameters of the incidental take permit required issuance of a section 10(a)(1)(B) scientific research permit).

16. For two significant early overviews of habitat conservation planning, see Michael J. Bean et al., Reconciling Conflicts Under The Endangered Species Act: The Habitat Conservation Planning Experience (World Wildlife Fund 1991), and Robert D. Thornton, *Searching for Consensus and Predictability: Habitat Conservation Planning Under the Endangered Species Act of 1973*, 21 Env't L. 605 (1991); *see also* Timothy Beatley, Habitat Conservation Planning: Endangered Species And Urban Growth (1994); Patrick Duggan, *Incidental Extinction: How the Endangered Species Act's Incidental Take Permits Fail to Account for Population Loss*, 41 Env't L. Rep. 10,628 (2011); Mark Maples, *Habitat Conservation Plans: Embracing Landowner Pragmatism and Quieting the Complexity of the Incidental Take Permit Process*; 1 Tex. A&M J. Prop. L. 245 (2013).

17. 16 U.S.C. § 1539(a)(2)(A)(i)–(iv).

After receipt of a permit application and an HCP that satisfies these criteria, and then after opportunity for public comment,[18] the Act instructs the Secretary to issue a section 10 permit if the Secretary finds that (1) the proposed taking will be incidental; (2) the applicant will, to the maximum extent practicable, minimize and mitigate the impacts of the taking; (3) the applicant will ensure adequate funding for the HCP; (4) the taking will not "appreciably reduce the likelihood of the survival and recovery of the species in the wild"; and (5) the applicant has agreed to implement such other measures, terms, and conditions as the Secretary deems necessary or appropriate.[19]

If the HCP is complex or involves multiple parties, the Services may require parties to the HCP to enter an implementing agreement (IA).[20] The IA serves as the contractual mechanism binding the parties to the terms of the IA and accompanying HCP.

6.3.1 Scope of an HCP

A single HCP may address one or many species, including both listed and nonlisted species.[21] Alternatively, an HCP may focus on particular habitat types and address all species within certain habitat types present in the plan area.[22] At a minimum, a permit applicant is well advised to include all listed plant[23] and wildlife

---

18. Section 10(c) of the Act requires that the Service ensure that the public has an opportunity to review the delineated area being addressed by the HCP. In *Gerber v. Norton*, 294 F.3d 173, 179, 184 (D.C. Cir. 2002), the court invalidated an HCP, in part, because the Service failed to make publicly available a map of the off-site mitigation. *See also* Friends of Animals v. Jewell, 824 F.3d 1033, 1041 (D.C. Cir. 2016) (holding section 10(c) "clearly creates a right to information" which plaintiffs may predicate standing upon if the Services intentionally or inadvertently withhold information).

19. 16 U.S.C. § 1539(a)(2)(B)(i)–(v). At least one court has rejected that this language operates as a nondiscretionary duty to issue the ITP. Sw. Ctr. for Biological Diversity v. Bartel, 470 F. Supp. 2d 1118, 1135 (S.D. Cal. 2006), *appeal dismissed and remanded*, 409 F. App'x 143 (9th Cir. 2011).

20. HCP Handbook, *supra* note 12, at 14-23.

21. *Id.* at 7-5 through 7-6 (addressing HCP species selection generally), and 7-6 (addressing non-ESA-listed species in an HCP); 89 Fed. Reg. 26,070, 26,072 (Apr. 12, 2024) (clarifying FWS's authority to issue permits for nonlisted species without including a listed species). Candidate conservation agreements are addressed in Section 6.4.

22. HCP Handbook, *supra* note 12, at 9-8 through 9-9 (addressing habitat-based goals).

23. Although plants generally are not the object of a section 10 permit (because the section 9 prohibitions against takings do not apply to plants), the Services cannot approve a section 10 permit for an action that would result in

species that might be taken incidentally during the life of the proposed project. Simply stated, the covered species should be identified clearly in the HCP and subsequent section 10 permit (or some other permit); failure to include all covered species that might subsequently be taken could result in enforcement, project delays, or even an injunction against the project.[24]

An HCP may be limited to a specifically identifiable action, such as the construction of residential properties,[25] or it may apply to broad categories of activities, such as county building permit programs or statewide logging activities affecting a listed species.[26] A section 10 permit for a "programmatic HCP," for example, might be issued to a county or state government, allowing entities subsequently permitted by the county or state government to conduct activities covered by the programmatic HCP and then avail themselves of incidental take protection under certain circumstances.[27] With respect to a programmatic section 10 permit issued by the National Marine Fisheries Service (NMFS), a person seeking permit coverage must apply for and receive a "certificate of inclusion."[28] In the case of an FWS-issued programmatic section 10 permit, the permit itself may identify persons under the jurisdiction of the permittee who are allowed to conduct activities under the permit, or the permittee may issue subsequent permits, through any "written instrument" consistent with implementation of the HCP.[29]

---

jeopardy to any listed species, including plants. HCP Handbook, *supra* note 12, at 7-2 through 7-5, 7-12, 16-5.

24. *Id.* at 3-7. See Chapter 4 for a discussion of actions prohibited by the ESA section 9. Regardless of an HCP's scope, all proposed activities must be consistent with and contemplated by the HCP and resulting section 10 permit for the shield against section 9 liability to apply. *See* Loggerhead Turtle v. Cnty. Council of Volusia Cnty., 148 F.3d 1231, 1242 (11th Cir. 1998).

25. *See, e.g.*, 88 Fed. Reg. 76,244 (Nov. 13, 2023) (noticing availability of a proposed HCP for residential development regarding the coastal California gnatcatcher).

26. See 86 Fed. Reg. 51,367 (Sept. 15, 2021) for an example of a statewide section 10 permit application and HCP. *See generally* Alejandro E. Camacho, Elizabeth M. Taylor & Melissa L. Kelly, *Lessons from Areawide, Multiagency Habitat Conservation Plans in California*, 46 Env't L. Rep. 10222 (2016).

27. *See* HCP Handbook, *supra* note 12, at 3-10. Such a regional-scale HCP was the subject of the litigation in *Southwest Center for Biological Diversity v. Bartel*, 470 F. Supp. 2d 1118 (S.D. Cal. 2006), *appeal dismissed and remanded*, 409 F. App'x 143 (9th Cir. 2011).

28. 50 C.F.R. § 222.307(f) (NMFS criteria for issuance of "certificates of inclusion").

29. *Id.* § 13.25(d), (e).

6.3.2 HCP Mitigation Requirements

The critical features of any HCP are the measures to "minimize and mitigate" the impacts of the proposed taking to the "maximum extent practicable."[30] The precise scope of this requirement is somewhat vague. Neither the ESA nor the section 10 regulations define "maximum extent practicable."[31] The Services require that mitigation be based on a "clear rationale" and that it be "commensurate with the impacts" addressed.[32] To demonstrate that mitigation is adequate, the applicant must either show (1) that the biological value that will be lost from covered activities will be fully replaced through implementation of conservation measures with equivalent biological value (meaning the impacts are fully offset, thereby meeting the "maximum extent practicable" standard) or (2) if HCP does not fully offset the impacts from the covered activity, that the minimization and mitigation measures provided in the HCP represent the most an applicant can practicably accomplish.[33]

For both analyses, the applicant must (1) estimate the type and amount of take expected from covered activities, and the impacts of such taking on the species or its habitat; (2) determine from a biological perspective how conservation measures in the HCP will minimize the impacts of the taking on the species' status and/or its habitat; and (3) determine from a biological perspective how conservation measures in the HCP will mitigate the remaining impact of the taking on the species' status or its habitat.[34]

To meet the "maximum extent practicable" standard, applicants must show that impacts are fully offset by comprehensively defining the impacts of the taking.[35] Rather than defining rigid

30. 16 U.S.C. § 1539(a)(2)(B).

31. *See* HCP Handbook, *supra* note 12, at 9-28. *See also* WildEarth Guardians v. U.S. Fish & Wildlife Serv., 622 F. Supp. 2d 1155, 1165 (D. Utah 2009) (citing Nat'l Wildlife Fed'n v. Norton, 306 F. Supp. 2d 920, 927 (E.D. Cal. 2004)).

32. HCP Handbook, *supra* note 12, at 9-2. Mitigation actions usually take one of the following forms: Avoiding the impact through project design (such as using seasonal restrictions or reducing the extent of the covered activity); minimizing the impact through best management practices (such as maintaining habitat connectivity and establishing buffer zones);minimizing the impacts of the taking by reducing or eliminating other threats; or mitigating or offsetting impacts by restoring degraded habitat, enhancing functional habitat, preserving habitat, creating new habitat, or translocating or repatriating species. *Id.* at 9-12 through 9-19.

33. *Id.* at 9-28 through 9-36.

34. *Id.*

35. The Services do not define the factors an applicant would need to assess to define impacts, rather the Services provide an in-depth list of questions for an

standards to determine when impacts are fully offset, the Services provide examples. For instance, the Services elaborate that when one hundred acres of a certain habitat are lost, those impacts can be fully offset if an applicant restores and protects, in perpetuity, at least 100 acres of that habitat type of at least equal biological value to the covered species before impacts occur.[36]

If impacts are not fully offset, the applicant must show that the proposed conservation measures minimize and mitigate to the maximum extent practicable, meaning the measures are "within [the applicant's] available means" and "the applicant can feasibly do no more to minimize or mitigate the impacts of the taking."[37] Applicants can make this showing by demonstrating that there are insufficient implementation options (for example, if an action results in habitat loss, an applicant might illustrate that it cannot acquire mitigation habitat within surrounding areas) or that financial constraints limit the applicant's ability to do more.[38] It is incumbent upon the Service to make a determination that no practicable alternative to the development plan exists that would minimize the taking of the species.[39]

The Services indicate that HCP mitigation programs are "multidisciplinary endeavors" and that they encourage "creative" yet balanced approaches.[40] These approaches must "carefully weigh the positive benefits of a potential creative approach against the possible negative repercussions, as well as the complexity of its implementation, legality, workload burden, and conservation contribution."[41] Nonetheless, mitigation should be as consistent as possible for the same species and the administrative record should support both the amount and level of mitigation ultimately required by the HCP. Federal courts generally review the administrative record for some "rational basis" to support any decision approving an HCP and issuing the associated section 10 permit.[42]

---

applicant to consider. *Id.* at 9-10.

36. *Id.* at 9-30.

37. *Id.* at 9-33 (citing Nat'l Wildlife Fed'n v. Norton, 306 F. Supp. 2d 920, 927 (E.D. Cal. 2004)) (holding that FWS appropriately required mitigation measures to correspond with the level of take by the proposed act).

38. *Id.*

39. *Id.* at 9-28. *See* Or.-Cal. Trails Ass'n v. Walsh, 467 F. Supp. 3d 1007, 1064 (D. Colo. 2020).

40. HCP Handbook, *supra* note 12, at 2-3 through 2-4.

41. *Id.*

42. Klamath-Siskiyou Wildlands Ctr. v. NMFS, 109 F. Supp. 3d 1238, 1244 (N.D. Cal. 2015) (overturning issuance of ITPs where FWS considered the conservation efforts of third parties not applying for the ITPs); Friends of Animals v.

This judicial review standard suggests that the record should contain some analysis of whether the amount or level of mitigation provided in the HCP is the maximum practicable.[43] The Services, moreover, may not justify their approval of an HCP on a mere speculative possibility of future actions (such as an unknown amount of funding from an unknown third party).[44]

6.3.3 No Surprises Policy and Adaptive Management

A section 10 HCP permit seeks to achieve two arguably competing goals. On the one hand, it should be flexible enough to adapt to changes in circumstances and new information regarding the needs of listed species. The Services generally emphasize the need to incorporate into decisions adequate mechanisms for adaptive management.[45] Conversely, applicants desire as much regulatory and economic certainty as they can secure, and for as long a period as possible. Yet Congress provided little guidance to the Secretary on how to balance these competing demands. Legislative history suggests only that the Secretary is vested with broad discretion and should address the situation by including in every long-term HCP "a procedure by which the parties will deal with unforeseen circumstances."[46] Courts appear to accept adaptive management provisions in an HCP, provided that the Service

---

Phifer, 238 F. Supp. 3d 119, 128 (D. Me. 2017) (upholding ITP even though incidental take of Canada lynx exceeded HCP estimates).

43. Sierra Club v. Babbitt, 15 F. Supp. 2d 1274, 1282 (S.D. Ala. 1998) (citing Sierra Club v. Marsh, 816 F.2d 1376 (9th Cir. 1987)) (action agency cannot be sure that project will not jeopardize species based upon promise of future mitigation measures); Nat'l Wildlife Fed'n v. Coleman, 529 F.2d 359 (5th Cir. 1976) (proposed actions by others do not ensure that a project will not jeopardize listed species). In *WildEarth Guardians v. U.S Fish & Wildlife Service*, the court rejected the argument that the ITP needed to identify a precise number of species covered by the take permit. 622 F. Supp. 2d 1155 (D. Utah 2009).

44. *Sierra Club v. Babbitt*, 15 F. Supp. 2d at 1282.

45. HCP Handbook, *supra* note 12, at 10-1 through 10-34. For one review of the program and its effectiveness, *see* Alejandro E. Camacho, *Can Regulation Evolve? Lessons from a Study in Maladaptive Management*, 55 UCLA L. Rev. 293 (2007). FWS has a technical guide for strategic habitat conservation that emphasizes the iterative process for habitat conservation strategies. U.S Fish & Wildlife Serv., Strategic Habitat Conservation Handbook: A Guide to Implementing the Technical Elements of Strategic Habitat Conservation (Version 1.0, Feb. 11, 2008), https://digitalmedia.fws.gov/digital/collection/document/id/901/.

46. H.R. Rep. No. 97-835, at 30 (1982), *reprinted in* 1982 U.S.C.C.A.N. 2860, 2872.

is not merely employing adaptive management as a surrogate for avoiding making difficult choices.[47]

In February 1998, FWS and NMFS promulgated the Habitat Conservation Plan Assurances (No Surprises) Rule.[48] This final rule formally implemented the FWS's no surprises policy, a policy described by one key Interior Department official as "the single most important catalyst in stimulating renewed interest in Habitat Conservation Planning."[49] The Services described the policy as follows:

> The No Surprises policy announced in 1994 provides regulatory assurances to the holder of a Habitat Conservation Plan (HCP) incidental take permit issued under section 10(a) of the ESA that no additional land use restrictions or financial compensation will be required of the permit holder with respect to species covered by the permit, even if unforeseen circumstances arise after the permit is issued indicating that additional mitigation is needed for a given species covered by a permit.[50]

The ITP operates as a firm arrangement between the permit holder and the government for species covered in the HCP; landowners properly implementing the terms of their HCP are shielded from being responsible for significant additional measures that may become necessary to respond to "unforeseen circumstances." This arrangement became further solidified once FWS issued a procedurally proper permit revocation rule, effectively providing that a permit would not be revoked unless the

---

47. In *National Wildlife Federation v. Babbitt,* 128 F. Supp. 2d 1274 (E.D. Cal. 2000), the court approved the adaptive management strategy, although it otherwise concluded that the ITP was too broad. *See also* NRDC v. Kempthorne, 506 F. Supp. 2d 322 (E.D. Cal. 2007); Sw. Ctr. for Biological Diversity v. Bartel, 470 F. Supp. 2d 1118 (S.D. Cal. 2006); Ctr. for Biological Diversity v. U.S. Fish & Wildlife Serv., 202 F. Supp. 2d 594 (W.D. Tex. 2002). Indeed, the absence of adaptive management could be problematic because one court suggested the need for adaptive management in lieu of what the court described as a "lock-in ineffective, unstudied, and inadequate mitigation" plan for the particular species for 50 years. Sw. Ctr. for Biological Diversity v. Bartel, 470 F. Supp. 2d 1118, 1146 (S.D. Cal. 2006), *appeal dismissed and remanded,* 409 F. App'x 143 (9th Cir. 2011).

48. 63 Fed. Reg. 8,859 (1998) (codified at 50 C.F.R. pt. 17) [hereinafter No Surprises Rule]. For the litigation surrounding the rule and a discussion of the rule, see *Spirit of the Sage Council v. Norton,* 294 F. Supp. 2d 67 (D.D.C. 2003), *appeal dismissed and orders vacated as moot,* 411 F.3d 225 (D.C. Cir. 2005).

49. Donald J. Barry, Opportunity in the Face of Danger: The Pragmatic Development of Habitat Conservation Plans, Keynote Address Before the West-Northwest Symposium (Mar. 1, 1997), *reprinted in* 4 Hastings W.-Nw. J. Env't L. & Pol'y 129, 130 (Summer 1998).

50. No Surprises Rule, *supra* note 48, 63 Fed. Reg. 8859 (1998).

permittee was not complying with its terms or if continuation of the permit might threaten to jeopardize the species.[51]

A few significant aspects of the no surprises policy are worth noting. First, the policy applies only to nonfederal parties seeking an ESA section 10(a)(1)(B) ITP;[52] second, the assurances provided to the permit holder are valid for the life of the permit and only with respect to species "adequately covered"[53] by the permit; third, the assurances provided to the permit holder are valid only when the HCP is being "properly implemented."[54] The larger issue, of course, is the scope and extent of the actual assurances provided to permit holders. The nature of the available assurances depends on whether a particular change in circumstances, affecting species covered by an HCP, is foreseeable or unforeseeable. Neither NMFS nor FWS define the term *foreseeable;* instead, the Services employ their respective definitions of the term *changed circumstances* for applying the No Surprises Rule. *Changed circumstances* means changes in circumstances affecting a species or geographic area covered by a conservation plan that can reasonably be anticipated by the plan's developers and the Service for which responses can be identified in a conservation plan (e.g., the listing of new species, effects of climate change, or a fire or other natural catastrophic event in areas prone to such events).[55]

And the term *unforeseen circumstances* is defined as changes in circumstances affecting a species or geographic area covered by a conservation plan or agreement that could not reasonably have been anticipated by plan or agreement developers and the Service at the time of the conservation plan's or agreement's

51. 69 Fed. Reg. 71,723 (Dec. 10, 2004); 69 Fed. Reg. 29,681 (May 25, 2004) (proposing permit revocation regulations); 69 Fed. Reg. 29,669 (May 25, 2004) (withdrawing certain permit revo-cation regulations); 64 Fed. Reg. 32,706 (June 17, 1999). The permit revocation survived a challenge based upon the argument that ITPs must promote the recovery of listed species. Spirit of the Sage Council v. Kempthorne, 511 F. Supp. 2d 31 (D.D.C. 2007). The court disagreed with other courts that suggested that HCPs must promote recovery, not just survival. *Id.* at 43 n.4.

52. No Surprises Rule, *supra* note 48, 63 Fed. Reg. at 8,868.

53. 50 C.F.R. § 17.22(b)(5); 50 C.F.R. § 17.32(b)(5); 50 C.F.R. § 222.307(g). The term *adequately covered* is defined in 50 C.F.R. §§ 17.3 and 222.102.

54. A *properly implemented conservation plan* is defined as "any conservation plan, implementing agreement and permit whose commitments and provisions have been or are being fully implemented by the permittee." 50 C.F.R. § 17.3.

55. 50 C.F.R. § 17.3 (FWS); 50 C.F.R. § 222.102 (NMFS).

negotiation and development, and that result in a substantial and adverse change in the status of the covered species.[56]

When developing an HCP, the parties should attempt to address all reasonably foreseeable changes in circumstances.[57] By definition, these changed circumstances are foreseeable, and when (or if) they occur during the life of the HCP, the permittee must address them as called for in the plan.[58] Rarely should a foreseeable change in circumstances not have been addressed in an HCP, but should such an event occur, the permittee will not be required to implement additional conservation and mitigation measures without its "consent."[59]

The import of unforeseen circumstances is that when and if they occur, the government may only require minimal additional measures of the permittee. The original terms of the HCP must be maintained to the maximum extent possible and, importantly, the Services may not require "commitments of additional land, water, or financial compensation or additional restrictions on the use of land, water, or other natural resources" without the permittee's consent.[60] The Services recognize that the needs of a species in such an instance may mandate that some action be taken on behalf of the species. As such, the Services noted in the No Surprises Rule that nothing in the rule should be read to limit or constrain any governmental entity (including the Services) from taking additional action at its own expense to protect or conserve a species included in an HCP.[61]

---

56. *Id.*

57. No Surprises Rule, *supra* note 48, 63 Fed. Reg. at 8863. The final No Surprises Rule is silent with respect to the extent of a party's obligation to address changes in circumstances. The supplementary information accompanying the final rule provides that reasonably foreseeable changes in circumstances "need to be addressed in an HCP," and that all reasonably foreseeable *circumstances, including natural* catastrophes that normally occur in the area, "should be addressed in the HCP." *Id.*

58. 50 C.F.R. § 17.22(b)(5)(i)–(ii) (FWS Regulations for Endangered Wildlife); 50 C.F.R. § 17.32(b)(5)(i)–(ii) (FWS Regulations for Threatened Wildlife); 50 C.F.R. § 222.307(g)(1), (2) (NMFS regulations).

59. 50 C.F.R. §§ 17.22(b)(5)(ii), 17.32(b)(5)(ii), 222.307(g)(ii).

60. 50 C.F.R. § 17.22(b)(5)(iii) (FWS); 50 C.F.R. § 222.307(g)(3) (NMFS).

61. 50 C.F.R. § 17.22(b)(6); 50 C.F.R. § 17.32(b)(6); 50 C.F.R. 222.307(h).

6.4 Enhancement of Survival and Conservation Benefit Agreements

Section 10(a)(1)(A)[62] of the ESA allows the Services to authorize otherwise prohibited acts when carried out to enhance the propagation or survival of a listed species. Examples of enhancement activities include capture, study, tagging, banding, and other scientific activities.

In addition, in 1999, FWS promulgated regulations for the use of safe harbor agreements (SHAs).[63] While an HCP is developed in concert with an application for an incidental take permit, an SHA was developed in conjunction with an application for an "enhancement of survival" permit. An SHA was a voluntary agreement, not necessarily provoked by immediate concerns over potential take liability associated with specific activities on private lands. Rather, the SHA-based enhancement of survival permit was appropriate when a landowner proposed activities that would restore, enhance, or maintain habitat for listed species, possibly increasing numbers of the particular species present on a landowner's private land. In exchange for the landowner's commitment to implement these species-friendly measures, the landowner would receive certain assurances limiting future land-use restrictions and was assured of some future incidental take of covered species, back down to an agreed-upon baseline level.

Corresponding to the FWS's agreements with private landowners to conserve candidate species on their property, NMFS created the candidate conservation agreement with assurances (CCAA).[64] For candidate species, or any "species that may become candidates in the near future or proposed for listing in the

62. 16 U.S.C. § 1539(a)(1)(A).

63. Announcement of Final Safe Harbor Policy, 64 Fed. Reg. 32,717 (June 17, 1999). The Services described the rules as "creating a new category of enhancement of survival permit." *Id.* at 32,722. Prior to the Services' implementation of a formal Final Safe Harbor Policy, the Services had operated implemented a safe harbor policy informally, so by August 1999, there were more than 40 SHAs in effect. U.S. Fish & Wildlife Serv., Safe Harbor Agreements for Private Property Owners, Questions & Answers (Sept. 1999).

64. Safe Harbor Agreement and Candidate Conservation Agreements with Assurances, 64 Fed. Reg. 32,706 (June 17, 1999). NMFS concurrently adopted the FWS policy regarding candidate conservation agreements, without promulgating formal rules. Announcement of Final Policy for Candidate Conservation Agreements with Assurances, 64 Fed. Reg. 32,726 (June 17, 1999). In 2004, FWS revised the CCAA regulations (Revisions to the Regulations, 69 Fed. Reg. 24,084 (May 3, 2004)). Then, in 2016, FWS announced a revised CCAA policy. Candidate Conservation Agreements with Assurances Policy, 81 Fed. Reg. 95,164 (Dec. 27, 2016).

near future,"[65] any nonfederal property owner that entered into a CCAA and implemented conservation measures on nonfederal property designed to benefit such species would receive assurances from the Services that additional conservation measures would not be required of the landowner, and that additional land, water, or resource restrictions would not be imposed on the landowner, should the species become listed.[66]

In 2024, FWS combined SHAs and CCAAs into a single agreement type called a "conservation benefit agreement."[67] FWS made this change to simplify the application process and encourage greater participation in voluntary conservation actions. As with SHAs and CCAAs, property owners[68] who enter a conservation benefit agreement receive assurances that they will not need to carry out any additional conservation measures beyond those set out in the conservation benefit agreement.[69]

Any person requesting a conservation benefit agreement-based permit must submit a permit application (FWS Form 3-200-54), a processing fee, and a conservation benefit agreement.[70] The conservation benefit agreement must include

- a complete description of the conservation measures, including the location of the activity or activities to be covered by the permit, and the intended outcome for the covered species;[71]
- the common and scientific names of the covered species;[72]
- the measurable biological goals and objectives of the conservation measures;[73]
- the baseline condition of the property or area to be enrolled in the conservation benefit agreement;[74]

65. 81 Fed. Reg. at 95,170.
66. *Id.* at 95,165–70.
67. Enhancement of Survival and Incidental Take Permits, 89 Fed. Reg. 26,070 (Apr. 12, 2024).
68. "A property owner, with respect to conservation benefit agreements and plans . . . means a person or other entity with a property interest (including owners of rights to water or other natural resources) sufficient to carry out the proposed activities, subject to applicable State, Tribal, and Federal laws and regulations." 50 C.F.R. § 17.3.
69. 89 Fed. Reg. at 26,072.
70. 50 C.F.R. § 17.22(c)(1).
71. *Id.* § 17.22(c)(1)(i).
72. *Id.* § 17.22(c)(1)(ii).
73. *Id.* § 17.22(c)(1)(iii).
74. *Id.* § 17.22(c)(1)(iv).

- a description of how the measures are reasonably expected to improve each covered species' existing baseline condition on the enrolled property and result in a net conservation benefit;[75]
- the steps the applicant will take to monitor and adaptively manage to ensure the conservation benefit agreement's goals and objectives are met, the responsibilities of all parties are carried out, and the conservation benefit agreement will be properly implemented;[76]
- a description of the enrollment process to provide neighboring property owners take coverage under the conservation benefit agreement, if applicable, or any other measures developed to protect the interests of neighboring property owners;[77]
- the applicant's choice between including authorization to return the enrolled property to baseline condition or forgoing that authorization;[78]
- any other measures that the Director may require as necessary or appropriate to meet the permit issuance criteria.[79]

To enter into a conservation benefit agreement, the applicant and FWS must determine the "baseline condition" of the property to be covered by the agreement.[80] The baseline determination allows the applicant to determine species-friendly measures or activities that are reasonably expected to accomplish a "net conservation benefit"[81] relative to the baseline conditions. This

75. *Id.* § 17.22(c)(1)(v).
76. *Id.* § 17.22(c)(1)(vi).
77. *Id.* § 17.22(c)(1)(vii).
78. *Id.* § 17.22(c)(1)(viii).
79. *Id.* § 17.22(c)(1)(ix).
80. "*Baseline condition* means population estimates and distribution or habitat characteristics across the enrolled property that currently sustains seasonal or permanent use by the covered species at the time a conservation benefit agreement is executed by the Service and the property owner . . . ." 50 C.F.R. § 17.3.
81. "*Net conservation benefit* means the cumulative benefit provided through implementation of a conservation benefit agreement that is designed to improve the existing baseline condition of a covered species by reducing or eliminating threats, or otherwise improving the status of covered species, minus the adverse impacts to covered species from ongoing land or water use activities and conservation measures, so that the condition of the covered species or the amount or quality of its habitat is reasonably expected to be greater with implementation of the agreement than without it. If the Service determines that the species and habitat are already adequately managed to the benefit of the species, a net conservation benefit will be achieved if the property owner commits to continuing

net conservation benefit need not be permanent, as landowners ultimately may degrade the habitat back down to the baseline.[82] Upon a finding that implementation of the conservation benefit agreement would provide a net conservation benefit, among other things,[83] FWS may issue a section 10(a)(1)(A) enhancement permit allowing the permittee to "incidentally"[84] take species covered by the agreement. The permit holder is then authorized to "continue ongoing activities . . . without concern that their activities may be curtailed by increasing populations or distribution of a listed species or a species that may become listed in the future."[85] The permit holder also is assured that no additional commitments of land, water, or financial resources will be required.[86]

The duration of a conservation benefit agreement and accompanying permit are within the Director's discretion, but they must be sufficiently lengthy to provide a net conservation benefit to species covered by the permit.[87] The Director will also consider the duration of the landowner's planned activities, uncertainties related to the impacts of the taking, and the positive and negative effects of the planned activities covered by the permit on the species covered by the conservation benefit agreement. Further, the

---

the species' management for a specified period of time, including addressing any likely future threats that are under the property owner's control, with the anticipation that the population will increase, habitat quality will improve, or both." 50 C.F.R. § 17.3.

82. The Services justify this aspect of conservation benefit agreements by noting allowing for increased flexibility may result in increased agreement participation. 89 Fed. Reg. at 26,071.

83. The Secretary may issue an enhancement of survival permit only upon finding that (1) the take will be incidental to an otherwise lawful activity or purposeful if it is necessary for the implementation of the conservation benefit agreement and will be in accordance with the terms of the agreement; (2) implementing the conservation benefit agreement's terms is reasonably expected to provide a net conservation benefit to the affected covered species on the enrolled property that is included in the permit and for each individual property within a programmatic conservation benefit agreement, based upon condition of the species or habitat, effects of conservation measures, and anticipated impacts of any permitted take; (3) the direct and indirect effects of any authorized take are unlikely to appreciably reduce the likelihood of survival and recovery in the wild of any listed species; (4) the conservation benefit agreement will not conflict with any ongoing conservation or recovery programs for listed species and the covered species included in the permit; and (5) the applicant is capable and can commit to upholding the conservation benefit agreement. 50 C.F.R. § 17.22(c)(2)(i)–(v).

84. A landowner cannot create a storehouse of specimens for later intentional "harvest" or take. Rather, the taking must be "incidental to otherwise lawful activities." 50 C.F.R. § 17.22(b)(2)(i).

85. 89 Fed. Reg at 26,072.

86. *Id.*; 50 C.F.R. § 17.22(c)(5)(i).

87. 50 C.F.R. § 17.22(c)(4).

conservation benefit agreement and accompanying permit may only be revoked under certain circumstances.[88]

Beyond these limited revocation criteria, however, an enhancement of survival permit may be revoked only after the Director, with the consent of the permit holder, "pursue[s] other appropriate options to avoid permit revocation," including extending or modifying the existing permit, capturing and relocating the species, compensating the property owner to forgo the activity, purchasing an easement or fee simple interest in the property, or arranging for a third-party acquisition of an interest in the property.[89]

A related tool is the candidate conservation agreement (CCA), designed to avoid the need for an ESA listing by having parties to the agreement engage in pro-conservation efforts. A CCA, unlike a conservation benefit agreement, does not result in the issuance of an enhancement of survival permit.[90] The Services' 2003 Policy for Evaluation of Conservation Efforts When Making Listing Determinations (PECE) promotes the development of CCAs, by taking into account CCAs when making listing decisions.[91] While it mostly serves as a mechanism for the Services to negotiate with federal or state land managers on how lands might be managed to promote species conservation, and possibly avert a listing, a CCA can apply to activities on both federal and nonfederal lands.[92]

---

88. Permits may be revoked if the covered activity appreciably reduces "likelihood of survival and recovery in the wild of any covered species"; or if the covered activity "[d]irectly or indirectly alter[s] designated critical habitat such that the value of that critical habitat is appreciably diminished for both the survival and recovery of a covered species." *Id.* § 17.22(c)(9).

89. *Id.* § 17.22(c)(9)(ii)

90. 89 Fed. Reg. at 26,086.

91. 68 Fed. Reg. 15,100 (Mar. 28, 2003). The PECE policy requires reasonable certainty that the conservation measures will be implemented and effective. *See generally* Hadassah M. Reimer & Murray D. Feldman, *Give PECE a Chance: Evaluating Conservation Programs to Avoid Endangered Species Act Listings*, 56 Rocky Mtn. Min. L. Inst. 21 (2010). CCAAs were promoted as a tool that could be used to avoid a listing decision, although their ability to do so is considered difficult to measure. *See* Timothy Male & Aimee Ford, *Landowner Incentives*, *in* Endangered Species Act: Law, Policy, and Perspectives 203 (Donald C. Baur & Ya-Wei Li eds., 3d ed. 2021).

92. *See* U.S. Fish & Wildlife Serv., *Using Existing Tools to Expand Cooperative Conservation for Candidate Species Across Federal and Non-Federal Lands*, https://www.fws.gov/sites/default/files/documents/CCA-CCAA-Final-Guidance.pdf (last visited Apr. 30, 2025).

6.5 Transferability

Many of these permits are transferable. For permits issued by FWS, for instance, transferability and other matters are generally governed by the general permit procedures in 50 C.F.R. part 13. Any transferees or successors to an individual holding a permit may avail themselves of the permit protections so long as they are otherwise qualified to hold such a permit[93] and provide adequate written assurances that they will fund and implement the terms of the permit.[94]

6.6 Conservation Banks

Building on the idea of mitigation banking in the wetlands area, FWS began to explore employing conservation banks as a mechanism for promoting species conservation. Conservation-bank-related guidance has a convoluted history. In 2003, FWS issued policy guidance intended to "provide a collaborative incentive-based approach to endangered species conservation."[95] Then, in 2008, FWS issued recovery credit guidance.[96] In 2016, FWS issued the ESA Compensatory Mitigation Policy clarifying FWS's expectations for all compensatory mitigation programs, including conservation banks.[97] FWS then withdrew this 2016 ESA Compensatory Mitigation Policy in 2018, leaving a 1981 Mitigation Policy operative instead.[98] In 2023, FWS announced a revised Compensatory Mitigation Policy and issuance of the ESA Compensatory

93. 50 C.F.R. § 13.25(b). *See also id.* § 13.21(c) (providing a list of factors that may disqualify one from receiving any FWS permit).

94. 50 C.F.R. §§ 13.24 (successors), 13.25 (transferees).

95. *See* Guidance for the Establishment, Use, and Operation of Conservation Banks (May 8, 2003), 68 Fed. Reg. 24,753, https://www.fws.gov/sites/default/files/documents/conservation-banking-guidance-2003-05-02.pdf.

96. *See* Notice of Availability of Recovery Crediting Guidance, 73 Fed. Reg. 44,761 (July 31, 2008); Notice of Availability for Draft Recovery Crediting Guidance, 72 Fed. Reg. 62,258 (Nov. 2, 2007).

97. Endangered Species Act Compensatory Mitigation Policy, 81 Fed. Reg. 95,316 (Dec. 27, 2016).

98. U.S. Fish and Wildlife Service Mitigation Policy, 83 Fed. Reg. 36,472 (July 30, 2018).

Mitigation Policy.[99] The 2023 ESA Compensatory Mitigation Policy clarifies the FWS's 2003 and 2008 Guidance on conservation banks and recovery crediting, and adopts the principles set forth in the general Mitigation Policy.[100] In the general Mitigation Policy, FWS identifies many "fundamental principles" including the requirement that FWS observe the mitigation hierarchy, meaning that minimizing harms is prioritized over compensatory mitigation measures. The Mitigation Policy also directs FWS to use the "best available science (including social and natural sciences and Indigenous Knowledge)."[101]

The Service has now approved more than 173 conservation banks nationwide, mostly in California, conserving roughly 260,000 acres.[102] An essential element of this program is that lands will be managed for their ecological value and protected through a conservation easement or other property instrument, and in return the bank owner will receive credits for the identified species, which credits can then be used as mitigation for those species elsewhere.[103]

6.7 Interagency Section 7 Consultation Requirement and NEPA

The decision to grant a section 10 incidental take permit must be made, in part, "using the same standard as found in section 7(a)(2) of the Act."[104] Thus, before issuance of any section 10 permit, the Secretary must determine that the contemplated taking "will not appreciably reduce the likelihood of the survival and recovery

99. U.S. Fish and Wildlife Service Mitigation Policy and Endangered Species Act Compensatory Mitigation Policy, 88 Fed. Reg. 31,000 (May 15, 2023); U.S. Fish & Wildlife Serv., Endangered Species Act Compensatory Mitigation Policy (May 2023, amended July 3, 2023), https://www.fws.gov/sites/default/files/policy/pdfs/FWS-ESA-Compensatory-Mitigation-Policy-amend_1.pdf; U.S. Fish & Wildlife Services, Mitigation Policy (May 2023), https://www.fws.gov/sites/default/files/policy/pdfs/FWS-Mitigation-Policy.pdf.

100. 88 Fed. Reg. 31,000.

101. Mitigation Policy, *supra* note 99, at 4.

102. 87 Fed. Reg. 45,076 (July 27, 2022).

103. U.S. Fish & Wildlife Serv., Conservation Banking Incentives for Stewardship (Sept. 2019); https://www.fws.gov/sites/default/files/documents/conservation-banking.pdf.

104. H.R. Conf. Rep. No. 97-835, at 29 (1982), *reprinted in* 1982 U.S.C.C.A.N. 2860, 2870.

of [any] species in the wild."[105] Because the issuance of a section 10 permit is a federal action, the issuing agency will engage in an internal section 7 consultation with itself to ensure that no species of animal or plant is jeopardized by issuance of the permit.[106] If the level of take authorized in the section 10 permit and embedded in the intra-service consultation biological opinion subsequently exceeds that which is allowed, the parties must reinitiate consultation, possibly necessitating the issuance of a new biological opinion.[107] The Service also must comply with the requirements of the National Environmental Policy Act (NEPA).[108] This may require the preparation of either an environmental assessment (EA) or an environmental impact statement (EIS), depending upon the nature of the proposed activities.[109] An HCP that qualifies as a low-effect HCP may be categorically excluded, however, from the requirement to prepare either an EA or an EIS.[110]

6.8 Other Specific Section 10 Exceptions

In addition to the more common incidental take and enhancement of survival permits, the ESA provides for a variety of exceptions applicable to specific situations, involving particular species, and in some cases applying only to particular persons.

For example, the ESA's hardship exemption provides that, under certain circumstances, the Secretary may, to minimize

105. 16 U.S.C. § 1539(a)(2)(B)(iv). *See generally* Oliver A. Houck, *The Endangered Species Act and Its Implementation by the U.S. Departments of Interior and Commerce*, 64 U. Colo. L. Rev. 277, 353–54 (1993) (discussing the overlap of sections 7 and 9 of the ESA).

106. HCP Handbook, *supra* note 12, at 6-4. The section 7 conference process applies to proposed species. 16 U.S.C. § 1536(c)(1).

107. *E.g.*, WildEarth Guardians v. U.S. Fish & Wildlife Serv., 622 F. Supp. 2d 1155, 1161 (D. Utah 2009) (noting that a new biological opinion had been issued); 50 C.F.R. § 402.16.

108. The Services may be required to comply with the National Historic Preservation Act, if applicable, as well as section 401 of the Clean Water Act, again if applicable. *See also* Medina Cnty. Env't Action Ass'n v. Surface Transp. Bd., 602 F.3d 687, 694–96 (5th Cir. 2010); San Luis & Delta-Mendota Water Auth. v. Jewell, 747 F.3d 581, 648 (9th Cir. 2014).

109. HCP Handbook, *supra* note 12, at 13-0 through 13-15.

110. Department of the Interior, *Department Manual, Part 516, Chapter 8: Managing the NEPA Process—U.S. Fish and Wildlife Service* (July 30, 2020), https://www.doi.gov/document-library/departmental-manual/516-dm-8-managing-nepa-process-us-fish-and-wildlife-service-0.

economic hardship, issue a permit exempting a person from application of the ESA's prohibitions for up to a year. The hardship exemption applies to situations in which a person has entered into a "contract with respect to a species" prior to publication in the *Federal Register* of notice of consideration of the species for listing, and prior to the final listing of the species, but only if application of the ESA's prohibitions would cause "undue economic hardship."[111]

In addition, section 10 of the ESA also authorizes trade in certain "pre-Act endangered species parts" (sperm whale oil and scrimshaw products);[112] certain takings and trade of listed species by Alaska natives;[113] and importation or possession of certain antique articles (at least 100 years old) composed of listed species.[114] ESA section 9 authorizes take in defense of human safety,[115] as well as activities associated with wildlife that was held in captivity or in a controlled environment, for noncommercial purposes, on December 28, 1973, or on the date the particular species was listed under the Act.[116] Finally, the ESA's takings prohibitions do not apply to raptors legally held in captivity or in a controlled environment on November 10, 1978, nor to the progeny of any such raptor.[117]

---

111. ESA section 10(b)(2) defines *undue economic hardship* to include economic loss: "(A) resulting from inability to.perform contracts with respect to species of fish and wildlife entered into prior to the date of publication in the *Federal Register* of a notice of consideration of such species as an endangered species; (B) to persons who for the year prior to the notice of consideration of such species . . . derived a substantial portion of their income from the lawful taking of the species; or (C) due to curtailment of certain subsistence takings of listed species." 16 U.S.C. § 1539(b)(2)(A)–(C).

112. 16 U.S.C. § 1539(f). For more about these exceptions, see Steven P. Quarles, Paul S. Weiland & Brian Ferrasci-O'Malley, *Another Take on "Take": The Section 9 Prohibition*, *in* ENDANGERED SPECIES ACT: LAW, POLICY, AND PERSPECTIVES 141, 151–68 (Donald C. Baur & Ya-Wei Li eds, 3d ed. 2021).

113. 16 U.S.C. § 1539(e) (defining *Alaska natives* to mean "any Indian, Aleut, or Eskimo who is an Alaskan Native who resides in Alaska; or any nonnative permanent resident of an Alaskan native village").

114. *Id.* § 1539(h).

115. See Chapter 4, Section 4.8.

116. 16 U.S.C. § 1538(b)(1).

117. *Id.* § 1538(b)(2)(A).

7 Section 7 Exemption Process

7.1 Overview

The exceptions to the Endangered Species Act's (ESA's) various prohibitions are limited and narrowly defined. Nonetheless, two circumstances exist when the ESA could allow the knowing elimination of an entire species. First, albeit highly unlikely, a person could lawfully kill even the last living member of a species in order to protect human safety.[1] Second, the Endangered Species Committee (ESC or "God Squad") may grant an exemption under section 7, allowing a particular federal project to proceed despite its destructive effect on a listed species, even if it would lead to the extinction of that species.[2] In an Executive Order "Declaring a National Energy Emergency," President Trump directed the Department of the Interior to convene the God Squad regularly, "unless otherwise required by law." The order also required all agencies involved in the God Squad to develop emergency energy consultation processes.[3]

In 1978, the Supreme Court held that federal actions that are likely to jeopardize the continued existence of listed species, or

---

1. *See* Chapter 4, Section 4.8.

2. *See generally* Jared des Rosiers, Note, *The Exemption Process Under the Endangered Species Act: How the "God Squad" Works and Why*, 66 Notre Dame L. Rev. 825 (1991). A 2019 study provides some data on how often disagreements surface about the effects of a federal action on a species, and the incidence of the need for the God Squad. *See* Michael J. Evans, Jacob W. Malcom & Ya-Wei Li, *Novel Data Show Expert Wildlife Agencies Are Important to Endangered Species Protection*, Nature Commc'ns, Aug. 1, 2019, https://www.nature.com/articles/s41467-019-11462-9.

3. Exec. Order No. 14156, 90 Fed. Reg. 8433, 8435 (Jan. 29, but signed Jan. 20, 2025).

that adversely modify or destroy critical habitat, may not proceed.[4] Congress responded to the Court's decision by creating the ESA section 7 exemption process to resolve conflicts between proposed federal actions and section 7's mandates.[5] The exemption process is available only in the rare instance when a section 7 consultation has yielded a determination both that a proposed federal action will jeopardize a listed species or will adversely modify critical habitat and that no reasonable and prudent alternatives to the proposed federal action exist.[6] Although few exemptions have been granted by the Endangered Species Committee,[7] and most contemporary observers believe that the process is no longer a viable option, the exemption process nevertheless remains available as a potential avenue for addressing otherwise irreconcilable conflicts between the needs of listed species and proposed federal activities.

7.2 Applying for an Exemption

Given the potential magnitude of an exemption decision, Congress narrowly defined who may apply for an exemption, and how and when an exemption application will be considered. The Fish and Wildlife Service (FWS) and the National Marine Fisheries Service (NMFS) likewise have promulgated extensive regulations governing nearly every aspect of the exemption process.[8]

---

4. Tenn. Valley Auth. v. Hill, 437 U.S. 153, 184–85 (1978).

5. H.R. Rep. No. 95-1627, at 13 (1978), *reprinted in* 1978 U.S.C.C.A.N. 9461, 9463. Congress streamlined the exemption process in 1982. 1982 Endangered Species Act Amendments, Pub. L. No. 97-304, *reprinted in* 1982 U.S.C.C.A.N. 1411.

6. See Chapter 5, Section 5.4 for a discussion of jeopardy BOs and RPAs.

7. The most recent vote exempted 13 Bureau of Land Management timber sales, allowing impacts to northern spotted owls. Endangered Species Committee Notice of Decision, 57 Fed. Reg. 23,405 (June 3, 1992). Prior to the spotted owl decision, the ESC voted to exempt the Grayrocks Reservoir project in Wyoming, allowing impacts to whooping cranes, but denied an exemption request to allow the Tellico Dam to proceed due to its impacts to the snail darter. *See generally* M. Lynn Corn, Betsy A. Cody, & Alexandra M. Wyatt, Cong. Rsch. Serv., R40787, Endangered Species Act: The Exemption Process 1, 11–18 (Jan. 27, 2017).

8. *See* 50 C.F.R. §§ 450–453.

7.2.1 Who May Apply for an Exemption

Three categories of persons may apply for a section 7 exemption: (1) a federal agency, (2) the governor of a state in which an agency action will occur, and (3) a permit or license applicant.[9] The phrase "permit or license applicant" is defined more narrowly in the exemption context than in the ESA section 7 consultation context;[10] only those individuals whose applications for federal permits or licenses have been denied on ESA section 7 grounds may apply for an exemption.[11] A private party whose proposed activities have no nexus to a federal project is not eligible to seek a section 7 exemption.

7.2.2 When to Apply for an Exemption

Section 7 consultation is a mandatory precursor to an application for an exemption.[12] The application must be submitted within 90 days "after the completion of the consultation process."[13] A permit or license applicant, however, may wait up to 90 days after the federal agency has formally denied the license or permit at issue before filing.[14] If an applicant chooses to seek administrative review of an agency's denial of a permit or license, the period for seeking an exemption is tolled, pending final disposition of the administrative appeal.[15] And an applicant may not simultaneously seek administrative review of a permit or license denial while applying for an exemption.[16]

7.2.3 Contents of the Exemption Application

An exemption application is mailed to the appropriate Secretary at the address provided for by regulation,[17] and must contain:

9. 16 U.S.C. § 1536(g)(1); 50 C.F.R. § 451.02(c).
10. See Chapter 5, Section 5.9 for a discussion of applicants in the section 7 consultation context.
11. 16 U.S.C. § 1536(g)(1); 50 C.F.R. §§ 450.01, 451.02(c).
12. 16 U.S.C. § 1536(g)(2)(A).
13. *Id.*
14. *Id.* § 1536(g)(2)(A); 50 C.F.R. § 451.02(d).
15. 16 U.S.C. § 1536(g)(2)(A); 50 C.F.R. § 451.02(d).
16. 50 C.F.R. § 451.02(d)(2).
17. *Id.* § 451.02(b).

- basic information identifying the exemption applicant;[18]
- a "comprehensive" description of the proposed action (and of the permit or license sought, when applicable);[19]
- a description of any remaining permit, license, or legal requirements that must be satisfied for the proposed action to proceed;[20]
- a description of the consultation process that preceded the exemption application;[21]
- copies of any biological assessment or biological opinion prepared;[22]
- a description of the considered alternatives to the proposed action;[23]
- a statement describing why the proposed action cannot be modified to avoid violating section 7(a)(2) of the ESA;[24]
- a description of the resources committed by the federal agency (or any permit or license applicant) to the proposed action subsequent to the initiation of consultation.[25]

An exemption application also must include a complete discussion or statement of:

- the nature and extent of the benefits of the proposed action;
- why the benefits of the project clearly outweigh the benefits of each considered alternative to the action;
- why none of the considered alternatives is reasonable and prudent;
- why the proposed action is in the public interest;
- why the action is of regional or national significance;
- mitigation and enhancement measures proposed to be undertaken if an exemption is granted.[26]

---

18. *Id.* § 451.02(e)(1) (requiring the exemption applicant to provide his or her name, mailing address, telephone number, and point of contact).
19. *Id.* § 451.02(e)(2)(i)–(ii), (3)(i)–(ii), (4)(i)–(ii).
20. *Id.* § 451.02(e)(2)(iii), (3)(iii), (4)(iii).
21. *Id.* § 451.02(e)(2)(iv), (3)(vii), (4)(vi).
22. *Id.* § 451.02(e)(2)(v)–(vi), (3)(v)–(vi), (4)(iv)–(v).
23. *Id.* § 451.02(e)(2)(vii), (3)(viii), (4)(vii).
24. *Id.* § 451.02(e)(2)(viii), (3)(ix), (4)(viii).
25. *Id.* § 451.02(e)(2)(ix), 3(x); (4)(ix).
26. *Id.* § 451.02(e)(5)(i)–(vi).

When the exemption applicant is a governor or a permit or license applicant, a copy of the application also must be provided (concurrent with filing the application) to the federal agency that denied the relevant license or permit.[27]

7.2.4 Initial Secretarial Action on the Application

Within ten days of receiving an exemption application, the Secretary must determine whether it contains all the required information.[28] If the Secretary rejects the application for lack of required information, the applicant may resubmit the application, but only within the original 90-day period provided for by regulation.[29] An exemption applicant, therefore, should consider submitting an application as soon as possible to allow time to cure any potential deficiencies. Upon receipt of the application, the Secretary will promptly transmit a copy to the Secretary of State,[30] publish notice of the application in the *Federal Register*,[31] and notify the governor of each affected state.[32]

7.3 The Exemption Process, Phase I: Consideration by the Secretary

Having determined that an exemption application contains all the required information, the Secretary must quickly turn to a more demanding, substantive examination of the consultation process that preceded the application. During this early phase of the process, the Secretary alone determines whether the application will be summarily denied or submitted to the ESC.

---

27. *Id.* § 451.02(e)(6).
28. *Id.* § 450.02(f).
29. *Id.* § 450.02(f)(2).
30. *Id.* § 450.02(g). This allows the Secretary of State to determine whether granting the exemption would violate treaties or other United States international obligations. *Id.* § 452.03(e).
31. 40 C.F.R. § 402.02(h). The *Federal Register* notice will summarize the information contained in the application and will designate a place where anyone may obtain a copy of the application. *Id.*
32. 50 C.F.R. § 451.03(b). After notification by the Secretary, the governor has ten days to submit recommendations of individuals that the state wishes to represent the state on the ESC. *Id.*

7.3.1 Threshold Determinations

Within 20 days after receiving an exemption application (or longer if the exemption applicant agrees), the Secretary must make the following three findings:

1. Whether any required biological assessment was conducted;
2. To the extent determinable within the time period provided, whether the federal agency or permit or license applicant has refrained from making irreversible or irretrievable commitments of resources; and
3. Whether the federal agency and any permit or license applicant have carried out consultation in "good faith" and have made reasonable and responsible efforts to develop and fairly consider modifications or reasonable and prudent alternatives to the proposed action.[33]

If the Secretary makes a negative finding on any of these three threshold issues, the Secretary must deny the application and terminate the exemption process.[34] The Secretary also must notify the applicant in writing of such a finding, and the Secretary's denial constitutes final agency action for purposes of judicial review.[35] Conversely, if the Secretary makes a positive finding with respect to each threshold criterion, the Secretary notifies the exemption applicant in writing that the application will be submitted to the ESC.[36]

7.3.2 Hearings

Having determined that the application meets the threshold criteria, the Secretary must designate an administrative law judge (ALJ) to preside over at least one public hearing on the application.[37] The ALJ must be someone uninvolved in the underlying ESA consultation and issue, and ex parte communications with the ALJ

33. 16 U.S.C. § 1536(g)(3); 50 C.F.R. § 452.03(a)(1)–(3).
34. 16 U.S.C. § 1536(g)(3)(B); 50 C.F.R. § 452.03(c).
35. 16 U.S.C. § 1536(g)(3)(B); 50 C.F.R. § 452.03(c).
36. 50 C.F.R. § 452.03(d).
37. 16 U.S.C. § 1536(g)(4); 50 C.F.R. § 452.05(a)(2).

are prohibited.[38] Although the Secretary sets the time period for conducting the hearing and closing the record,[39] the ALJ presides over the hearing, and is responsible for conducting any prehearing conference, ruling on motions, and determining whether the evidence offered is "relevant, material, and reliable."[40] The ALJ possesses broad latitude in conducting the hearing, and may subpoena the production of evidence and compel witness attendance and testimony.[41]

The hearing itself, to the extent practicable, must be conducted in accordance with the Administrative Procedure Act (APA),[42] and must be open to the public.[43] The parties to the hearing consist of the exemption applicant, the federal action agency proposing the underlying action, the Service (NMFS or FWS), and intervenors whose motions to intervene have been granted.[44] At all times, the exemption applicant bears the burden of going forward with evidence to show that the criteria for exemption are met.[45] The hearing does not culminate in an ALJ's decision. Rather, the ALJ's responsibilities are fulfilled by certifying the record and transmitting it to the Secretary.[46] The Secretary bases a report on the record produced at the hearing, but may direct the ALJ to reopen the record and obtain additional information.[47]

7.3.3 The Secretary's Report

After receiving the ALJ's hearing record and transcript, and within 140 days from the date the Secretary initially determined that the threshold criteria for an eligible exemption had been met, the

38. 50 C.F.R. § 452.07.
39. *Id.* § 452.05(a)(3).
40. *Id.* § 452.05(b), (d)(1).
41. *Id.* § 452.05(g).
42. 16 U.S.C. § 1536(g)(4), (6). The Ninth Circuit overturned a 5–2 grant of an exemption to the Bureau of Land Management for certain timber sales, 57 Fed. Reg. 23,405 (June 3, 1992), because of impermissible ex parte contacts. Portland Audubon Soc'y v. Endangered Species Comm., 984 F.2d 1534 (9th Cir. 1993).
43. 16 U.S.C. § 1536(g)(8); 50 C.F.R. § 452.05(f).
44. 50 C.F.R. § 452.06. The ALJ must approve a party's motion to intervene upon a finding that the intervenor would contribute to a fair determination of the issues. *Id.*
45. 50 C.F.R. § 452.05(e).
46. *Id.* § 452.08.
47. *Id.*

Secretary must submit a report to the ESC.[48] The report must discuss and summarize the following:

- the availability of reasonable and prudent alternatives to the proposed action;
- the nature and extent of the benefits of the proposed action;
- the nature and extent of the benefits of alternative courses of action consistent with conserving the species or its critical habitat;
- whether the proposed action is of national or regional significance;
- whether the proposed action is in the public interest;
- appropriate and reasonable mitigation and enhancement measures;
- whether the federal agency and permit or license applicant, if any, have refrained from making any irreversible or irretrievable commitment of resources.[49]

The next stage of the exemption process may now proceed, and the ESC must make a decision.

7.4 The Exemption Process, Phase II: The Endangered Species Committee

Congress created the ESC as "an administrative court of last resort."[50] Having been kept informed of the Secretary's progress in preparing his or her report,[51] the ESC must vote, and the mem-

48. 16 U.S.C. § 1536(g)(5); 50 C.F.R. § 452.08(b). The 140-day time limit may be modified by mutual agreement of the Secretary and the exemption applicant. 16 U.S.C. § 1536(g)(5).

49. 16 U.S.C. § 1536(g)(5)(A)–(D); 50 C.F.R. § 452.04(a)(1)–(7).

50. Portland Audubon Soc'y v. Endangered Species Comm., 984 F.2d 1534, 1541 (9th Cir. 1993) (quoting S. Rep. No. 97-418, at 17 (1982)) (emphasis in original omitted).

51. *See, e.g.*, 16 U.S.C. § 1536(g)(4) (requiring that the hearing set by the Secretary be held "in consultation with" the members of the ESC); H.R. Rep. No. 97-567, at 29 (1982), *reprinted in* 1982 U.S.C.C.A.N. 2807, 2828–29 (noting that Congress intended the ESC to be fully informed and "thoroughly familiar" with the background evidence by the time it receives the Secretary's report).

bers of this cabinet-level body must be personally accountable for their votes; no member may delegate his or her vote to anyone.[52]

7.4.1 The Committee

The ESC is composed of the following members:

- The Secretary of Agriculture
- The Secretary of the Army
- The Chairman of the Council of Economic Advisors
- The Administrator of the Environmental Protection Agency
- The Secretary of the Interior
- The Administrator of the National Oceanic and Atmospheric Administration (NOAA)
- One individual from each affected state[53]

The Secretary of the Interior serves as the chair of the ESC,[54] and five members of the committee constitute the required quorum.[55] With respect to members from affected states, when more than one state is involved, the state members collectively have one vote on the committee and must determine among themselves how it will be cast.[56]

7.4.2 The Exemption Decision

Upon receipt of the Secretary's report, the ESC must, within 30 days, determine whether to grant the exemption.[57] Within this 30-day window, the ESC considers the report and may gather additional information on its own initiative;[58] the ESC may solicit written submissions from interested persons[59] and may even hold

52. 16 U.S.C. § 1536(e)(10); 50 C.F.R. § 453.05(c).
53. 16 U.S.C. § 1536(e)(3).
54. *Id.* § 1536(e)(5)(B).
55. *Id.* § 1536(e)(5)(A).
56. 50 C.F.R. § 453.05(d).
57. 16 U.S.C. § 1536(h)(1).
58. *Id.* § 1536(h)(1)(A) (ESC may base its decision on the report of the Secretary and "such other testimony or evidence as it may receive.").
59. 50 C.F.R. § 453.04(a).

its own informal hearing.[60] The committee's hearing must be open to the public, and is governed by the provisions of the APA applicable to formal adjudications, including the prohibition on ex parte communications.[61] The committee shall grant an exemption if at least five members agree that:

- there are no reasonable and prudent alternatives to the agency action;
- the benefits of such action clearly outweigh the benefits of alternative courses of action consistent with conserving the species or its critical habitat, and such action is in the public interest;
- the action is of regional or national significance; and
- neither the federal agency concerned nor the exemption applicant made any irreversible or irretrievable commitment of resources.[62]

Once granted, an exemption is generally permanent in nature and covers all listed species that might be affected by the action, whether or not those species were covered in the biological assessment.[63]

7.4.3 Mitigation and Enhancement

When granting an exemption, the ESC must specify reasonable mitigation and enhancement measures to be implemented by the exemption applicant.[64] For example, when the ESC exempted 13 Bureau of Land Management (BLM) timber sales in 1992, the ESC required the BLM to mitigate the impacts of these sales on

60. *Id.* § 453.04(b).

61. Portland Audubon Soc'y v. Endangered Species Comm., 984 F.2d 1534, 1549 (9th Cir. 1993).

62. 16 U.S.C. § 1536(h)(1)(A); 50 C.F.R. § 453.03(a)(1). *See* Endangered Species Committee Notice of Decision, 57 Fed. Reg. 23,405 (June 3, 1992) (applying the exemption criteria to deny exemption to 31 of 44 BLM timber sales).

63. 16 U.S.C. § 1536(h)(2); 50 C.F.R. § 453.03(c). Such blanket and permanent exemptions are available only if a BA was actually prepared. Likewise, an exemption may be declared temporary in nature if it would result in the extinction of species not considered during consultation. 16 U.S.C. § 1536(h)(2); 50 C.F.R. § 453.03(c).

64. 16 U.S.C. § 1536(h)(1)(B) and 50 C.F.R. § 450.01 (providing examples of appropriate mitigation and enhancement measures).

northern spotted owls by implementing the final recovery plan for the owl.[65] The exemption applicant is responsible for the cost of implementing mitigation and enhancement measures, and must report annually on its compliance efforts until all mitigation and enhancement measures have been completed.[66]

7.5 Special Cases

The ESA recognizes three circumstances when the normal exemption rules do not apply. First, in any area declared by the president to be a major disaster area, the president may exempt from the ESA any project to repair or replace public facilities, if (1) "necessary to prevent the recurrence of such a natural disaster and to reduce the potential loss of human lives," and (2) the situation is an emergency that does not allow the ordinary procedures to be followed.[67] Second, the ESC must grant an exemption whenever the Secretary of Defense finds that such exemption is necessary for reasons of national security.[68] Finally, the ESC is prohibited from even considering an exemption application if the Secretary of State determines that granting the exemption would result in a violation of an international treaty or other international obligations of the United States.[69]

65. 57 Fed. Reg. at 23,408.

66. 16 U.S.C. § 1536(*l*). *E.g.*, ANNUAL REPORT ON ENDANGERED SPECIES ACT EXEMPTION, 64 Fed. Reg. 9,153 (Feb. 24, 1999) (summarizing implementation of mitigation and enhancement measures for Grayrocks Reservoir exemption).

67. 16 U.S.C. § 1536(p).

68. *Id.* § 1536(j); 50 C.F.R. § 453.03(d).

69. 16 U.S.C. § 1536(i); 50 C.F.R. § 452.03(e).

8 Federal Interaction with States and Tribes

8.1 Overview

States historically managed and protected wildlife in the United States.[1] Yet, since the passage of the first major national wildlife statute (the Lacey Act) in 1900,[2] Congress repeatedly has demonstrated its willingness to protect wildlife and habitat through federal legislation. Federal wildlife agencies now work closely with state wildlife agencies and play a major role in American wildlife conservation.

The Endangered Species Act (ESA), therefore, contemplates that states would play a role in helping conserve species. Nearly every major section of the ESA contains a provision recognizing the states' role in species conservation.[3] Indeed, the Act's

---

1. *See generally* MICHAEL J. BEAN & MELANIE ROWLAND, THE EVOLUTION OF NATIONAL WILDLIFE LAW (3d ed. 1997); ERIC T. FRYFOGLE, DALE D. GOBLE & TODD A. WILDERMUTH, WILDLIFE LAW: A PRIMER (2019); John Nagle, *The Original Role of States in the Endangered Species Act*, 53 IDAHO L. REV. 385 (2017); *see also* John R. Ernst, *Federalism and the Act, in* BALANCING ON THE BRINK OF EXTINCTION: THE ENDANGERED SPECIES ACT AND LESSONS FOR THE FUTURE 98 (Kathryn A. Kohm ed., 1993).

2. 16 U.S.C. § 701.

3. The ESA defines the term *State* to include "any of the several states, the District of Columbia, the Commonwealth of Puerto Rico, American Samoa, the Virgin Islands, Guam, and the Trust Territory of the Pacific Islands." 16 U.S.C. § 1532(17). The ESA also separately defines the term *State agency* to mean "any State agency, department, board, commission, or other governmental entity which is responsible for the management and conservation of fish, plant, or wildlife resources within a State." *Id.* § 1532(18). Some of the ESA's state role provisions refer to the States themselves and others to the State agency. *See, e.g., id.* § 1535(a) (calling for cooperation with the States); § 1533(i) (calling for Secretary's written justification to "the State agency" when the Secretary adopts a regulation under section 4 that "is in conflict with such comments" of a State agency submitted on the proposed regulation); *see also* San Luis & Delta-Mendota Water Auth. v. Badgley, 136 F. Supp. 2d 1136, 1151 (E.D. Cal. 2000) (holding that FWS violated ESA in listing decision where FWS did not submit the required section 4(i)

legislative history demonstrates Congress's expectation that successful implementation of the ESA involves a good working arrangement between federal agencies and states.[4] Section 6 of the Act, in particular, encourages states to take an active role in the development and implementation of conservation programs. The table at the end of this chapter illustrates the statutory role of states in ESA activities.

8.2 The ESA as a Valid Exercise of Congressional Commerce Power

In 1997, the D.C. Circuit noted that 521 of the then 1,082 listed species existed wholly within the boundaries of single states.[5] Some, therefore, might question Congress's authority to regulate activities with respect to these intrastate species. Courts uniformly have held that the ESA is a valid exercise of Congress's power under the Constitution's commerce clause, and any state law that provides less protection to listed species is preempted.

Federal courts have long held that Congress's commerce clause power is a valid basis for federal wildlife legislation,[6] including the ESA.[7] But after the Supreme Court held that the federal Gun-Free School Zones Act of 1990 exceeded the congressional commerce clause authority,[8] some thought that the ESA, at least as applied to purely intrastate species, might be vulnerable to a constitutional challenge. In 1995, the National Association of Home Builders, along with other building industry plaintiffs, filed

---

written justification to the California Department of Fish and Game); Alaska Oil & Gas Ass'n v. Jewell, 815 F.3d 544, 562 (9th Cir. 2016) (court "may not assess the substantive adequacy of the agency's responses to the [state agency] comments because the ESA does not specify what the substance of a written justification must be").

4. *See* H.R. Conf. Rep. No. 93-740 (1973), *reprinted in* 1973 U.S.C.C.A.N. 3001.

5. Nat'l Ass'n of Home Builders v. Babbitt, 130 F.3d 1041, 1052 (D.C. Cir. 1997).

6. *Id.* at 1054 n.15 (discussing cases upholding the Migratory Bird Treaty Act, the Lacey Act, and the Eagle Protection Act as valid exercises of Congress's commerce clause authority).

7. Palila v. Haw. Dep't of Land & Nat. Res., 471 F. Supp. 985, 992–95 (D. Haw. 1979) (holding that ESA protection of the palila, a bird found only in Hawaii, was a valid exercise of the commerce power).

8. United States v. Lopez, 514 U.S. 549 (1995).

suit alleging that application of the ESA's section 9 prohibitions against take were unconstitutional as applied to the endangered Delhi Sands flower-loving fly.[9] The plaintiffs argued that because the fly was located entirely within an eight-mile radius in two California counties, Congress's protection of the fly did not amount to a valid exercise of its commerce clause power. The D.C. Circuit disagreed and, citing the legislative history of the ESA, held that the loss of "biodiversity itself" has a substantial effect on interstate commerce;[10] the de minimis impact on commerce from individual circumstances (such as protection of a particular species of fly) "is of no consequence."[11] As such, protection of listed species in the "aggregate" bears a substantial relationship to interstate commerce and the use of the channels of interstate commerce.[12] Other courts similarly have rejected constitutional challenges.[13]

8.3 Preemption of State Law

ESA section 6(f)[14] explicitly preempts state laws inconsistent with the Act. On this basis, for programs related to importation and exportation of as well as commerce in listed species, state laws or regulations that prohibit what is allowed by the ESA, or that allow what is prohibited by the ESA, are void.[15] With respect to take

9. *Nat'l Ass'n of Homebuilders,* 130 F.3d at 1045.

10. *Id.* at 1052–54.

11. *Id.* at 1046.

12. *Id.*

13. *See* People for the Ethical Treatment of Property Owners (PETPO) v. U.S. Fish & Wildlife Serv., 852 F.3d 990, 1004 (10th Cir. 2017); San Luis & Delta-Mendota Water Auth. v. Salazar, 638 F.3d 1163, 1175–77 (9th Cir. 2011); Alabama-Tombigbee Rivers Coal. v. Kempthorne, 477 F.3d 1250, 1277 (11th Cir. 2007); GDF Realty Invs., LTD v. Norton, 326 F.3d 622 (5th Cir. 2003); Rancho Viejo, L.L.C. v. Norton, 323 F.3d 1062 (D.C. Cir. 2003); Gibbs v. Babbitt, 214 F.3d 483 (4th Cir. 2000). Courts continue to hold that the ESA protects purely intrastate species: recently, the Eastern District of North Carolina has made successive holdings that the ESA protects a population of fewer than 20 red wolves located solely on North Carolina's Albemarle Peninsula. *See* Red Wolf Coal. v. United States Fish & Wildlife Serv., No. 2:20-CV-75-BO, 2021 U.S. Dist. LEXIS 12061 (E.D.N.C. Jan. 21, 2021); *see also* Kathryn E. Kovacs, *The Origins of Federal Wildlife Regulation Under the Commerce Clause*, 45 Harv. Env't L. Rev. Online 35 (2021).

14. 16 U.S.C. § 1535(f).

15. *Id.* For example, in a long-running dispute, courts have held that, because FWS has authorized import of alligator and crocodile products under special rules that permit taking and trade of listed species in certain circumstances, section 6(f)

of listed species, the Act provides that state laws may be more restrictive than the exemptions or permits allowed by the ESA, but may not be less restrictive.[16]

Section 6(g)(2) of the Act,[17] however, contains a provision apparently modifying section 6(f). Section 6(g)(2) provides that the Act's takings prohibitions do not apply with respect to the taking of listed species within any state that is, at the time of the taking, a party to a section 6(c) cooperative agreement, "except to the extent that the taking . . . is contrary to the law of such state."[18] In the only reported decision directly addressing this contradiction, the District of Montana federal district court ruled that section 6(f)'s explicit preemption of "less restrictive" state laws, combined with the Act's overriding goal of species conservation, meant that federal takings prohibitions applied in a "cooperative agreement state" despite a less restrictive state law.[19]

8.4 Section 6 Cooperative Agreements

Section 6 of the ESA provides for federal funding of state conservation programs benefiting endangered fish, wildlife, and plants.[20] The ESA cooperative agreement program was considered by Congress to be "essential" to an adequate endangered species program.[21] Any state with an "adequate and active" program

preempts a California law banning such imports. *See* April in Paris v. Bonta, 2023 U.S. Dist. LEXIS 38322 (E.D. Cal. Mar. 6, 2023).

16. *Id.* In one interesting case, a court determined that regulations promulgated pursuant to another federal statute, the Animal Welfare Act, which also dealt with endangered species, were regulations that "implemented" the ESA for purposes of preemption. In Def. of Animals v. Cleveland Metroparks Zoo, 785 F. Supp. 100 (N.D. Ohio 1991).

17. 16 U.S.C. § 1535(g)(2).

18. *Id.* § 1535(g)(2)(A).

19. Swan View Coal., Inc. v. Turner, 824 F. Supp. 923 (D. Mont. 1992). For divergent views of this holding, see Temple Stoellinger, *Wildlife Issues Are Local—So Why Isn't ESA Implementation?*, 44 Ecol. L.Q. 681, 708–09 (2017); Michael J. Bean & Melanie J. Rowland, Evolution of National Wildlife Law 270 (3d ed. 1997).

20. 16 U.S.C. § 1535(c). See 50 C.F.R. pt. 81 for FWS regulations implementing the Cooperative Agreement Program of ESA section 6(c). NMFS is bound by the Department of Commerce's general regulations and guidelines for cooperative agreements, notably at 15 C.F.R. pt. 24.

21. H.R. Conf. Rep. No. 93-740 (1973), *reprinted in* 1973 U.S.C.C.A.N. 3001, 3005.

for endangered and threatened species conservation[22] is entitled to enter into a cooperative agreement with the Secretary; states with cooperative agreements are eligible to receive as much as a 90 percent federal contribution toward the cost of implementing conservation measures.[23] In 1994, the Fish and Wildlife Service (FWS) and the National Marine Fisheries Service (NMFS) promulgated a policy statement reaffirming the agencies' commitment to meeting the ESA section 6(a) requirement of cooperating, to the maximum extent practicable, with the states in carrying out the ESA program; it revised this policy in 2016, observing that the revision reflected "a renewed commitment by the Services and State fish and wildlife agencies to work together in conserving America's imperiled wildlife."[24] Both Services have entered into agreements with states, and NMFS has its own guidance document for the criteria governing these agreements.[25] At least one

22. The Act provides a detailed list of requirements for an adequate state program. *See* 16 U.S.C. §§ 1535(c)(1) (for fish and wildlife), 1535(c)(2) (for plants). Requirements for state programs pertaining to plants differ from those for fish and wildlife; plant programs need not include land acquisition. *Id.* § 1535(c)(2)(A)–(D).

23. For programs addressing species of interest to only one state, the federal contribution of funds is limited to 75 percent. *Id.* § 1535(d)(2)(i). With respect to joint agreements among states having a common interest in one or more listed species, the federal contribution of funds may be increased to 90 percent. *Id.* § 1535(d)(2)(ii). For information about the section 6 grant program, see U.S. Fish & Wildlife Serv., Cooperative Endangered Species Conservation Fund Grants: Section 6 of the Endangered Species Act, https://www.fws.gov/media/cooperative-endangered-species-conservation-fund-grants-section-6-endangered-species-act; NOAA Fisheries, ESA Section 6 Program: Cooperation with States, https://www.fisheries.noaa.gov/national/endangered-species-conservation/endangered-species-act-section-6-program-cooperation.

24. Revised Interagency Cooperative Policy Regarding the Role of State Agencies in Endangered Species Act Activities, 81 Fed. Reg. 8,663, 8,664 (Feb. 22, 2016). The revised policy directs FWS and NMFS to increase collaboration with state agencies to conserve species before they require ESA protection, including through Candidate Conservation Agreements with Assurances with nonfederal landowners; to increase collaboration on listing and recovery, including use of Safe Harbor Agreements with nonfederal landowners; and to avoid duplication of effort where the Services and states have similar permitting authority for activities related to listed species. The revised policy came on the heels of a lawsuit brought by Alaska claiming that in designating polar bear critical habitat, FWS had failed to satisfy section 6(a)'s requirement that it cooperate with states to the maximum extent practicable. *See* Alaska Oil & Gas Ass'n v. Salazar, 916 F. Supp. 2d 974, 997 (D. Alaska 2013), *rev'd and remanded sub nom.* Alaska Oil & Gas Ass'n v. Jewell, 815 F.3d 544 (9th Cir. 2016). The district court rejected Alaska's argument, deferring to FWS under *Auer v. Robbins*, 519 U.S. 452 (1997), and the Ninth Circuit avoided Alaska's "maximum extent practicable" argument; *see generally* Temple Stoellinger et al., *Improving Cooperative State and Federal Species Conservation Efforts*, 20 Wyo. L. Rev. 183 (2020).

25. *See* NOAA Fisheries, Cooperation with the States: The ESA Section 6 Program Application Guidance for States (n.d.), https://media.fisheries.noaa.gov/dam-migration/application_guidelines_for_states.pdf.

state has explored a creative section 6 cooperative agreement that includes the sharing of section 10 permitting responsibilities: in 2012, Florida finalized a cooperative agreement that gave the Florida Fish and Wildlife Conservation Commission authority to issue incidental take permits for federally listed species under criteria more stringent than those governing FWS's issuance of an incidental take permit—though the applicant could also seek a permit under the federal process in ESA section 10(a)(1)(B).[26]

8.5 Role of Tribal Governments

Beginning in the 1990s, the Services began to explore how to involve Tribal governments in aspects of the ESA decision-making process. This led to the development of the Joint Secretarial Order on American Indian Tribal Rights, Federal-Tribal Trust Responsibilities, and the Endangered Species Act (Secretarial Order No. 3206).[27] In the June 1997 Order, the Secretaries committed to "carry out their responsibilities under the [ESA] in a manner that

26. The 2017–18 amendment to Florida's section 6 cooperative agreement retains this provision permitting the state wildlife agency to issue incidental take permits. *See* FWS & Florida Wildlife Conservation Commission, Cooperative Agreement for the Conservation of Endangered Fish and Wildlife (Apr. 13, 2018), https://myfwc.com/media/25356/co-op-agreement-usfws-section-6.pdf. The 2012 Florida cooperative agreement additionally aimed to integrate the incidental take permitting process with landscape conservation cooperatives (LCCs), public-private partnerships established in 2009 by Department of the Interior Secretarial Order No. 3289. LCCs were intended to transcend political boundaries and employ holistic, collaborative, and adaptive principles to improve land, water, wildlife, and cultural resource management. Since 2018, LCCs no longer have federal government support under that name, although FWS's Science Applications program has continued to support regional conservation partnerships replicating the function of LCCs. *See* FWS, 2021 Report to the Committees on Appropriations on FWS's Support of the Next Generation of Landscape Conservation, https://www.fws.gov/sites/default/files/documents/FWS%20LCC%20Report.pdf.

27. *See generally* Marren Sanders, Implementing the Federal Endangered Species Act in Indian Country: The Promise and Reality of Secretarial Order 3206 (Joint Occasional Papers on Native Aff., 2007); Charles F. Wilkinson, *The Role of Bilateralism in Fulfilling the Federal-Tribal Relationship: The Tribal Rights-Endangered Species Secretarial Order,* 72 Wash. L. Rev. 1063 (1997). For a discussion of the role of tribes under the ESA, see Mary Gray Holt, *Indian Rights and the Endangered Species Act, in* Endangered Species Act: Law, Policy, and Perspectives 127 (Donald C. Baur & Wm. Robert Irvin eds., 2d ed. 2010). *See also* Secretarial Order 3225 (Jan. 19, 2001) (clarifying application of Secretarial Order 3206 to Alaska Natives whose subsistence hunting can be exempt from the prohibitions on taking endangered and threatened species, see 16 U.S.C. § 1539(e), and consultation requirements involved in determining that exemption).

harmonizes the Federal trust responsibility to tribes, Tribal sovereignty and the statutory missions of the Departments and that strives to ensure that the Indian tribes do not bear a disproportionate burden for the conservation of listed species so as to avoid or minimize the potential for conflict and confrontation." That commitment was underscored when President Clinton issued Executive Order No. 13,175, in November 2000, confirming that federal agencies must consult and coordinate with Indian tribes on policies that impact Indian communities.[28] And on December 1, 2011, Interior Secretary Salazar issued Secretarial Order 3,317, updating, expanding, and clarifying the Department's policy on "consultation with American Indian and Alaska Native tribes," and acknowledging "that the provisions for conducting consultation in compliance with Executive Order . . . 13175 . . . are expressed in the Department of the Interior Policy on Consultation with Indian Tribes."[29]

The federal government has since clarified and refined these initial efforts to better coordinate wildlife and habitat protections with tribes. In 2016, for example, the Secretaries clarified that Secretarial Order 3,206, which provides that critical habitat shall not be designated on Tribal land "unless it is determined essential to conserve a listed species," does not negate the Secretaries' statutory obligations to designate critical habitat.[30] Also in 2016, FWS released a revised Native American Policy designed to guide FWS in consulting with tribes, coordinating management of fish and wildlife, facilitating tribes' access to sacred and culturally important sites under FWS control, and encouraging mutual exchange of knowledge.

The Services are also, at time of publication, bound by new executive memoranda requiring increased coordination with tribes, particularly in light of the federal trust responsibility to tribes and Executive Order No. 13,175's consultation requirement. In

28. 65 Fed. Reg. 67,249–52 (Nov. 9, 2000).

29. Secretarial Order 3317 is available at https://www.doi.gov/document-library/secretary-order/3317-department-interior-policy-consultation-indian-tribes. The current status of this Secretarial Order is unclear: the order is labeled "archived" on the Department of the Interior's website but it has not, as of spring 2025, been publicly rescinded.

30. 81 Fed. Reg. 7,226, 7,230–31 (Feb. 11, 2016). FWS has excluded from critical habitat Tribal land where the tribe has developed a management plan for that species. *See, e.g.*, 78 Fed. Reg. 344, 374 (Jan. 3, 2013) (excluding portions of the Navajo and Southern Ute reservations from designation of critical habitat for Southwestern willow flycatcher).

2021, President Biden issued a memorandum requiring all agencies to develop detailed plans to implement EO 13,175,[31] and in 2022, President Biden issued a memorandum outlining uniform standards for such consultation.[32] These policies have particular relevance to the Services because federal wildlife protections, including the ESA, frequently intersect with treaty rights or other rights reserved by tribes.[33] In 2022, the Secretary of the Interior and FWS released new policies on Tribal co-management of habitat and wildlife,[34] and the administration reported that in 2023 alone it had signed more than 190 land, water, or wildlife co-stewardship or co-management agreements with tribes.[35] These agreements build on long-standing co-management practices, among them, for example, FWS's decades-long co-management of salmon with tribes in the Pacific northwest.[36] Also, FWS maintains a Tribal Wildlife Grant Program for federally recognized

31. 86 Fed. Reg. 7,491–92 (Jan. 26, 2021).

32. 87 Fed. Reg. 74,479–83 (Nov. 30, 2022).

33. Some litigants have argued that treaty rights conflict with federal or state wildlife protections. *See* United States v. Dion, 476 U.S. 734 (1986); Puyallup Tribe v. Washington Game Dep't, 391 U.S. 392 (1968); United States v. Turtle, 365 F. Supp. 3d 1242 (M.D. Fla. 2019). In 2021, the Department of Interior's Office of the Solicitor withdrew three opinions analyzing whether and how federal conservation statutes limit tribes' reserved hunting and fishing rights. Among the now-obsolete opinions is Solicitor Opinion M-36926, a 1980 opinion addressing the application of the ESA to treaty hunting and fishing rights. Relying on *Dion*, the 2021 opinion concludes that the ESA did not abrogate treaty hunting and fishing rights. However, citing *Turtle*, the 2021 opinion maintains the federal government's official position that it "has the authority to enforce the ESA against Tribal members." Solicitor's Opinion M-37063, Withdrawal of Solicitor Opinion M-36936, M-36926, and M-27690 (Jan. 15, 2021).

34. *See* Dep't of the Interior, 502 DM 1 Collaborative and Cooperative Stewardship with Tribes and the Native Hawaiian Community (Nov. 30, 2022); U.S. Fish & Wildlife Serv., Director's Order No. 227, Fulfilling the Trust Responsibility to Tribes and the Native Hawaiian Community, and Other Obligations to Alaska Native Corporations and Alaska Native Organizations, in the Stewardship of Federal Lands and Waters (Sept. 8, 2022).

35. *See* Biden-Harris Administration Announces New Actions and Historic Progress Supporting Tribal Nations and Native Communities Ahead of Third Annual White House Tribal Nations Summit (Dec. 6, 2023), https://bidenwhitehouse.archives.gov/briefing-room/statements-releases/2023/12/06/fact-sheet-biden-%E2%81%A0harris-administration-announces-new-actions-and-historic-progress-supporting-tribal-nations-and-native-communities-ahead-of-third-annual-white-house-tribal-nations-summit/.

36. *See generally* Michael C. Blumm, Daniel J. Rohlf & Adam Eno, *A Half-Century of Pacific Salmon Saving Efforts: A Primer on Law, Policy, and Biology*, 64 Nat. Res. J. 137 (2024).

tribes,[37] and NMFS, too, provides opportunities for grants to such tribes, commensurate with the section 6 grant program.[38]

While some statutes governing the environment have their own Tribal consultation requirements, the "ESA does not contain similar consultation requirements."[39] Thus, the consultation requirements binding the Services are derived from executive order, particularly Executive Order 13,175; specific obligations incurred in treaties conducted with particular tribes; the United States' trust responsibility to tribes;[40] and statutes other than the ESA that impose consultation requirements on certain actions the Services take—among them, for example, the National Historic Preservation Act.[41]

FWS's Tribal Consultation Handbook provides detailed guidance regarding procedures for consulting with tribes in compliance with these multifaceted requirements. That handbook incorporates and is intended to expand on the Department of the Interior's Policy on Consultation with Indian Tribes, which has been updated more recently than FWS's handbook.[42] Under those policies, FWS must consult with tribes where a "departmental action with Tribal implications" occurs.[43] Such actions include

37. *See* U.S. Fish & Wildlife Serv., Tribal Wildlife Grants, https://www.fws.gov/service/tribal-wildlife-grants (last visited Apr. 30, 2025).

38. *See* NMFS, NOAA Fisheries Serv., Species Recovery Grants to Tribes, https://www.fisheries.noaa.gov/grant/species-recovery-grants-tribes (last updated Nov. 26, 2024).

39. Ctr. for Biological Diversity v. Salazar, No. 10-2130-PHX-DGC, 2011 U.S. Dist. LEXIS 138307, at *31 (D. Ariz. Nov. 30, 2011).

40. Seminole Nation v. United States, 316 U.S. 286, 296–97 (1942) ("In carrying out its treaty obligations with the Indian tribes, the Government is something more than a mere contracting party . . . it has charged itself with moral obligations of the highest responsibility and trust."); *but see* Arizona v. Navajo Nation, 599 U.S. 555, 563 (2023) ("To maintain [a breach-of-trust claim], the Tribe must establish, among other things, that the text of a treaty, statute, or regulation imposed certain duties on the United States."); Gros Ventre Tribe v. United States, 469 F.3d 801, 812 (9th Cir. 2006) (though "the United States does owe a general trust responsibility to Indian tribes," "unless there is a specific duty that has been placed on the government with respect to Indians, this responsibility is discharged by the agency's compliance with general regulations and statutes not specifically aimed at protecting Indian tribes").

41. *See* Wishtoyo Found. v. U.S. Fish & Wildlife Serv., No. CV 19-03322-CJC(ASx), 2019 U.S. Dist. LEXIS 229219 (C.D. Cal. Dec. 18, 2019) (discussing FWS's consultation obligations under the National Historic Preservation Act, in context of a tribe's assertion that the California condor is a traditional cultural property).

42. Dep't of the Interior, 512-DM-4 (Nov. 30, 2022).

43. FWS, Tribal Consultation Handbook, 12 (Oct. 2018).

a "[d]epartmental regulation, rulemaking, policy, guidance, legislative proposal, plan, programmatic or operational activity, or grant or funding formula changes that may have a substantial direct effect on a Tribe in matters" implicating (1) Tribal cultural practices, lands, treaty rights, resources, ancestral lands, sacred sites, and traditional areas of cultural or religious importance on federally managed lands and waters; (2) the tribe's ability to govern itself; (3) the tribe's formal relationship with FWS; or (4) any action proposed by a nonfederal entity that requires agency action by FWS, unless the tribe is a party to the action.[44]

FWS views "the entire range of [ESA] activities" as departmental actions with Tribal implications."[45] Thus, for "candidate conservation, the listing process, section 7 consultation, habitat conservation planning, recovery, and law enforcement, the Service will consult and collaborate with Tribal governments when developing plans and regulations."[46] The precise details of FWS's consultation are beyond the scope of this book.[47] In general, consultation should begin early in the Services' process toward taking action under the ESA. FWS may use proactive engagement with tribes to develop a list of tribes that are usually consulted on certain actions in certain regions.[48] Any notice of invitation to consult on a particular action should give relevant tribes "sufficient information on the topic . . . in an accessible language and format" as well as "context for the consultation topic."[49] For

44. Dep't of the Interior, *supra* note 42, at 1–2.

45. FWS, Native American Policy, 510 FW 1, 3 (Jan. 20, 2016).

46. *Id.* Importantly, where the Services offer a biological opinion intended to guide another agency's compliance with the ESA, the action agency will engage in consultation with tribes.

47. For more detailed treatment of consultation, see, *e.g.*, FWS, Tribal Consultation Handbook 14–24 (Oct. 2018 update) (laying out FWS's consultation process), App'x B (describing laws governing FWS consultation with tribes), App'x E (sample letter to tribes inviting consultation); Working Group of the Memorandum of Understanding Regarding Interagency Coordination and Collaboration for the Protection of Tribal Treaty and Reserved Rights, Best Practices for Identifying and Protecting Tribal Treaty Rights, Reserved Rights, and Other Similar Rights in Federal Regulatory Actions and Federal Decision-Making (Nov. 30, 2022). *See also* Benjamin Barron Richardson, *Interpreting Consultation: U.S. Fish & Wildlife Service and Native American Perceptions of Engagement Practices*, W. Vir. U. Rsch. Repository (unpublished dissertation) (2016); Steven K. Albert, *American Indian Perspectives on the Endangered Species Act*, 9 Buffalo Env't L.J. 175 (2002).

48. *See, e.g.*, FWS, Tribal Consultation Handbook, *supra* note 47, App'x E.

49. Executive Memorandum on Uniform Standards for Tribal Consultation, 87 Fed. Reg. 74,479, 74,480 (Nov. 30, 2022).

example, FWS invited tribes to consult on its 2022 12-month finding for gray wolves in the western United States through a letter explaining the impetus for consultation, setting forth two meetings FWS would convene to consult with tribes, and providing contact information and a means to submit written comments.[50] "Meaningful consultation," a phrase used in Executive Order 13,175, has become the shorthand for the requirements placed on agencies after they initiate consultation. Because the ESA does not require consultation with tribes, litigation challenging FWS's consultation procedures is often brought under a statute that itself requires consultation.[51]

At least some literature has addressed the effects, negative and positive, of the ESA on tribes.[52] The ESA generally benefits species in the United States, preserving animal and plant life that may be important to tribes. But while the ESA exempts from its take prohibitions "any Indian, Aleut, or Eskimo who is an Alaskan Native who resides in Alaska,"[53] it does not exempt from the take prohibitions subsistence, cultural, or religious use of listed animals or plants by tribes in the lower 48 states. The Supreme Court, for example, has held that the ESA as well as the Bald and Golden Eagle Protection Act abrogate treaty rights to hunt protected species beyond the borders of tribes' reservations.[54] Increased attention to co-management and consultation may palliate some of the ESA's negative effects on tribes and Tribal governance while accentuating its benefits to species.

---

50. FWS, Invitation to Consult on 12-Month Finding for Gray Wolves in the Western United States (Apr. 27, 2022).

51. *See, e.g.*, Wishtoyo Found. v. U.S. Fish & Wildlife Serv., No. CV 19-03322-CJC (ASx), 2019 U.S. Dist. LEXIS 229219 (C.D. Cal. Dec. 18, 2019) (National Historic Preservation Act claim); Confederated Tribes & Bands of the Yakama Nation v. U.S. Fish & Wildlife Serv., No. 1:14-CV-3052-TOR, 2015 U.S. Dist. LEXIS 38800 (E.D. Wash. Mar. 20, 2015) (same).

52. *See, e.g.*, Anna V. Smith, *The Endangered Species Act's complicated legacy in Indian Country*, High Country News (Dec. 1, 2023); R.L. Stoney Burk, *The Endangered Species Act: Should It Affect Indian Hunting and Fishing Rights?*, 2 Pub. Land L. Rev. 123 (1981).

53. 16 U.S.C. § 1538(a).

54. United States v. Dion, 476 U.S. 734 (1986).

ESA Activities and the Respective Roles of States

ESA Activity	State Role
Section 4 Listing and Critical Habitat Designations	Secretary must take into account efforts of the states to protect species, prior to making a listing determination. (16 U.S.C. § 1533(b)(1)(A))
	Secretary must give actual notice of any proposed listing, de-listing or critical habitat designation to the relevant state wildlife agency and counties in which a species is believed to occur, and must invite comments from the state agency. (16 U.S.C. § 1533(b)(5)(A)(ii))
	Secretary must give actual notice of any emergency listing to the relevant state wildlife agency. (16 U.S.C. § 1533(b)(7)(D))
	Secretary must provide state with written justification upon Secretary's failure to adopt a state's comments or petition with respect to listing, critical habitat, or Section 4(d) rule designation. (16 U.S.C. § 1533(i))
Section 6 Agreements	States may enter into cooperative agreements with the Secretary, whereby the federal government contributes 75–90 percent of covered conservation program costs. (16 U.S.C. § 1535(c) & (d)(2))
	States may enter into management agreements for the administration and management of areas for the conservation of listed species. (16 U.S.C. § 1535(b))
Section 6 Land or Water Acquisition	Secretary must consult with states before acquiring any land or water for conservation of listed species. (16 U.S.C. § 1535(a))

(continued)

ESA Activities and the Respective Roles of States *(continued)*

ESA Activity	State Role
Section 7 Consultation	Governor of a state that may ultimately wish to apply for a Section 7 exemption, pursuant to ESA Section 7(g), may (in cooperation with the Secretary) prepare a biological assessment with respect to a particular proposed federal action. (16 U.S.C. § 1536(c)(2))
	Interagency consultation is to ensure that agency action is not likely to result in the destruction or adverse modification of habitat of such species [consulted upon] which is determined by the Secretary, after consultation as appropriate with affected States, to be critical. (16 U.S.C. § 1536(a)(2))
Section 7 Exemption Process	Governor of an affected state may apply for an exemption and initiate the Endangered Species Committee process. (16 U.S.C. § 1536(g)(1))
	One individual from each affected state may participate as a member of the Endangered Species Committee. (16 U.S.C. § 1536(e)(3)(G))
Section 8 International Conventions	Provisions relating to the Western Hemisphere Convention do not affect state authority, jurisdiction, or responsibility regarding resident fish and wildlife. (16 U.S.C. § 1537a(e)(4))
Section 9 Prohibited Acts with Respect to Listed Plants	The ESA prohibits damage to endangered plants when done in knowing violation of state laws. (16 U.S.C. § 1538(a)(2)(B))
Section 10 Permits	State may apply for and hold takings permits; in some cases, persons regulated by the state may avail themselves of the takings allowed pursuant to the permit. (See Chapter 6)
Section 11 Enforcement	Secretary may, by agreement, utilize state personnel and resources to enforce the ESA. (16 U.S.C. § 1540(e)(1))

9 International Application of the ESA

9.1 Overview

"A primary factor bringing about the near extinction of many animals has been the demand created by the international trade in animals and animal products."[1] The Endangered Species Act (ESA), not surprisingly, reflects this appreciation and implements aspects of the United States' commitment to protecting species worldwide. Congress, in the opening subsection of the ESA, recognized the United States' "international commitments"[2] with respect to conservation of fish, wildlife, and plants, and it further declared that the United States "has pledged itself as a sovereign state in the international community" to conserve to the extent practicable listed species pursuant to:

- migratory bird treaties with Canada and Mexico;
- the Migratory and Endangered Bird Treaty with Japan;
- the Convention on Nature Protection and Wildlife Preservation in the Western Hemisphere (the Western Hemisphere Convention);
- the International Convention for the Northwest Atlantic Fisheries;
- the International Convention for the High Seas Fisheries of the North Pacific Ocean;

1. Lewis Regenstein, The Politics of Extinction: The Shocking Story of the World's Endangered Wildlife 120 (1975).
2. 16 U.S.C. § 1531(a)(5).

- the Convention on International Trade in Endangered Species of Wild Fauna and Flora (CITES); and
- other international agreements.[3]

In the Act's second subsection, Congress expressly declared that one of the purposes of the ESA is to take such steps as may be appropriate to achieve the purposes of these listed treaties and conventions.[4] To that end, the ESA contains several provisions specifically addressing international concerns. In addition, some, but not all, of the Act's general provisions apply outside U.S. boundaries. Finally, the ESA formally implements two of the referenced conventions: CITES and the Western Hemisphere Convention.[5] The ESA, on the whole, represents a clear demonstration of a "congressional commitment to worldwide conservation efforts."[6]

9.2 International Applicability

Generally, federal statutes are presumed to apply only within the territorial jurisdiction of the United States, and courts require a clear expression of congressional intent to apply a statute beyond U.S. boundaries.[7] And, while the ESA contains various references to international agreements and concerns, most of its principal provisions apply only within the United States, its territorial waters, or upon the "high seas."[8] The following sections summarize those aspects of the ESA that have some role in the international arena.

3. *Id.* § 1531(a)(4).
4. *Id.* § 1531(b).
5. See Section 9.5 for a discussion of CITES and the Western Hemisphere Convention.
6. Defs. of Wildlife v. Lujan, 911 F.2d 117, 123 (8th Cir. 1990), *rev'd on other grounds,* 504 U.S. 555 (1992).
7. Morrison v. Nat'l Australia Bank Ltd., 130 S. Ct. 2869, 2878 (2010).
8. The term *high seas* is not defined in the ESA or its implementing regulations.

9.3 Listing of Species

The ESA, like its predecessor statute, the Endangered Species Conservation Act of 1969,[9] authorizes the listing of any species of fish, wildlife, or plant, without regard to whether a species' range lies within the United States. Of the more than 1,900 species on the endangered or threatened list, roughly one-fourth occur outside the United States.[10] The ESA, therefore, provides some guidance for the listing of foreign species. For example, when considering any listing, the Secretary must take into account the efforts being made by any foreign nation or political subdivision of a foreign nation to protect the species within any area under its jurisdiction, or on the high seas.[11] In addition, if the Secretary proposes a regulation to implement a listing decision, the Secretary must, insofar as practicable, give notice of the proposed regulation to each foreign nation where the species is believed to occur, or whose citizens harvest the species on the high seas, and the Secretary must invite the comment of such nations on proposed listing regulations.[12] A recent and high-profile initiative involved efforts to strengthen protection for African Elephants.[13]

9.4 Limits on the ESA's Applicability

For the most part, the ESA's section 7 obligations, its requirements for designating critical habitat, and the need to establish recovery plans do not apply to activities abroad. To begin with, the ESA section 4 provision governing the designation of critical habitat is

9. Pub. L. No. 91-135, 83 Stat. 275 (1969).

10. U.S. Fish & Wildlife Serv., Species Reports, https://ecos.fws.gov/ecp/report/species-listings-foreign?statusCategory=Listed (last visited Apr. 30, 2025).

11. 16 U.S.C. § 1533(b)(1)(A).

12. *Id.* § 1533(b)(5).

13. FWS, Revision to the Section 4(d) Rule for the African Elephant, 89 Fed. Reg. 22,522 (Apr. 1, 2024). For another recent listing, see FWS, Threatened Species Status with Section 4(d) Rule for Egyptian Tortoise, 88 Fed. Reg. 19004 (Mar. 30, 2023). When the Service proposed downgrading the Northern DPS of the southern subspecies of the scarlet macaw, and allowed a 4(d) rule that would avoid the need for a permit for certain imports, a court remanded but did not vacate the rule. Friend of Animals v. Williams, 628 F. Supp. 3d 71 (D.D.C. 2022), 2024 WL 3359507 (D.D.C. July 10, 2024) (after remand upholding the rule), *appeal pending in* No. 24-5278 (D.C. Cir.).

silent with respect to designations of lands in foreign nations. Yet, with the implicit approval of Congress,[14] the Services expressly addressed this issue, by declaring through regulation that "critical habitat shall not be designated within foreign countries or in other areas outside the United States' jurisdiction."[15] Next, section 4 recovery plans similarly are not prepared for foreign species. This reflects the practical reality that the United States would have no means of implementing management activities abroad.

Finally, the ESA's section 7 consultation provision and substantive mandate do not expressly address whether they apply to federal agency actions carried out in foreign countries.[16] The joint consultation regulations promulgated by the Services in 1978 extended the scope of section 7 to foreign countries,[17] but the Services reversed themselves in the 1986 (and still current) regulations, concluding that section 7 extends only to federal actions carried out in whole or in part by federal agencies in the United States or upon the high seas.[18] The Services justified this change in approach based upon "the apparent domestic orientation of the consultation and exemption processes," and because of potential "interference with the sovereignty of foreign nations."[19] One federal appeals court held that the 1986 regulations improperly limited the geographic scope of section 7,[20] but the U.S. Supreme Court reversed the decision on procedural grounds, concluding that the plaintiffs lacked standing.[21] The 1986 rule limiting section 7 to the United States and the high seas still applies.

---

14. *See* H.R. Rep. No. 97-567, at 20 (1982), *reprinted in* 1982 U.S.C.C.A.N. 2807, 2820 (agreeing with the Department of the Interior's Solicitor's Office that critical habitat designation in foreign countries or on the high seas would be "inappropriate").
15. 50 C.F.R. § 424.13(h).
16. See Chapter 5 for a discussion of the section 7 consultation process.
17. 43 Fed. Reg. 874 (1978).
18. 50 C.F.R. § 402.02.
19. Preamble to Final Rule, 51 Fed. Reg. 19,926, 19,929 (1986).
20. *See* Defs. of Wildlife v. Lujan, 911 F.2d 117, 122–25 (8th Cir. 1990).
21. Defs. of Wildlife v. Lujan, 504 U.S. 555 (1992). Concurring, Justice Stevens disagreed with the majority's opinion on standing, but on the merits expressed the view that section 7 does not apply to activities in foreign countries. 504 U.S. at 581 (Stevens, J., concurring).

9.5 Implementation of CITES and the Western Hemisphere Convention

A detailed discussion of international wildlife treaties and conventions is beyond the scope of this book. Indeed, several chapters would be necessary to fully explain the operation of CITES,[22] its complicated import/export requirements, and its permit application processes. This section provides a brief overview of the significant aspects of CITES and the Western Hemisphere Convention,[23] with an emphasis on the role of the ESA as the implementing statute for each.

9.5.1 CITES

The idea of an international agreement arose in the 1960s and resulted in CITES, in force since 1975,[24] with a membership that now includes 185 parties.[25] CITES broadly proclaims the parties' recognition of the need to protect "wild fauna and flora in their many beautiful and varied forms"[26] and translates this lofty goal into more detailed requirements, creating an intricate regulatory scheme governing international trade in wildlife and plants. Section 8a of the ESA formally implements CITES for the United

22. Convention on International Trade in Endangered Species of Wild Fauna and Flora, Mar. 3, 1973, 27 U.S.T. 1087, T.I.A.S. No. 8249 [hereinafter CITES]. For an overview of CITES, see https://cites.org/eng/disc/text.php; https://www.fws.gov/international-affairs/cites (last visited Apr. 30, 2025). *See also* Holly Wheeler, W. Michael Young & Russell Husen, *The Convention on International Trade in Endangered Species of Wild Fauna and Flora, in* Endangered Species Act: Law, Policy, and Perspectives 291 (Donald C. Baur & Ya-Wei Li eds., 3d ed. 2021); Michael De Alessi, *Protecting Endangered Species at Home and Abroad: The International Conservation Effects of the Endangered Species Act and Its Relationship to CITES, in* Rebuilding the Ark: New Perspectives on Endangered Species Act Reform 201 (Jonathan H. Adler ed., 2011).

23. Convention on Natural Protection and Wildlife Preservation in the Western Hemisphere, Oct. 12, 1940, 56 Stat. 1354, T.S. No. 981.

24. *Id.* art. XXII, 27 U.S.T. at 1115. *See generally* Willem Wijnstekers, The Evolution of CITES (CITES Secretariat, 9th ed. 2011).

25. FWS, CITES, https://www.fws.gov/international-affairs/cites/cop; CITES, List of Contracting Parties, https://cites.org/eng/disc/parties/index.php (last visited Apr. 30, 2025).

26. CITES, *supra* note 22, 27 U.S.T. at 1091.

States.[27] In particular, CITES requires that each party designate a Management Authority and a Scientific Authority, and ESA section 8a(a) designates the Secretary of the Interior as both the Management Authority and the Scientific Authority.[28] Sections 8 and 8a of the ESA, moreover, create a multilayered approach to conserving listed species abroad, including committing the United States to the "worldwide" protection of listed species, authorizing financial assistance to foreign countries,[29] and directing the encouragement of foreign conservation efforts as well as bilateral or multilateral agreements with foreign nations.[30]

Similar to the ESA, CITES applies only to certain designated, or listed, species.[31] While the ESA creates two lists of covered species (endangered and threatened), CITES contains three separate lists, denoted simply as appendices I, II, and III.[32] Different regulatory requirements apply to species listed in each appendix. CITES now protects several thousand species of animals, and many thousands of species of plants.[33]

Species are added to or removed from appendices I and II only by a two-thirds vote of the parties present and voting at a particular conference of the parties,[34] but any party may unilaterally add species to or remove species from appendix III.[35] Appendix I species are those threatened with extinction and that are or may be affected by trade; these species are subject to "particularly strict regulations."[36] Appendix II species are those that may not

27. 16 U.S.C. § 1537a(a)–(d) (establishing the Secretary of the Interior as the "Management Authority" and the "Scientific Authority" pursuant to CITES).

28. *See* 50 C.F.R. § 23.6.

29. 16 U.S.C. § 1537a(a). This provision applies to species listed by the United States as endangered or threatened pursuant to section 4 of the ESA.

30. 16 U.S.C. § 1537(b).

31. *Id.* § 1537. Section 8, as originally passed, applied only to fish and wildlife species; Congress authorized plant conservation efforts abroad in 1979. Pub. L. No. 96-159, § 5, 93 Stat. 1228 (1979).

32. *See* 50 C.F.R. § 23.4.

33. For CITES information and species, see https://cites.org/eng. See also the checklist of CITES species at https://cites.org/eng/disc/species.php.

34. CITES, *supra* note 22, art. XV, 27 U.S.T. at 1110–12. When FWS proposes changes to the appendices, it provides the public with notice and opportunity to comment on any proposed amendments at the next Conference of the Parties. *See, e.g.,* Conference of the Parties to the Convention on International Trade in Endangered Species of Wild Fauna and Flora (CITES); Twentieth Regular Meeting: Taxa Being Considered for Amendments to the CITES Appendices, 89 Fed. Reg. 105,074 (Dec. 26, 2024).

35. CITES, *supra* note 22, art. XVI, 27 U.S.T. at 1113–14.

36. *Id.* art. II(1), 27 U.S.T. at 1092.

yet be threatened with extinction but that may become so without strict regulation of trade in those species.[37] Finally, appendix III species are any species identified by any convention party as being subject to regulation within its jurisdiction and for which the convention party needs the cooperation of other parties in the control of trade.[38] Because CITES emphasizes species threatened by trade, the ESA lists of endangered and threatened species do not perfectly overlap with the three CITES appendices. Also, "CITES allows for downlisting to Appendix II (and therefore, to trade of) threatened and endangered species if it can be shown that trade is *not detrimental* to the survival of the species," while the ESA "requires that permits to import threatened and endangered species will only be issued when it can be demonstrated that trade will result in *enhancing the survival* of the species."[39]

Any person engaging in international trade involving species listed under CITES must comply with detailed permitting requirements.[40] ESA section 9(c) expressly makes unlawful any trade in, or possession of, any specimen of fish, wildlife, or plant in violation of CITES. Before the Management Authority will issue a permit for any appendix I or appendix II species, CITES requires that the Scientific Authority for the country of export make certain determinations, such as that such export will not be "detrimental to the survival of that species" (a non-detriment finding).[41] The

37. *Id.* art. II(2)(a), 27 U.S.T. at 1092. In a provision analogous to the ESA's provision for listing species similar in appearance to endangered or threatened species, Appendix II may also include species that must be subject to regulation in order to control trade in other Appendix II species. *Id.* art. II(2)(b).

38. *Id.* art. 11(3), 27 U.S.T. at 1092.

39. De Alessi, *supra* note 22, at 206.

40. See 50 C.F.R. pt. 23 for permitting requirements for importing, exporting, reexporting, or possessing species listed under CITES. The International Affairs program in the Service notes that it reviews and issues roughly 20,000 permits annually. https://www.fws.gov/international-affairs/permits. *See also* Revision of Regulations Implementing the Convention on International Trade in Endangered Species of Wild Fauna and Flora (CITES), 72 Fed. Reg. 48,402 (Aug. 23, 2007) (final rule). FWS subsequently revises its permitting regulations in response to changes following the Conference of the Parties. *E.g.*, FWS, Implementing the Convention on International Trade in Endangered Species of Wild Fauna and Flora (CITES; Updates Following the Eighteenth Meeting of the Conference of the Parties (CoP18) to CITES, 87 Fed. Reg. 10073 (Feb. 23, 2022); Revisions of Regulations Implementing the Convention on International Trade in Endangered Species of Wild Fauna and Flora (CITEs), 79 Red. Reg. 30400 (May 27, 2014). The program also may preempt inconsistent state laws. *See* Man Hing Ivory & Imps., Inc. v. Deukmejian, 702 F.2d 760 (9th Cir. 1983); H.J. Justin & Sons, Inc. v. Deukmejian, 702 F.2d 758 (9th Cir. 1983).

41. CITES, *supra* note 22, art. IV, 27 U.S.T. at 1095.

Secretary's determination must be based upon the best available biological information derived from professionally accepted wildlife management practices, and estimates of population size are not required.[42] In the United States, the U.S. Department of Agriculture Animal Health Inspection Service inspects plants that are being imported or exported, sometimes inspecting over 50 million listed plants a year. Failure to secure the necessary and timely export permit may result in civil forfeiture in the United States when a party seeks to import the regulated specimen.[43] And export permits are to be granted only if the Management Authority has determined that the specimen was obtained in accordance with the laws of the country.[44]

A variety of special issues and rules apply to particular specimens being imported or exported. Captive breeding operations, for instance, for some specimens are treated separately.[45] In a highly publicized example, the Fish and Wildlife Service (FWS) had excluded certain specimens of U.S. captive-bred live wildlife and sport-hunted trophies of the scimitar-horned oryx, addax, and dama gazelle from the take and export prohibitions under the ESA, but later had to remove this exclusion after a court held that the exclusion had been improperly adopted.[46] Imported sport trophies present another unique problem.[47] Species listed on appendix I and endangered under the ESA require an import

42. 16 U.S.C. § 1537a(c).

43. *See* Conservation Force v. Salazar, 646 F.3d 1240 (9th Cir. 2011) (challenging civil forfeiture of leopard skin and skull as violating the Civil Asset Forfeiture Reform Act of 2000).

44. *See* Castlewood Prods., LLC v. Norton, 365 F.3d 1076 (D.C. Cir. 2004).

45. *See* 50 C.F.R. § 17.21(g) (allowing take, trade, and commercial activity when the purpose of such activity is to enhance the propagation or survival of the affected species). *See generally* Wheeler et al., *supra* note 22, at 323–24.

46. *See* 77 Fed. Reg. 431 (Jan. 5, 2012); Friends of Animals v. Salazar, 626 F. Supp. 2d 102 (D.D.C. 2009). *Cf.* 50 C.F.R. § 17.21(h). After many years, the Service added the three African antelope species to the ESA list and included an exemption (allowing take, trade, transportation, and sale) for captive-bred populations undertaken in compliance with certain requirements. 70 Fed. Reg. 52,310, 52,319 (Sept. 2, 2005); *see also* Safari Club Int'l v. Salazar, 852 F. Supp. 2d 102 (D.D.C. 2012).

47. *See* Wheeler et al., *supra* note 22, at 325–26 (discussing trade in hunting trophies). FWS has been reluctant to issue section 10 permits for importing sport hunting trophies. *See* FWS, Draft Policy for Enhancement-of-Survival Permits for Foreign Species Listed Under the Endangered Species Act, 68 Fed. Reg. 49,512 (Aug. 18, 2003); *see also* Conservation Force v. Salazar, 851 F. Supp. 2d 39 (D.D.C. 2012) (noting delay in issuing wood bison trophies and remanding back to Service decision to deny import permits); Conservation Force v. Salazar, 811 F. Supp. 2d 18 (D.D.C. 2011) (markhor importation permits).

permit, with exacting standards. For some specimens, the Secretary moreover will only allow the importation upon certain conditions and findings, such as upon an enhancement finding for importing specimens of sport-hunted African elephants.[48]

9.5.2 Western Hemisphere Convention

In addition to implementing CITES, section 8a of the ESA[49] implements the Western Hemisphere Convention. The Secretary of the Interior, in cooperation with the Secretary of State, acts on behalf of the United States in all issues respecting the Western Hemisphere Convention.[50] Though in place since 1940, the Western Hemisphere Convention went largely unnoticed for a while.[51] Congress specifically directed the Secretary of the Interior to take such steps as are necessary to implement the Western Hemisphere Convention, including but not limited to:

1. Cooperating with other parties and international organizations to develop personnel, resources, and programs to facilitate implementation of the convention;
2. Identifying species of birds that migrate between the United States and other contracting parties, and taking steps to conserve these species; and
3. Identifying measures necessary and appropriate to implement provisions of the convention addressing the protection of wild plants.[52]

---

48. *See, e.g.*, Ctr. for Biological Diversity v. Bernhardt, 2021 WL 2482088 (D. Ariz. June 17, 2021) (procedural issues in a challenge to leopard import permits), *sub. op.* Ctr. for Biological Diversity v. Haaland, 695 F. Supp. 3d 110 (D. Ariz. 2023); Franks v. Salazar, 816 F. Supp. 2d 49 (D.D.C. 2011); *see also* Marcum v. Salazar, 810 F. Supp. 2d 56 (D.D.C. 2011) (involving attempt to import hunted African elephants from Zambia and concluding that challenges to permit denials may not be brought under the ESA citizen suit provision).

49. 16 U.S.C. § 1537a(e).

50. *Id.*

51. For a discussion of the Western Hemisphere Convention, see Mark C. Trexler & Laura H. Kosloff, *International Implementation: The Longest Arm of the Law? in* BALANCING ON THE BRINK OF EXTINCTION: THE ENDANGERED SPECIES ACT AND LESSONS FOR THE FUTURE 114 (Kathryn A. Kohm ed., 1993).

52. 16 U.S.C. § 1537a(e)(2).

9.6 Prohibited Acts

Section 9 of the ESA limits the scope of prohibited take of listed species of fish or wildlife to the United States, its territorial seas, and the high seas.[53] But the Act also broadly prohibits certain other types of activities, such as the import, export, and "foreign commerce"[54] of listed species. ESA section 9(c) also makes unlawful and a violation of the ESA any trade or possession of species in violation of CITES.[55] "A specimen that has been traded contrary to CITES becomes contraband at the time it enters the jurisdiction of the United States."[56] This does not, however, expand the reach of the Act beyond the United States, because it still only applies these prohibitions to "person[s] subject to the jurisdiction of the United States."[57] But if trade in the specimen is not prohibited under CITES, and the species is listed under the ESA, a party can import the specimen if they satisfy the requirements of ESA section 10 or section 4(d).[58]

In addition, although the Secretary may, after consultation with the Secretary of State or the Secretary of Treasury, as appropriate, conduct law enforcement investigations in foreign countries,[59] jurisdictional realities limit the extent to which the Act's prohibitions apply.

---

53. *Id.* § 1538(a)(1)(B), (C). *See* 18 U.S.C. § 5 (defining *United States* for purposes of criminal jurisdiction); *id.* § 7 (defining *special maritime and territorial jurisdiction of the United States*).

54. *See generally* 16 U.S.C. § 1538(a), (b), (d); *see also* 16 U.S.C. § 1532(9) (defining *foreign commerce* very broadly to include transactions between persons in foreign countries).

55. 16 U.S.C. § 1538(c). *See also id.* § 1540(a)(1), (2) (prescribing civil and criminal penalties for violation of ESA section 9(c)); United States v. Place, 693 F.3d 219 (1st Cir. 2012) (crime to violate CITES regulations).

56. 72 Fed. Reg. at 48,405.

57. 16 U.S.C. §§ 1538(a)(1), (2), 1538(g).

58. In December 2024, the Fish and Wildlife Service published a fact sheet on understanding CITES and the limitations after import of Appendix-1 species. U.S. Fish & Wildlife Service, Understanding CITES: Use After Import of Wildlife Specimens of CITES Appendix-1 Species (Dec. 2024), https://www.fws.gov/sites/default/files/documents/2024-12/factsheet-use-after-import-cites-appendix-i-dec-2024.pdf. There are exemptions from import requirements, but one court rejected the notion that a defendant could themselves decide whether their activity is exempt. United States v. Martinez, 2022 WL 17100684 (S.D. Fla. Nov. 22, 2022) (discussing declaration at customs).

59. 16 U.S.C. § 1537a(d).

10 Experimental Populations

10.1 Overview

As discussed in Chapter 3, section 7(a)(1)[1] of the Endangered Species Act (ESA) directs all federal agencies to carry out programs for the conservation of endangered species. The ESA defines *conservation* to include "live trapping, and transplantation."[2] Early efforts to relocate endangered species were often plagued by staunch local opposition concerned with the strict take prohibitions applicable to the relocated species.[3] But more recently, resource agencies have touted the potential efficacy for increasing relocation efforts.[4] Indeed, Colorado voters passed a ballot measure designed to reintroduce wolves onto state lands in Western

---

1. 16 U.S.C. § 1536(a)(1).

2. *Id.* § 1532(3).

3. *See* H.R. Rep. No. 97-567, at 17 (1982), *reprinted in* 1982 U.S.C.C.A.N. 2807, 2817 ("Another shortcoming of the Act is its tendency to discourage voluntary introduction of species in areas of their historic range. State F&W agencies had probed the feasibility of introducing such experimental populations, but they feared political opposition to reintroducing species unless some assurances were simultaneously extended to prevent the creation of Endangered Species Act problems."). *See generally* Mimi S. Wolok, *Experimenting with Experimental Populations,* 26 Env't L. Rep. 10,018 (1996).

4. The recovery program for the black-footed ferret, for instance, is tied to reintroduction efforts. *E.g.*, U.S. Fish & Wildlife Serv., Endangered and Threatened Wildlife and Plants; Revision of the Nonessential Experimental Population of Black-Footed Ferrets (Musteia nigripes) in the Southwest, 88 Fed. Reg. 69045 (Oct. 3 2023) (expanding black-footed ferret reintroduction); Western Watersheds Project v. Vilsack, 696 F. Supp. 3d (D. Wyo. 2023) (involving U.S. Forest Service land plan amendment and impact on the species). *See also* FWS, Northern Cascades Grizzly Bear 10(j) Rule, 89 Fed. Reg. 26982 (May 3, 2024); U.S. Fish & Wildlife Serv., Endangered and Threatened Wildlife and Plants; Revision to the Nonessential Experimental Population of the Mexican Wolf, 87 Fed. Reg. 39348 (2023).

Colorado, with five wolves introduced into the Rockies in late 2023.[5] As of the summer 2023, the Services had established over 60 experimental populations.[6]

In 1982, Congress amended the ESA to "relax certain restrictions" governing experimental populations, with the goal of encouraging private support for reintroduction efforts.[7] Through ESA section 10(j),[8] Congress established a flexible approach for the reintroduction of endangered and threatened species. As discussed in this chapter, the degree of protection afforded an "experimental population" under section 10(j) can vary considerably, depending on whether the particular population is designated as "essential" or "nonessential." Also, because experimental populations are classified as "threatened"[9] rather than as "endangered" species, special regulations under section 4(d) (applicable to threatened species) may be tailored to address the needs of each particular species, as well as any concerns of the public. Since inception of the experimental population program, the Fish and Wildlife Service (FWS) has exercised its authority judiciously and generally avoids designating essential experimental populations.[10]

---

5. AP, *Colorado Releases First 5 Wolves in Reintroduction Plan*, Greenwire, Dec. 19, 2023. One court reports how "[t]he reintroduction of the gray wolf in Colorado has been a matter of controversy for a number of years, with valid interests and concerns raised on each side of the equation." Gunnison Country Stockgrowers' Ass'n, Inc. v. U.S. Fish & Wildlife Serv., 707 F. Supp. 3d 1056 (D. Colo. 2023) (denying a TRO). The experimental population program has recently generated interest from some in Congress. *See* Michael Doyle, *Panel Puts Heat on ESA "Experimental" Wildlife Moves*, E&E Daily, Mar. 5, 2025.

6. *See* CRS, In Focus: Experimental Populations Under the Endangered Species Act, July 27, 2023.

7. H.R. Rep. No. 97-567, *supra* note 3, at 33, 1982 U.S.C.C.A.N. at 2833. *See also* Wyo. Farm Bureau Fed'n v. Babbitt, 199 F.3d 1224, 1231 (10th Cir. 2000).

8. 16 U.S.C. § 1539(j).

9. *Id.* § 1539(j)(2)(C).

10. Congress expected that "in most cases experimental populations will not be essential." H.R. Conf. Rep. No. 97-835, at 34 (1982). The designations are in 50 C.F.R. §§ 17.84, 17.85. NMFS has been less active in developing experimental populations, but efforts exist. *See, e.g.,* Omnibus Public Land Management Act of 2009, Pub. L. No. 111-11, § 10011 (Mar. 30, 2009) (regarding California Central Valley spring-run chinook salmon reintroduction into San Joaquin River); 76 Fed. Reg. 28,715 (May 18, 2011) (proposed rule for designation of nonessential experimental population for Middle Columbia River steelhead above the Pelton Round Butte Hydroelectric Project).

10.2 Establishing an Experimental Population

Section 10(j) authorizes the Secretary to establish an experimental population of a listed species. An experimental population is defined as "any population (including any offspring arising solely therefrom) authorized by the Secretary for release . . . but only when, and at such times as, the population is wholly separate geographically from nonexperimental populations of the same species."[11] When establishing an experimental population, the Secretary may authorize the transportation and release of any "population (including eggs, propagules, or individuals) of an endangered or threatened species outside its current range."[12] Before authorizing the release of any experimental population, however, the Secretary must employ the "best scientific and commercial data available," determine if the release will further the species' conservation,[13] and consider

- the possible adverse effects on existing populations resulting from removal of individuals, eggs, or propagules for introduction elsewhere;
- the likelihood that the experimental population will become established and survive in the foreseeable future;
- the relative effects that the experimental population will have on the recovery of the species; and
- the effects of existing or anticipated federal, state, or private activities within or adjacent to the experimental population area.[14]

---

11. 16 U.S.C. § 1593(j)(2). U.S. Fish & Wildlife Service regulations further define an experimental population as an introduced and/or designated population (including any offspring arising solely therefrom) that has been so designated in accordance with the procedures of this subpart but only when, and at such times as, the population is wholly separate geographically from nonexperimental populations of the same species. Where part of an experimental population overlaps with nonexperimental populations of the same species on a particular occasion, but is wholly separate at other times, specimens of the experimental population will not be recognized as such while in the area of overlap. That is, experimental status will be recognized only outside the area of overlap. Thus, such a population will be treated as experimental only when the times of geographic separation are reasonably predictable; e.g., fixed migration patterns, natural or manmade barriers. A population is not treated as experimental if total separation will occur solely as a result of random and unpredictable events. 50 C.F.R. § 17.80(a). *See also* 50 C.F.R. § 222.501(a) (NMFS experimental population definition).

12. 16 U.S.C. § 1539(j)(2)(A).

13. *Id.* See Chapter 2, Section 2.3 for a discussion of "best scientific and commercial data available."

14. 50 C.F.R. § 17.81(b)(1)–(4).

The release area must be "suitable natural habitat" outside of the species' "current natural range." Until 2023, FWS regulations provided that an experimental population had to be within the "probable historic range" of the species, unless such habitat has been "unsuitably and irreversibly altered or destroyed," in which case a release may occur in areas not formerly occupied by the species.[15] The revised 2023 regulations removed the requirement tethering experimental populations to their historic range.[16] FWS considered this change necessary to respond to the effects of climate change on suitable habitat areas.[17] If an experimental population is proposed to be introduced outside of its historical range, however, the revised regulations require that FWS consider the potential adverse effects to the ecosystem.[18]

The Secretary must follow the informal rulemaking process under the Administrative Procedure Act (APA) when establishing an experimental population, and any such regulation must contain the following:

- appropriate means to identify the experimental population, its location, migration, numbers, and so forth;
- management restrictions, protective measures, or other special management concerns; and
- a process for the periodic review and evaluation of the success or failure of the release and the effect of the release on the conservation and recovery of the species.[19]

And when developing and implementing an experimental population rule, the Secretary has committed to consulting with all affected stakeholders.[20] Also, the regulation may establish any applicable prohibitions,[21] as discussed later in this chapter.

Specimens collected for relocation may come from any existing population of the species, including populations not currently

---

15. *Id.* § 17.81(a) (2022).
16. U.S. Fish & Wildlife Serv., Designation of Experimental Populations, 88 Fed. Reg. 42,642 (July 3, 2023).
17. *Id.*
18. *Id.* at 42,651–52 (amending 50 C.F.R. § 17.81(b)). NMFS's regulations differ slightly from those of FWS and NMFS previously required a consideration of the effect on the ecosystem. 50 C.F.R. § 222.502(a) (2022).
19. 50 C.F.R. § 17.81(c)(1), (3), (4).
20. *Id.* § 17.81(e). The Secretary's decision to propose an experimental population triggers the National Environmental Policy Act. *E.g.*, Forest Guardians v. U.S. Fish & Wildlife Serv., 611 F.3d 692, 700 (10th Cir. 2010).
21. 50 C.F.R. § 17.82.

listed under the Act.[22] Section 10(a)(1)(A) research permits and "enhancement of survival" permits[23] are the vehicles used to authorize activities necessary to collect, relocate, establish, and maintain an experimental population, while avoiding inadvertent injury to the species as a whole.[24]

10.3 Essential Versus Nonessential Experimental Populations

Prior to authorizing the release of any experimental population, the Secretary must determine whether the population is "essential to the continued existence of an endangered species or a threatened species."[25] An *essential experimental population* is one "whose loss would be likely to appreciably reduce the likelihood of the survival of the species in the wild"; and "[a]ll other experimental populations are to be classified as nonessential."[26] The two primary regulatory distinctions between essential and nonessential experimental populations are found in application of the Act's critical habitat and section 7 consultation provisions.

10.4 Geographic Separation

A population designated as experimental remains so only at such times as the population is "wholly separate geographically from non-experimental populations of the same species."[27] The issue of geographic overlap between experimental populations and natural populations of the same species was considered by Congress

22. United States v. McKittrick, 142 F.3d 1170, 1174 (9th Cir. 1998) (Secretary does not have to deplete endangered or threatened populations in order to gather individuals for creation of an experimental population).

23. See Chapter 6, Section 6.4 for a discussion of enhancement of survival permits.

24. 50 C.F.R. § 17.81(d); *see* 16 U.S.C. § 1539(d) (providing that no section 10 permit may be issued if doing so would operate to the disadvantage of the species).

25. 16 U.S.C. § 1539(j)(2)(B); 50 C.F.R. § 17.81(c)(2).

26. 50 C.F.R. § 17.80(b). *See also id.* § 222.501(b) (NMFS definition).

27. 16 U.S.C. § 1539(j)(1).

when enacting the experimental population provision.[28] Congress was concerned about the need to "protect natural populations and . . . avoid potential complicated problems of law enforcement" triggered by experimental populations.[29] It noted that when such overlap occurs, the experimental population designation does not apply within the area of overlap, and thus the full protections afforded a listed, nonexperimental population apply to both the naturally occurring population and the reintroduced population. Conversely, when the sporadically overlapping populations are geographically separated, the reintroduced population is afforded the reduced level of protection of an experimental population, but only when the times of geographical separation are "reasonably predictable" and not a result of "random and unpredictable events."[30]

FWS interprets the geographic overlap concept as applying to populations, not individual members of the species, such as lone dispersers. This interpretation has been affirmed in two cases involving the reintroduction of gray wolves.[31] In 1994, FWS promulgated final rules authorizing the establishment of an experimental population of gray wolves in Yellowstone National Park, central Idaho, and southwestern Montana.[32] In *Wyoming Farm Bureau,* the Tenth Circuit upheld FWS's determination that the ESA's geographic separation requirement applies only to "population" overlap and not to overlap with "lone dispersers" or individuals of a species.[33] The naturally occurring, individual wolves in the reintroduction area did not amount to a population, and thus the reintroduced wolves remained "wholly separate geographically" from any known *population* of naturally occurring wolves. The Tenth Circuit again deferred to the Secretary's interpretation for the reintroduction of the northern Aplomado falcon.[34] The Ninth Circuit reached the same conclusion in an ESA section 9 criminal case.[35] On appeal of his conviction for unlawfully tak-

---

28. H.R. Rep. No. 97-567, at 33–34 (1982), *reprinted in* 1982 U.S.C.C.A.N. 2833.
29. *Id.*
30. *Id.; see also* 50 C.F.R. § 17.80 (largely mirroring H.R. Rep. No. 97-567).
31. United States v. McKittrick, 142 F.3d 1170, 1175 (10th Cir. 1998); Wyo. Farm Bureau Fed'n v. Babbitt, 199 F.3d 1224, 1234–37 (10th Cir. 2000).
32. 59 Fed. Reg. 60,252 (1994) (codified at 50 C.F.R. § 17.84(1)).
33. *Wyo. Farm Bureau,* 199 F.3d at 1233–36.
34. Forest Guardians v. U.S. Fish & Wildlife Serv., 611 F.3d 692 (10th Cir. 2010).
35. *McKittrick,* 142 F.3d 1170.

ing, possessing, and transporting a gray wolf (a member of the same experimental population at issue in *Wyoming Farm Bureau),* defendant McKittrick challenged the validity of the experimental population designation. In upholding McKittrick's conviction, the appeals court deferred to FWS's interpretation that the "wholly separate geographically" requirement applies only to populations, not to individual animals.[36]

10.5 Critical Habitat

The Secretary may designate critical habitat for an essential experimental population, but not for nonessential experimental populations.[37]

10.6 Section 7 Consultation

For purposes of the consultation provisions of ESA section 7,[38] nonessential experimental populations are treated as species proposed to be listed, except for nonessential populations occurring within a national park or a national wildlife refuge.[39] Sections 7(a)(1) and 7(a)(2) apply to populations inside units of a national park or wildlife refuge. For populations outside any national park or wildlife refuge, neither a section 7 consultation nor the section 7 prohibition against jeopardy is required for federal actions affecting nonessential experimental populations. Instead, the less stringent section 7(a)(4) "conferencing" requirement applies to proposed actions that are "likely to jeopardize" a nonessential population.[40] Section 7(a)(4) requires that federal agencies "confer" with the Service on proposed actions that are likely to jeopardize the continued existence of a species proposed for listing,

36. *Id.* at 1175 ("sporadic sightings of isolated indigenous wolves in the release area, lone wolves, or 'dispersers,' do not constitute a population").

37. 16 U.S.C. § 1539(j)(2)(C)(ii); 50 C.F.R. § 17.81(g).

38. 16 U.S.C. § 1536(a)(2). See Chapter 5, Section 5.4 for a discussion of ESA section 7 consultation.

39. 16 U.S.C. § 1539(j)(C)(i); 50 C.F.R. § 17.83(a).

40. 16 U.S.C. § 1536(a)(4). See Chapter 5, Section 5.7 for a discussion of ESA section 7 conferencing.

but the results of this conference are advisory and do not prohibit agency actions. By contrast, experimental populations determined to be essential to the survival of a species are treated as any other threatened species for section 7 purposes.[41]

10.7 Special Rules with Respect to Experimental Populations

Each member of an experimental population, whether essential or nonessential, is treated as a threatened species.[42] In Congress's view, such a designation "grants the Secretary broad flexibility in promulgating regulations to protect such species," and these regulations "can even allow the taking of threatened animals."[43] For example, Congress noted that special regulations associated with experimental populations could allow for such activities as the inadvertent take of experimental fish species by fishermen seeking other species in the same body of water, or the taking of predators such as wolves, if depredations occur or if the release of a population would continue to be frustrated by public opposition.[44] In *Gibbs v. Babbitt,*[45] the Fourth Circuit upheld a special regulation for the taking of the experimental population of red wolves. When an issue surfaces about the possible "taking" of an experimental population species, the inquiry is whether any special rule under section 4(d) for that species has been violated rather than a generic inquiry into whether a "take" has occurred under section 9 of the Act.[46]

---

41. 50 C.F.R. § 17.83(b).
42. 16 U.S.C. § 1539(2)(C).
43. H.R. Rep. No. 97-567, *supra* note 3, 1982 U.S.C.C.A.N. at 2834 ("the committee fully expects that there will be instances where the regulations allow for the incidental take of experimental populations . . . [and] that, where appropriate, the regulations could allow for the directed taking of experimental populations").
44. *Id.*
45. 214 F.3d 483 (4th Cir. 2000).
46. *See, e.g.*, Humane Soc'y of the U.S. v. Klenzie, 333 F. Supp. 3d 1236, 1241, 1260–61 (D.N.M. 2018).

11 Citizen Suits, Standing, and Procedure

11.1 Overview

Generally, the Secretaries of the Interior, Commerce, Agriculture, and Treasury, and the U.S. Coast Guard all enforce aspects of the Endangered Species Act (ESA).[1] But Congress also intended to facilitate enforcement by allowing private citizens to act as "private attorneys general."[2] ESA section 11(g)[3] allows "any person"[4] to bring suit in federal district court to enforce the Act.[5] This chapter discusses the statutory scope of ESA section 11(g), as well as its constitutional and procedural limitations. Although the ESA's citizen suit provision is premised on the belief that citizens can hold government enforcement agencies accountable, the process requires that citizens initiating such lawsuits have proper standing and give appropriate pre-suit notice.

1. 16 U.S.C. § 1540(e), (h); *id.* § 1532(14) (definition of "Secretary" in Act).

2. Bennett v. Spear, 520 U.S. 154, 165 (1997). Over the more than 50 years since Congress included citizen-suit provisions in various environmental statutes, including the ESA, litigants have repeatedly claimed that these provisions are unconstitutional because they usurp Article II powers. *See generally* Jeffrey S. Miller & Brooke S. Donner, *The Constitutionality of Citizen Suit Provisions in Federal Environmental Statutes*, 27 J. Env'T L. & Litig. 401 (2012).

3. 16 U.S.C. § 1540(g).

4. *See id.* § 1532(13) (defining *person* broadly).

5. 16 U.S.C. § 1540(g)(3)(A). *See also id.* § 1540(g)(1) (providing that the district court shall have jurisdiction, without regard to the amount in controversy or the citizenship of the parties).

11.2 Scope of ESA Section 11(g)

The ESA's citizen suit provision grants district courts jurisdiction over suits when the relevant agency has neglected a nondiscretionary duty.[6] Also under section 11(g), any person may "commence a civil suit on his own behalf" to attempt to enjoin any entity alleged to be in violation of various provisions of the Act.[7] The citizen suit provision specifically allows suits:

> (A) To enjoin any person, including the United States and any other governmental instrumentality or agency (to the extent permitted by the 11th Amendment to the Constitution) who is alleged to be in violation of any provision of [the ESA or its regulations]; or
> (B) To compel the Secretary to apply [section 4(d) or section 9 prohibitions] with respect to the taking of any resident endangered species or threatened species within any state; or
> (C) Against the Secretary where there is alleged a failure of the Secretary to perform any act or duty under [section 4 of the Act] which is not discretionary with the Secretary.[8]

Subsection (A) enables private parties to enforce the ESA against any party regulated by the Act, including private entities and government agencies.[9] Any violation of the Act or its regulations is actionable under subsection (A), except that for actions against the Secretaries of the Interior or Commerce, citizen suits are generally limited under section 11(g) to the discrete subject matter outlined in subsections (B) and (C)—that is, section 9 and section 4(d) enforcement and nondiscretionary actions under section 4 of the Act.[10] Challenges to the Secretaries' implementation or "administration" of the Act are not reviewable under ESA

6. *Id.* § 1540(g)(1)(C) (authorizing suit "where there is alleged a failure of the Secretary to perform any act or duty under section 1533 of this title which is not discretionary with the Secretary"). *See also* Save the Bull Trout v. Williams, 51 F.4th 1101, 1109 (9th Cir. 2022) (noting that "[a]s a result, federal courts must assess the merits of an ESA claim in order to determine their jurisdiction over it").

7. *Id.* § 1540(g)(1).

8. *Id.* § 1540(g)(1)(A)–(C).

9. *Id.*

10. *See, e.g.*, Bennett v. Spear, 520 U.S. 154, 172 (1997) (concluding that critical habitat designation under section 4(d)(2) of the Act is a nondiscretionary action reviewable under the citizen suit provision).

section 11(g).[11] In some circumstances, actions not reviewable under section 11(g) may be reviewed under the Administrative Procedure Act.[12]

11.3 60-Day Notice Requirement

As a general rule, ESA section 11(g) citizen suits may not be commenced prior to 60 days after written notice has been given to the Secretary and to any alleged violator intended to be a defendant in the lawsuit.[13] A few exceptions exist. No notice, for instance, is required for actions challenging the grant of an exemption by the Endangered Species Committee.[14] Also, an action may be brought immediately after notification of the alleged violation when the violation would immediately affect a legal interest of the plaintiff.[15] This includes actions alleging that the Secretary has failed to perform a nondiscretionary duty under ESA section 4, which actions may proceed "immediately" after notification to the Secretary if there is an "emergency posing a significant risk to the

11. *Id.* at 173–75 (concluding that allegations regarding the Secretary's failure to perform his duties as administrator of the Act are not reviewable under section 11(g)). *See also* Salmon Spawning & Recovery All. v. U.S. Customs & Border Prot., 550 F.3d 1121, 1129 (Fed. Cir. 2008) (citizen suit provision not available to challenge implementation and enforcement of the Act).

12. *Bennett*, 520 U.S. at 175 ("Nothing in the ESA's citizen-suit provision expressly precludes review under the APA, nor do we detect anything in the statutory scheme suggesting a purpose to do so."). *See also* Pacificans for a Scenic Coast v. Cal. Dep't of Trans., 204 F. Supp. 3d 1075, 1090, 1098 (N.D. Cal. 2016) (a Biological Opinion that relied on a "vague and speculative mitigation measure" that was not under a project proponent's control violated the procedural requirements of the ESA and hence was arbitrary and capricious under the APA).

13. 16 U.S.C. § 1540(g)(2)(A), (B), (C). The "appropriate" Secretary must be provided notice. *See* Hawksbill Sea Turtle v. Fed. Emergency Mgmt. Auth., 126 F.3d 461, 473 (3d Cir. 1997) (because the Departments of Interior and Commerce shared jurisdiction over sea turtles, notification of only the Secretary of the Interior, and not the Secretary of Commerce, was insufficient to meet the 60-day notice requirement). No action may be commenced under subsections 1540(g)(1)(A) or (B) if the Secretary has commenced action to impose a penalty or is diligently prosecuting the violator. 16 U.S.C. §§ 1540(g)(2)(A)(iii), 1540(g)(2)(B)(ii).

14. *Id.* § 1536(m).

15. 43 U.S.C. § 1349(a)(3); *see also* Brown v. Offshore Specialty Fabricators, Inc., 663 F.3d 759, 768 (2011) (describing and rejecting plaintiffs' claim that their rights were immediately affected by defendant's conduct); Pac. Nw. Venison Producers v. Smitch, 20 F.3d 1008 (9th Cir. 1994) (dismissal of plaintiffs' ESA claim for lack of notice would be unjust because it would have precluded timely relief to save breeding season).

well being of any species."[16] Potential litigants should be aware that the emergency exception to the 60-day notice requirement is strictly limited to alleged failures of the Secretary to perform *non-discretionary* acts under section 4 (listing, critical habitat, recovery planning) of the ESA.[17]

The purpose of the 60-day notice requirement is to afford the recipient advance notice of perceived violations of the statute and to ensure that they are given an opportunity to review their actions and take corrective measures if warranted.[18] The 60-day notice provision, therefore, establishes a "litigation-free window" allowing parties time to resolve disputes short of litigation.[19] Since the Supreme Court's discussion of notice requirements in *Hallstrom v. Tillamook County,*[20] lower courts are increasingly demanding strict compliance with such statutory notice requirements.

A proper 60-day notice must sufficiently alert the recipient of the actual alleged violation so that the recipient may attempt to abate the violation.[21] The notice must be "sufficiently specific to

---

16. 16 U.S.C. § 1540(g)(2)(C). *See* Me. Audubon Soc'y v. Purslow, 672 F. Supp. 528, 531 (D. Me. 1987) (dismissing suit against developer who was planning to subdivide property near bald eagle nest for failure to provide 60-day notice and holding that Congress did not intend to "grant citizen plaintiffs immediate enforcement power").

17. *E.g.*, Salmon Spawning & Recovery All. v. U.S. Customs & Border Prot., 532 F.3d 1338 (Fed. Cir. 2008). Courts have distinguished emergencies in the listing context from those in the notice context. *See* Ctr. for Biological Diversity v. Bernhardt, 2021 WL 1565787 (D. Nev. Apr. 21, 2021) (though the Secretary of the Interior had already denied plaintiff's petition for emergency listing "and signaled its position that an emergency [in the listing context] does not exist," an emergency in the notice context existed, and plaintiffs could sue immediately after filing notice, because the "pleadings demonstrate[d] a well-founded concern for the species, and all parties acknowledge the steep decline in the [Tiehm's] buckwheat's population").

18. Water Keeper All. v. U.S. Dep't of Def., 271 F.3d 21, 29–30 (1st Cir. 2001); Sw. Ctr. for Biological Diversity v. Bureau of Reclamation, 143 F.3d 515, 521 (9th Cir. 1998). Crucially, the violation must have occurred before the notice of intent is given; "pre-violation notice" is not notice under the ESA's citizen suit provision. *See* Friends of Animals v. Ashe, 51 F. Supp. 3d 77, 84 (D.D.C. 2014).

19. *Sw. Ctr. for Biological Diversity*, 143 F.3d at 521.

20. 493 U.S. 20 (1989) (in case involving RCRA's citizen suit provision, comparable to the ESA's citizen suit provision, Court held that failure to provide notice mandates dismissal of the case).

21. *See* Klamath-Siskiyou Wildlands Ctr. v. MacWhorter, 797 F.3d 645, 651 (9th Cir. 2015). For a more fine-grained understanding of required elements of a notice, courts have turned to an analogous notice provision in the Clean Water Act, which unlike the ESA's notice provision has an implementing regulation. *See id.* at 650 (relying on cases interpreting the CWA's notice provision but noting that, because the ESA's notice provision lacks implementing regulations, "to the degree that the CWA implementing regulation might be thought to require more specific notice than would be required under the [ESA], standing alone, we are not

inform the alleged violator about what it [was] doing wrong" in order that the violator knows what corrective actions may be taken.[22] Courts typically require that letters give notice of the asserted violation and intent to sue.[23] Likewise, "comments" submitted in a formal rulemaking process do not meet the Act's notice requirement "no matter how vehemently it [the comment] may have conveyed the party's intention to go to court if the rule ultimately adopted were not to [the commentor's] liking."[24] Some courts hold that the particular plaintiffs must be identified in a required notice letter.[25] And an otherwise adequate notice that is provided fewer than 60 days prior to commencement of the lawsuit is generally insufficient to meet the requirements of the Act.[26] Failure to satisfy the substantive and timing requirements for a valid 60-day notice may result in dismissal of the suit, though most courts now understand the notice requirement to be a "mandatory claims-processing rule, not a jurisdictional predicate."[27] Potential ESA

---

bound to adopt that more demanding requirement"); *see also* 40 C.F.R. § 135.3(a) (CWA regulations interpreting notice provision).

22. Ctr. for Biological Diversity v. EPA, 316 F. Supp. 3d 1156, 1170 (N.D. Cal. 2018) (internal quotation marks omitted); *see Sw. Ctr. for Biological Diversity*, 143 F.3d at 521 (notice was insufficient where letters sent to agencies did not reveal that plaintiff had a grievance, which was the basis for suit, regarding a specific bird species' habitat in the Lake Mead delta).

23. Save the Yaak Comm. v. Block, 840 F.2d 714, 721 (9th Cir. 1988), *overruled on other grounds*, Cascadia Wildlands v. Scott Timber Co., 105 F.4th 1144, 1153 (9th Cir. 2024) (notice was also insufficient in that it was never sent to the Secretary). *But cf.* Marbled Murrelet v. Babbitt, 83 F.3d 1068, 1072–73 (9th Cir. 1996) (notice was adequate to support suit based on ESA section 7, even though the focus of the letter was on ESA section 9 violations and section 7 was mentioned in only one part of the letter).

24. Humane Soc'y of the U.S. v. Lujan, 768 F. Supp. 360, 362 (D.D.C. 1991).

25. *See* N.M. Citizens for Clean Air & Water v. Espanola Mercantile Co., 72 F.3d 830, 833 (10th Cir. 1996); Wash. Trout v. McCain Foods, Inc., 45 F.3d 1351, 1354–55 (9th Cir. 1995).

26. *See* Me. Audubon Soc'y v. Purslow, 907 F.2d 265 (1st Cir. 1990) (filing suit one day after providing notice was clearly insufficient); Protect Our Eagles' Trees (POETS) v. City of Lawrence, 715 F. Supp. 996, 998 (D. Kan. 1989) (16 days' notice of lawsuit was insufficient). *But cf.* Sierra Club v. Block, 614 F. Supp. 488, 492 (D.D.C. 1985) (court allowed citizen suit to proceed in spite of only 35 days' notice because (1) the defendant agencies had responded to the notice of intent in writing, stating that they were not reconsidering their position, and (2) the defendants were not prejudiced).

27. Cascadia Wildlands v. Scott Timber Co., 105 F.4th 1144, 1153 (9th Cir. 2024) (reversing holding in Save the Yaak Comm. v. Block, 840 F.2d 714, 721 (9th Cir. 1988) that the notice requirement is jurisdictional but reiterating that "failure to strictly comply with the notice requirement acts as an absolute bar to bringing suit under the ESA" (internal quotation marks omitted)). *See also* Sierra Club v. Yeutter, 926 F.2d 429, 437 (5th Cir. 1991) ("section 1540(g)(2)(A), though clearly mandatory, is not jurisdictional in the strict sense of the term, and hence may not be availed of for the first time on appeal by an appellant seeking reversal of an

citizen suit plaintiffs, therefore, should send a notice at least 60 days prior to commencing an action. The notice should (1) be clearly identified as a 60-day notice under ESA section 11(g), (2) identify the particular plaintiff(s) on whose behalf the notice is provided, (3) clearly discuss all issues that the party believes could be the basis of a future lawsuit, and (4) be served upon the relevant Secretary and any other alleged ESA violator.

11.4 APA Review as an Alternative to an ESA Citizen Suit

The Administrative Procedure Act (APA) provides a right to judicial review of any "final agency action for which there is no other adequate remedy in a court."[28] Certain final actions of the Secretary that are not reviewable under ESA section 11(g)(1)(B) or (C) are reviewable under the APA. For example, in *Bennett v. Spear,* the Supreme Court held that alleged deficiencies in a final biological opinion (BO) prepared by the Fish and Wildlife Service (FWS) were not reviewable under ESA section 11(g), but that the BO represented final agency action reviewable under the APA.[29]

One important aspect of APA review of secretarial decisions under the ESA is that, unlike citizen suit review, the APA does not require 60 days' notice prior to filing suit. In one informative post-*Bennett* case, the Ninth Circuit held that an environmental plaintiff's challenge to the adequacy of a BO was an APA claim, and that therefore the ESA citizen suit 60-day notice requirement was

---

adverse trial court judgment on that basis"); *but see* Hawksbill Sea Turtle v. Fed. Emergency Mgmt. Auth., 126 F.3d 461, 471 (3d Cir. 1997) (holding ESA notice requirement jurisdictional).

28. 5 U.S.C. § 704. Because "the APA applies only where there is 'no other adequate remedy in a court,'" courts have held that where the ESA's citizen-suit provision provides a remedy "the APA does not apply." W. Watersheds Project v. Kraayenbrink, 632 F.3d 472, 497 (9th Cir. 2011) (citing 5 U.S.C. § 704).

29. Bennett v. Spear, 520 U.S. 154, 174–79 (1997). *See generally* Sam Kalen, *Standing on Its Last Legs:* Bennett v. Spear *and the Past and Future of Standing in Environmental Cases,* 13 J. Land Use & Env't L. 1 (1997). *See also* Earth Island Inst. v. Albright, 147 F.3d 1352, 1357–58 (Fed. Cir. 1998) ("maladministration" of the ESA is not reviewable under ESA section 11(g), but rather under the APA); Conservation Force v. Salazar, 2012 WL 1059732 (D.D.C. 2012) (challenges to FWS's decisions to deny import permits are not properly citizen suit cases; they must instead be brought under the APA).

inapplicable.[30] Conversely, the court also ruled that claims filed in the same lawsuit against two federal action agencies (the Bureau of Reclamation and the U.S. Army Corps of Engineers) were ESA citizen suit claims and subject to the 60-day notice requirement.[31]

Plaintiffs, however, should be cautious if they presume that they have a choice between APA or ESA citizen suit review. If an action may proceed pursuant to ESA section 11(g), a plaintiff should proceed in compliance with section 11(g) and, indeed, may prefer to do so. And little is likely to be accomplished if plaintiffs attempt to circumvent the notice requirements of the ESA by merely "re-styling their claims to fit within the APA."[32] Likewise, for actions not reviewable as section 11(g) citizen suits, plaintiffs must satisfy the APA's requirement that the "action" being challenged is "final" and therefore otherwise reviewable.[33] Perhaps because of the benefits of proceeding under section 11(g), it has become common practice even in APA-styled claims for plaintiffs to comply with the section 11(g) notice requirements, possibly with the goal of securing attorneys' fees under the citizen suit provision.[34]

30. Am. Rivers v. NMFS, 126 F.3d 1118, 1124–25 (9th Cir. 1997).

31. *Id.* at 1125. Whether under ESA section 11(g) or the APA, parties should ensure that a court of appeals does not otherwise have exclusive jurisdiction over particular agency decisions. *See* Am. Bird Conservancy v. FCC, 545 F.3d 1190 (9th Cir. 2008) (ESA citizen suit lawsuit could not be brought in district court when court of appeals exercises exclusive jurisdiction over actions of the FCC).

32. Citizens Interested in Bow Run, Inc. v. Edrington, 781 F. Supp. 1502 (D. Or. 1991).

33. *Bennett,* 520 U.S. at 175. A recent decision of the Ninth Circuit hinged on whether a recovery plan adopted for the grizzly bear in accord with ESA section 4(f) was final agency action. *See* Ctr. for Biological Diversity v. Haaland, 58 F.4th 412 (9th Cir. 2023). Because FWS was not required to abide by the recovery plan, the plan did not meet the Supreme Court's definition, from *Bennett v. Spear,* of final agency action as, in part, action by which rights or obligations have been determined, or from which legal consequences will flow.

34. The Ninth Circuit has suggested in at least one instance that distinguishing between ESA and APA cases is not all that significant. W. Watersheds Project v. Kraayenbrink, 632 F.3d 472, 481 (9th Cir. 2011) ("Irrespective of whether an ESA claim is brought under the APA or the citizen-suit provision, the APA's 'arbitrary and capricious' standard applies; and, an agency's 'no effect' determination under the ESA must be upheld unless arbitrary and capricious."). But case law in that circuit reveals possibly important divergence between ESA and APA cases. First, the ESA specifically provides that litigants in ESA citizen suits may be awarded attorneys' fees. 16 U.S.C. § 1540(g)(4). The APA, by contrast, does not include an attorneys' fees provision, though such fees may be available in certain APA suits under the fee-shifting provision of the Equal Access to Justice Act (EAJA), 28 U.S.C. § 2412. Second, different forms of evidence are admissible in claims brought as ESA citizen suits versus under the APA. The Ninth Circuit has not clearly resolved the question whether review of ESA citizen suit claims should be limited to the administrative record, as the APA requires, or should be evaluated

11.5 Standing

Article III of the Constitution requires that a party satisfy the "irreducible constitutional minimum" of standing to ensure that there is a proper case or controversy, and the ESA does not otherwise relax the constitutionally minimum standing requirements.[35] Courts also apply the additional APA requirement that a plaintiff be within the *zone of interest* of the ESA, "an issue that requires [courts] to determine, using traditional tools of statutory interpretation, whether a legislatively conferred cause of action ["arguably" under modern caselaw] encompasses a particular plaintiff's claim."[36] The so-called zone-of-interest test initially had limited standing in ESA cases to persons seeking to further the environmental and conservation goals of the Act. Since the Supreme Court's 1997 decision in *Bennett v. Spear,* however, the zone-of-interest test generally no longer inhibits ESA citizen suits, though it remains applicable to suits brought under the APA alleging violations of the ESA.[37]

---

with any admissible evidence, as in non-APA civil suits. In *Kraayenbrink,* considering an ESA citizen suit, the Ninth Circuit held that it "may consider evidence outside the administrative record for the limited purposes of reviewing" the citizen-suit claim. *Id.* at 479 (citing Washington Toxics Coalition v. EPA, 413 F.3d 1024, 1034 (9th Cir. 2005)); *but see* Karuk Tribe of Cal. v. United States Forest Serv., 681 F.3d 1006, 1017 (9th Cir. 2012) (holding, without citing *Washington Toxics* or *Kraayenbrink,* that an ESA citizen suit was a "record review case"). "*Kraayenbrink* has not been consistently applied and district courts in [the Ninth] [C]ircuit appear somewhat split as to the broader implications of *Washington Toxics* and *Kraayenbrink.*" *See* Riverkeeper v. Nat'l Marine Fisheries Serv., No. 6:21-cv-00034-AA, 2023 U.S. Dist. LEXIS 109532, at *5 (D. Or. June 26, 2023) (collecting cases and holding that review of ESA citizen suits is not confined to an administrative record). Other circuits have not considered this issue in such detail, but district courts in the Fourth Circuit have held that review in ESA citizen suits is limited to the record. *See, e.g.,* Am. Canoe Ass'n, Inc. v. EPA, 46 F. Supp. 2d 473, 476 (E.D. Va. 1999).

35. Lujan v. Defs. of Wildlife, 504 U.S. 555, 560 (1992) (reaffirming the applicability of Article III standing requirements and denying standing to environmental plaintiffs seeking to challenge FWS/NMFS rule excluding agency actions carried out abroad from ESA section 7 consultation).

36. Lexmark Int'l, Inc. v. Static Control Components, Inc., 572 U.S. 118, 127 (2014). The Court previously referred to the zone-of-interest test as among the "self-imposed" limits on the exercise of federal jurisdiction referred to collectively as "prudential" standing requirements. *Bennett,* 520 U.S. at 163–64.

37. *Bennett,* 520 U.S. at 164 ("the ESA's citizen-suit provision . . . negates the zone-of-interests test (or, perhaps more accurately, expands the zone of interests)" by permitting "any person" to bring suit); Seafreeze Shoreside v. Dep't of the Interior, 123 F.4th 1, 15–20 (1st Cir. 2024) (omitting consideration of the zone-of-interest test in determining ESA citizen suit standing, but holding that "[a]n APA claimant must establish that the claim arguably falls within the zone of interests to be protected or regulated by the underlying statute").

11.5.1 Article III Standing

In a 1992 case challenging the Services' regulations excluding agency actions carried out abroad from ESA section 7 consultation requirements, the Supreme Court reiterated the Article III requirements for standing.[38] Article III standing requires satisfying three elements:

1. The plaintiff must have suffered an "injury in fact."
2. There must be a causal connection between the injury and the conduct complained of.
3. It must be likely that the injury will be redressed by a decision favorable to the plaintiffs.[39]

More than one court has observed that "standing is not a concept that can be defined by strict metes and bounds and is not susceptible to facile application; so litigation about standing often results in a close call."[40] Although a detailed discussion of Article III standing is beyond the scope of this book,[41] any person filing or defending against an ESA citizen suit must have at least a general understanding of the three-prong test for Article III standing articulated in *Defenders of Wildlife*. And parties should appreciate that questions of Article III standing can be raised at any time during a proceeding and that the conditions for standing "must remain extant at all stages of review, not merely at the time the complaint is filed."[42]

---

38. *Def. of Wildlife*, 504 U.S. at 560.

39. *Id.* In multi-plaintiff litigation, if for each claim one plaintiff shows constitutional and zone-of-interests standing, the court need not address whether other plaintiffs have standing to raise that claim. In re Polar Bear ESA Listing and Section 4(d) Rule Litigation, 794 F. Supp. 2d 65, 82 n.21 (D.D.C. 2011), *aff'd on other grounds*, 720 F.3d 354 (D.C. Cir. 2013).

40. Pac. N.W. Generating Coop. v. Brown, 38 F.3d 1058, 1066 (9th Cir. 1994) (citations omitted).

41. *See generally* Robin Kundis Craig, *Removing "The Cloak of Standing Inquiry": Pollution Regulation, Public Health, and Private Risk in the Injury-in-Fact Analysis*, 29 CARDOZO L. REV. 149 (2007); Cass R. Sunstein, *What's Standing After* Lujan*? Of Citizen Suits, "Injuries," and Article III*, 91 MICH. L. REV. 163 (1992).

42. Coastal Env't Rights Found. v. Naples Rest. Grp., Ltd. Liab. Co., 115 F.4th 1217, 1221 (9th Cir. 2024). *See also* Pac. Rivers Council v. U.S. Forest Serv., 2012 WL 336133 (9th Cir. Feb. 3, 2012) (standing challenged for the first time on appeal); Ctr. for Biological Diversity v. Kempthorne, 588 F.3d 701, 707 (9th Cir. 2009) (standing challenged in secondary briefing on appeal); W. Watersheds Project v. Kraayenbrink, 632 F.3d 472, 482 (9th Cir. 2011) (where government declined to defend regulations on appeal, defendant-intervenors could continue to defend them but were, for the first time, required to establish standing).

11.5.1.1 Prong 1: "Injury in Fact"

To have an injury in fact, a plaintiff must have suffered an invasion of a legally protected interest that is both (1) concrete and particularized and (2) actual or imminent, as opposed to merely "conjectural" or "hypothetical."[43] Even though "purely aesthetic" interests are legally cognizable for purposes of standing,[44] plaintiffs must show some actual and imminent injury to their aesthetic (or other) interests.[45] For example, in *Defenders of Wildlife,* the plaintiffs alleged that the Secretaries' failure to apply ESA section 7 consultation requirements abroad would injure Defenders of Wildlife members who had visited, and planned to return to, Sri Lanka and Egypt (the sites of two proposed federal projects) to observe endangered wildlife.[46] The Court, however, noted

---

43. *Defs. of Wildlife*, 504 U.S. at 560. Even State plaintiffs alleging special solicitude for standing purposes must establish a concrete injury. *See* Wyoming v. U.S. Dep't of the Interior, 674 F.3d 1220 (10th Cir. 2012); Del. Dep't of Nat. Res. & Env't Control v. FERC, 558 F.3d 575, 579 n.6 (D.C. Cir. 2009); Arizona v. Mayorkas, 584 F. Supp. 3d 783, 800 (D. Ariz. 2022) ("Whatever its contours, the special solicitude doctrine cannot be some sort of magic wand that a state can wave over an otherwise inadequate record to automatically cure standing defects that would be fatal to a private litigant.").

44. *Defs. of Wildlife*, 504 U.S. at 563–64 (citing Sierra Club v. Morton, 405 U.S. 727 (1972)). *See also* Summers v. Earth Island Inst., 555 U.S. 488, 494 (2009). An injury-in-fact may be aesthetic and/or psychological. Animal Legal Def. Fund v. Glickman, 154 F.3d 426, 430–31 (D.C. Cir. 1998) (en banc) ("Because USDA regulations permit the nonhuman primates in zoos, such as the Long Island Game Farm and Zoological Park to be housed in isolation, Marc Jurnove was exposed to and will be exposed in the future to behaviors exhibited by these animals which indicate the psychological debilitation caused by social deprivation. Observing these behaviors caused and will cause Marc Jurnove personal distress and aesthetic and emotional injury."). But witnessing a contested action without evidence of aesthetic injury may not suffice. *See* Am. Soc'y for Prevention of Cruelty to Animals v. Feld Ent., Inc., 659 F.3d 13 (D.C. Cir. 2011); *see also* Wilderness Soc'y v. Rey, 622 F.3d 1251 (9th Cir. 2010). And courts have expressed skepticism that a plaintiff has standing through aesthetic injury when that injury was self-inflicted through, for example, travel to a polluted site. *See* Ctr. for Biological Diversity v. United States EPA, 937 F.3d 533, 540 (5th Cir. 2019).

45. *See, e.g.*, Humane Soc'y of the U.S. v. Hodel, 840 F.2d 45, 52 (D.C. Cir. 1988) (plaintiffs adequately alleged injury based upon FWS decision to open wildlife refuges to hunting, thereby "forcing members to witness animal corpses and environmental degradation . . . [and] depleting the supply of animals and birds refuge visitors seek to view"). The Supreme Court has indicated that even when a party invokes standing based on a procedural injury, it must still have some concrete interest. *See* Summers v. Earth Island Inst., 555 U.S. 488, 496 (2009). This is often satisfied with a proximity to the area. *E.g.*, Sierra Club v. U.S. Army Corps of Eng'rs, 645 F.3d 978 (8th Cir. 2011) (proximity and engagement in bird watching and other activities).

46. An organization or association has standing to bring suit on behalf of its members when (1) its members would otherwise have standing to sue in their own right; (2) the interests it seeks to protect are germane to the organization's purpose;

that the mere fact that the plaintiffs had visited those locations in the past to observe endangered animals, and planned to return "someday," was simply not sufficient to show actual or imminent injury.[47] Likewise, the Court rejected the plaintiffs' purportedly novel "animal nexus" or "vocational nexus" theories, holding that injury cannot be shown merely because one has an interest—even a professional interest—in observing an animal.[48]

Since the Court's decision in *Defenders of Wildlife,* plaintiffs in ESA cases arguably have become adept at successfully articulating the necessary Article III injury to establish standing. Examples of such injuries include injury to the ability to observe and study wolves;[49] injury to economic interests, such as receipt of a water supply from Bureau of Reclamation reservoirs;[50] and injury to property, based upon a showing of past flooding and an increased threat of future flooding.[51] Yet in *Summers v. Earth Island Institute,*[52] the Court reaffirmed the importance of establishing a temporal or geographic nexus of the plaintiff to the area arguably adversely affected by the defendant's alleged conduct.

---

and (3) neither the claim asserted nor the relief requested requires the participation of individual members in the lawsuit. Friends of the Earth, Inc. v. Laidlaw Env't Serv., 528 U.S. 167, 181 (2000); Hunt v. Wash. State Apple Advertising Comm'n, 432 U.S. 333, 343 (1977).

47. *Defs. of Wildlife*, 504 U.S. at 564. Had the plaintiffs demonstrated "concrete" plans to visit Sri Lanka or Egypt (by establishing travel dates, for example), the Court might have determined that an imminent injury existed. *Id.*

48. *Id.* at 566 n.3.

49. Wyo. Farm Bureau Fed'n v. Babbitt, 987 F. Supp. 1349, 1359 (D. Wyo. 1997) (holding that plaintiffs who demonstrated actual plans to use specific areas of Idaho had standing to challenge the government's reintroduction of wolves into those areas), *rev'd on other grounds*, 199 F.3d 1224 (10th Cir. 2010). *See also* Strahan v. Coxe, 939 F. Supp. 963, 978 (D. Mass. 1996), *aff'd in part, vacated in part,* 127 F.3d 155 (1st Cir. 1997) (holding that plaintiff, a conservation biologist engaged in whale research, would be injured by harm to whales in Massachusetts waters, where he regularly observed whales).

50. Bennett v. Spear, 520 U.S. 154 (1997).

51. Glover River Org. v. U.S. Dep't of the Interior, 675 F.2d 251, 254 (10th Cir. 1982) (standing ultimately denied on causation and redressability grounds). *See also* Bldg. Indus. Ass'n v. Babbitt, 979 F. Supp. 893, 899 (D.D.C. 1997) (plaintiffs presented adequate evidence that listing of fairy shrimp had depressed land values and had halted or impeded development, thereby causing injury).

52. 555 U.S. 488, 494–95 (2009). *See also* Glynn Env't Coal., Inc. v. Sea Island Acquisition, LLC, 26 F.4th 1235, 1242 (11th Cir. 2022) (though wetland was on private property, a plaintiff need not physically step foot on or use a wetland to have an aesthetic interest in it, and viewing the wetland created such interest). *See generally* Bradford Mank, *Revisiting the* Lyons *Den:* Summers v. Earth Island Institute*'s Misuse of* Lyons*'s "Realistic Threat" of Harm Standing Test,* 42 ARIZ. ST. L.J. 837 (2010).

11.5.1.2 Prong 2: "Causation"

Plaintiffs must show a causal connection between their injury and the conduct complained of.[53] An "attenuated chain of conjecture" is not enough;[54] the injury suffered must be "fairly traceable to the challenged action of the defendant, and not the result of the independent action of some third party not before the court."[55] Courts, for instance, may reject causation where plaintiffs appear to rely on "speculation" about what future parties not before the court will do, particularly when subsequent actions by those parties will otherwise trigger federal involvement.[56]

Causation may be absent when the injury is the result of the independent action of a third party; however, the "fairly traceable" requirement does not mean that the defendant's actions that caused the injury must be the very last step in a chain of causation.[57] For example, even though a BO issued under section 7 is "advisory" and does not mandate particular action agency activity,[58] the fact that a BO has a "powerful coercive effect on the action agency"[59] is generally sufficient to support an allegation that its issuance causes injury. Similarly, industry plaintiffs have successfully argued that the Secretary's decision to list a species had a "determinative or coercive effect" on other agencies (the Army Corps of Engineers, for example), which in turn forced the plaintiff to incur costs and delays or injury.[60] When the actions of a third party cause an injury, and those actions would not occur

53. *Defs. of Wildlife*, 504 U.S. at 560 (Court did not rule on whether plaintiffs met the requirement for causation, instead dismissing the action for failure to show injury and redressability).

54. Salmon Spawning & Recovery All. v. Gutierrez, 545 F.3d 1220, 1228 (9th Cir. 2008) (citing Ecological Rights Found. v. Pac. Lumber Co., 230 F.3d 1141, 1152 (9th Cir. 2000)).

55. *Id.* Multiple concurrences and dissents accompanying a recent en banc decision of the Fifth Circuit address traceability at length. *See* Env't Tex. Citizen Lobby, Inc. v. ExxonMobil Corp., 123 F.4th 309 (5th Cir. 2024) (especially Davis, J., concurring and Jones, J, dissenting).

56. Ctr. for Biological Diversity v. U.S. Dep't of the Interior, 563 F.3d 466, 479 (D.C. Cir. 2009).

57. *Bennett*, 520 U.S. at 168–69.

58. See Chapter 5, Section 5.4 for a discussion of section 7 consultation and biological opinions.

59. *Bennett*, 520 U.S. at 169.

60. Bldg. Indus. Ass'n v. Babbitt, 979 F. Supp. 893, 899 (D.D.C. 1997). *But cf.* Glover River Org. v. U.S. Dep't of the Interior, 675 F.2d 251, 255 (10th Cir. 1982) (holding that the causal link between listing of the leopard darter and the loss of federal funding for proposed dam projects was "far too speculative to support standing").

but for the actions of the defendant, sufficient causation exists to support standing.[61] Assuming that the defendant's actions can fairly be said to have caused the plaintiff's injury, a plaintiff must still meet the third prong of Article III standing: redressability.

11.5.1.3 Prong 3: "Redressability"

Courts will adjudicate a case only if the plaintiff's injury can be redressed by a favorable decision of the court.[62] The legal standard for redressability is that it be "likely," as opposed to merely "speculative," that a favorable decision will redress the plaintiff's asserted injury.[63] *Bennett v. Spear* and *Defenders of Wildlife* provide two examples of the Supreme Court's treatment of redressability in ESA cases. In *Bennett,* the plaintiff ranchers and irrigation districts challenged the validity of a BO, which had concluded that operation of the Klamath Irrigation Project by the Bureau of Reclamation would jeopardize the continued existence of two listed species.[64] The government argued that the proximate cause of any harm to the plaintiffs (through reductions in water deliveries) would be a decision by the Bureau of Reclamation regarding water allocations, and not the BO itself.[65] Although the Court agreed that an action agency is technically free to disregard a BO and proceed with its own proposed action, the Court noted the "virtually determinative effect" of BOs on agency actions, as well as the fact that the BO at issue contained an incidental take statement, a violation of which would be a violation of section 9 of the ESA.[66] Given that the Bureau of Reclamation had operated the Klamath Project in the same manner throughout the 20th century until receipt of the BO, the Court held that without the BO the Bureau would not likely impose water level restrictions; and if the plaintiffs were to succeed in having the BO overturned, their injuries "likely" would be redressed.[67]

---

61. Strahan v. Coxe, 939 F. Supp. 963, 978–79 (D. Mass. 1996) (operations of licensed commercial fishing and whale-watching vessels, which injure whales, are fairly traceable to the defendant issuing licenses for such activity).
62. Lujan v. Defs. of Wildlife, 504 U.S. 555, 561 (1992).
63. *Id.*
64. Bennett v. Spear, 520 U.S. 154 (1997).
65. *Id.* at 168.
66. *Id.* at 169–71.
67. *Id.*

In *Defenders of Wildlife,* conversely, the plaintiffs mounted a programmatic challenge to the Services' regulation rendering the section 7 consultation process inapplicable to federal agency actions in foreign countries. The Supreme Court held that invalidation of the regulation would not redress the plaintiffs' claimed injuries to environmental interests in Sri Lanka and Egypt.[68] The Court concluded that even if the plaintiffs prevailed on the merits and the Secretary was ordered to promulgate new regulations applying section 7 consultation abroad, redress of the respondents' injuries would require other, nonparty agencies to take action (i.e., to terminate funding of foreign projects pending consultation).[69] Because the nonparty agencies would not have been bound by the new regulation, and because the agencies had provided only a fraction (10 percent) of the funding for the foreign projects in question, the Court held that it was "entirely conjectural" whether the activity that affected the respondents would be altered or affected by the promulgation of new section 7 regulations.[70]

Together, *Bennett* and *Defenders of Wildlife* serve as useful preliminary guides for any party wishing to establish, or refute, standing in any ESA lawsuit.[71] In some situations, however, a lack of redressability also might suggest that the case is no longer ripe, or possibly that it has become moot.[72]

---

68. *Defs. of Wildlife,* 504 U.S. at 568–69.

69. *Id.* at 571.

70. *Id.*

71. *See also Glover River Org.*, 675 F.2d at 255 (plaintiffs could not show that, absent the listing of the leopard darter, certain flood control projects would be undertaken; thus, delisting of the darter would not redress plaintiffs' injuries). Where a procedural right is at issue, a plaintiff "need not establish the likelihood that the agency would render a different decision after going through the proper procedural steps." Ctr. for Biological Diversity v. Exp.-Import Bank of the United States, 894 F.3d 1005, 1013 (9th Cir. 2018). Still, a plaintiff must show that the claimed injury would not occur if the court ruled in its favor. *Id.* (holding that an injury is redressable where the defendant has direct regulatory authority over the violator, even though, in this case, the Export-Import Bank did not exercise such authority over liquid natural gas projects near the Great Barrier Reef).

72. *See* Marcum v. Salazar, 810 F. Supp. 2d 56 (D.D.C. 2011); Rio Grande Silvery Minnow v. Bureau of Reclamation, 601 F.3d 1096 (10th Cir. 2010); Klamath Tribes v. U.S. Bureau of Reclamation, 2023 U.S. Dist. LEXIS 198398, at *35 (D. Or. Sept. 11, 2023).

Table of Cases

Index